THE
COMPOSER'S
LANDSCAPE

THE
COMPOSER'S
LANDSCAPE

THE PIANIST AS EXPLORER

*Interpreting the Scores
of Eight Masters*

CAROL MONTPARKER

AMADEUS
PRESS

AN IMPRINT OF HAL LEONARD CORPORATION

Published in 2014 by Amadeus Press
An Imprint of Hal Leonard Corporation
7777 West Bluemound Road
Milwaukee, WI 53213

Trade Book Division Editorial Offices
33 Plymouth St., Montclair, NJ 07042

Printed in the United States of America

Book design by Michael Kellner

Music engraving in Appendix A (pp. 179–211) and Appendix B (pp. 213–248) by Staccato Media Group, Inc.
Music engraving on pp. 109–110 by Jeffrey Reid Baker

Library of Congress Cataloging-in-Publication Data

Montparker, Carol, author.
 The composer's landscape : the pianist as explorer, interpreting the scores of eight masters / Carol Montparker.
    pages cm
 Includes bibliographical references and index.
 ISBN 978-1-57467-452-1
 1. Piano music--Interpretation (Phrasing, dynamics, etc.) 2. Piano music--Analysis, appreciation. 3. Piano music--18th century--History and criticism. 4. Piano music--19th century--History and criticism. I. Title.
 ML700.M66 2014
 786.209--dc23
                        2014020447

www.amadeuspress.com

Every book I write is for Ernest.

Also in memory of my late parents, Edward and Grace Mont, and my two great teachers, Leopold Mittman and Josef Fidelman.

Don't only practice your Art
But force your way into its secrets
For it and knowledge
Can raise men to the Divine.

—LUDWIG VAN BEETHOVEN

CONTENTS

ACKNOWLEDGMENTS

I am grateful to the Steinway Piano Company, for their kindness to me, most specifically in providing me with the most beautiful pianos to play, along with their support for my lecture-performance series, "The Composer's Landscape." Special thanks to Dan Miceli, Gordon McNelly, and Barry Tognolini.

Thanks to Jeffrey Reid Baker, pianist, composer, and audio engineer, for his indispensable assistance in many of the technological facets of my recording work. Thanks to James Rohner, former publisher at the Instrumentalist Company, who hired me many years ago as an editorial assistant at *Clavier* magazine, a position that ultimately led to that of senior editor, and the chance to interview countless great artists.

Thanks to the community of piano teachers, students, and music lovers who came and supported my programs; especially to my own wonderful students with their constant support and interest in my projects, my thanks for their inspiration and love.

A grateful thanks to Jessica Burr, my editor at Amadeus Press, for her patience and guidance through tricky new electronic territories, and her expert and intuitive suggestions. Also to Barbara Norton for her hard work on my manuscript. My special thanks and appreciation to Michael Kellner for his beautiful design of this volume.

To my beloved friend Andrea Klepetar-Fallek, special thanks for her generous support, in this case by making the acquisition of the autograph manuscripts from the Pierpont Morgan Library's archives altogether possible; and for certain essential phone calls in German to archives in Europe. Also, my grateful acknowledgments go to Nicole Kämpken at Beethoven-Haus in Bonn, the Riemenschneider Bach Institute at Baldwin Wallace University Conservatory, and the Irving S. Gilmore Library at Yale University for permission to reprint pages from autograph manuscripts.

Mostly, my love and gratitude go to my wonderful husband, Ernest Taub, for assisting me in innumerable ways, always lovingly, making everything possible.

Ludwig van Beethoven, sketches for the slow movement of Piano Sonata No. 29 in B-flat Major ("Hammerklavier"), Opus 106; autograph manuscript (1818?). The Pierpont Morgan Library, New York, Cary 550.

INTRODUCTION

When a piano performance (or a piece of visual art, or, for that matter, a book) is presented to the public, it is unlikely that the struggles to achieve that finished product will be fully understood. The essays and explorations in this volume attempt to describe the process by which a pianist prepares and develops an interpretation. By focusing on works written by eight great composers, I have tried to define the many elements that determine a performer's final artistic choices. How does a musician resolve questions of style and technique (for which there are countless options) while staying within the historical context of that composer and at the same time maintaining the freedom of recreative expression? What are the particular challenges unique to each composer? And how do we approach their scores with optimum comprehension?

While these matters might be of interest to music lovers and concert-goers, they are of *essential* importance to those of us who are actively engaged in the work of presenting music to the public—performing pianists, piano students, and teachers—all of whom participated in the series of lectures, performances, and workshops called "The Composer's Landscape" that I presented as a Steinway Artist in conjunction with the Steinway Piano Company.

The essays in this book had their origin in those events. At each of the two-hour workshops I discussed a single composer and the essential elements and exigencies of performing his piano works, and followed the discussion with a performance of major works by that composer.

In the second half of the program, three or four pianists or piano students whom I had selected, then performed the pieces they were working on, after which I coached them in front of the auditors.

As a pianist and music journalist for many years, I have been fortunate to share musical ideas with, and sometimes to be coached by, not only my own great teachers, but the many renowned concert artists I have met writing feature stories for *Clavier*. One day, while working on this book, I suddenly realized that I had an almost-forgotten wealth of material that would supplement my own observations and opinions in these essays; there they were, lying on the shelves of our home library—past issues of *Clavier* containing the almost two hundred discussions and articles I had done. I call them "discussions" because I was encouraged by the pianists whom I was interviewing to participate fully, and so I did. Our talks were deep, thorough, and thoughtful dialogues. We played on the tables of restaurants or on the pianos in their studios to illustrate points. I believe that my enthusiastic participation was catalytic and yielded richer results for the final article.

Each article had a shelf life of about a month until the next issue arrived, but the wisdom shared and recorded is worth preserving. So I reread the magazine pieces and excised relevant segments, weaving them into the eight chapters presented here. I am grateful, retrospectively, for the scholarship, insight, wit, and ideas offered by so many pianists on the subject of performance and understanding the scores—just as I was when the meetings took place. Their opinions are, of course, as valuable and pertinent now as they were at the time the interviews were conducted.

I decided to add, as an appendix, the entirety of two exciting projects I did for *Clavier*. One was entirely devoted to discussions of the Chopin *Barcarolle*, Opus 60, with seven world-famous pianists each lending their thoughts and analysis to this eight-minute work, possibly the greatest of Chopin's compositions. The other is a similar project, with the Chopin Ballade No. 4, Opus 52, as the work-in-focus—with five more concert pianists. The amazing thing is that none of the pianists ever repeated any of the others; in fact there were some amusing contradictions. (I have included updates on each participating pianist's career in the appendices.)

The important point here is that, while they stay within the boundaries of the score, the interpretive ideas put forth from one artist to the next have an amazingly wide range of validity. The discussions I had with them couldn't be more essential and germane to the whole point of this book. I have had many requests from individual musicians and readers over the years to copy and send them the texts of the Barcarolle and Fourth Ballade articles (actually four articles, as each set of conversations was divided between two consecutive issues of *Clavier*). Looking back, I am ever more grateful for the excellent job done by the *Clavier* editorial staff in formatting the material for these comprehensive studies.

During the two years since the "Composer's Landscape" series ended at Steinway, I have also received requests to continue the series or to make available the talks and recordings of the performances and sessions. My hope is that this book will closely recapture the pleasure and value of the live events.

A few words and metaphors will explain why I gave the series the name "The Composer's Landscape." Music is a language, and that language has a very broad spectrum. Often referred to as "the universal language," still it encompasses many styles, genres, and dialects. Not only does each composer write in a unique language, but performing artists have to learn to "speak" and "sing" in these various tongues. Very often pianists find that they are fluent and conversant in many composers' languages—but not all. Very few pianists play every composer equally convincingly. Even if we are lucky enough to be born with talent, it usually has a territorial boundary, as my great teacher Leopold Mittman put it.

To my eyes, a page from any score is a landscape, with its own contours and terrain, that is directly related to the language of that composer—a kind of visual depiction of the language. When a musician beholds a page from a Schumann score, it has an altogether different look from a page of Mozart; it can be as different as a jungle is from a well-tended garden, and an experienced musician can glance at a page and discern which composer wrote it, just from the appearance of the writing style.

Yes, there is the same system of notation: notes, clefs, phrase marks, dynamics, lines and spaces, and so on. But what gets much more complex is the "topography": the shapes—the peaks and depths, the patches of bramble or thickets to plow through, the open plains to traverse, the circuitous routes of the melodic lines, the clotted harmonies, the busy thoroughfares where all the voices converge, the layers of their importance, and the depth of meanings, stacked like the geological strata of a canyon, through which we must dig in order to get to the core of truth. We must, in essence, be explorers and, for me, the metaphor of landscape works so well that I could find endless parallels between the manuscript and any kind of geographical terrain.

Most concerts are eclectic and varied. This series proved to be a rare opportunity to present and examine one composer at a time and take note of the extraordinary and essential elements that distinguish one composer's landscape from the next, and what the unique challenges are for the explorer-pianist.

Generally what I am discussing here is published music, in the standard editions from which we work. Very few of us have had the opportunity and thrill of viewing original autographed manuscripts held in archives and music libraries around the world. But I have been fortunate to view some precious and hallowed pages in exhibits and in preparation for an article I did in *Clavier* called "The Creative Impulse"

(January 1982). There is something deeply stirring about examining the raw stuff of a great manuscript and trying to project oneself back to the action of creation: an angry impulse that caused a careless blot of ink to fall on the paper along with an indication for *rinforzando* in the Liszt Sonata, or an exquisitely scribbled sea-spray of a scale dabbed in by Chopin in a polonaise. These I perused in awe at an exhibit of forty-three manuscripts, "Piano Manuscripts of Two Centuries," at the J. P. Morgan Library many years ago.

As I sauntered reverently from one showcase to the next, from Mozart's elegant hand all the way across time to Webern's unexpressive and stodgy notations, the temptation might have been to draw conclusions about temperament and mood from the style of script, in a sort of graphological analysis. But I now believe that although one might find conveniently credible correlations to support such conjecture, there are even more surprising contradictions. Beethoven, who was known to have carefully formulated rational schemes in his head before putting them on paper, had an impetuous hand; and Mozart, from whom the music poured almost faster than he could jot it down, with hardly an imperfection to emend, notated in rational and consistent penmanship.

Moreover, what might seem to represent a certain trait to one viewer comes across quite differently to another. In his account of this exhibit, Donal Henahan, then chief music critic of *The New York Times*, described the sober Brahms manuscript as frivolous and charming, while I felt it revealed a peasantlike bluntness. In short, such explicit deductions, while an amusing pastime, are in all likelihood entirely invalid.

There are, however, some things a serious student or fancier of musical artifacts can learn from these wondrous pages. Sometimes there are clear changes, neatly, even artistically crosshatched out (as by Chopin, for example). Sometimes the ink is entirely different halfway through the page, from which one might wonder whether there was a flagging of the imagination or a distraction. Often the very strokes of the pen recreate the natural flow of the music (as described, for example, in the Beethoven chapter). We can see the backward slant of Schubert's handwriting, and, with the manuscripts in varying stages of alteration, we sense the composer's restless dissatisfaction and soul-searching.

The very good news for me was that, thanks to a generous gift from a dear friend, I was able to acquire photos of beautiful pages from original autograph manuscripts held in the J. P. Morgan Library's collection, in the Beethoven-Haus in Bonn, and in the Riemenschneider Bach Institute of each of the composers discussed in this book. While these original scores ignite the imagination, yield a primal feeling of connection with the composer, and arouse fantasized glimpses of the surly Beethoven scribbling passionately into the night in the flickering candlelight or the frail, consumptive Chopin on Majorca or at Nohant, what truly interests me for this book are the ideas and meanings we pianists can deduce from the music.

As a musician and as a pianist (a subspecies of musician), I would like to say a few words about the attached CD. I have had to select the shorter works from my "Composer's Landscape" series in order to produce a sort of sampler to accompany this book. (Mendelssohn's *Variations sérieuses* were omitted owing to space considerations.) And so the longer, later Beethoven sonatas and the Schumann *Fantasie*, *Kreisleriana*, and the *Symphonic Etudes*, all included in the series, had to wait for the forthcoming audiobooks that will follow this volume.

All of the performances are either from live events or recorded at home by myself on a small Zoom system. They were then placed onto a CD by an audio technician who adjusted and equalized the volume levels, spaced the tracks, and even tried to remove the sound of a truck going by on Fifty-seventh Street during a recital at Steinway Hall. I did not want to use a splicing-and-dicing studio. These are my honest, spontaneous, and *human* accounts of these beloved works. To be sure, the end product is not as polished as discs from commercial companies;

there will be differences of sound between the various halls and between the instruments on which the pieces were recorded, not to mention the odd mis-struck note; but if I did not feel them to be worthy of being heard, I would not have presented them here.

I am a musician who loves to write; I do not pretend to be a scholar or a theoretician. All of my observations and suggestions contained in this book are empirically based—in other words, experiential, pragmatic, experimental, and intuitive, and drawn from my many years of performing, listening, teaching, reading (both music literature and books), and those countless rarified discussions. They are offered in the same spirit as all the work I have done: to share and communicate, with the hope that it has value for others.

—CAROL MONTPARKER

Johann Sebastian Bach, Praeludium in D Minor from the *Well-Tempered Clavier*, Book 1, in the *Klavierbüchlein für Wilhelm Friedemann Bach*; autograph manuscript (begun in Cöthen on January 22, 1720). Courtesy of The Irving S. Gilmore Library, Yale University, New Haven, Connecticut.

1

BACH (1685–1750)

Nothing in musical literature, except perhaps the thirty-two Beethoven sonatas and his sixteen string quartets, are as monumental a musical gift to mankind as the two books of forty-eight preludes and fugues of *The Well-Tempered Clavier* by Johann Sebastian Bach. They have been referred to as the "Old Testament" and "sacred scriptures"—attempts to describe the manifest magnificence of these works. And indeed, to many of us they are nothing less than a miracle.

Throughout my long musical life I have been making a pilgrimage through both volumes, and although I have read through all forty-eight, to date I have performed only about three-quarters of them. As in all of Bach keyboard music, very few details besides the notes were indicated by the composer, and so the keyboardist must draw from both imagination and scholarship in order to make stylistic decisions regarding ornamentation, phrasing, articulation, dynamics, and so on. These choices still remain, as they were in the Baroque period, the measure of the artist, and they provide enormous creative potential and challenge. The pianist faces a page of the score, the "landscape," with countless choices of colors, timbres, and tempi from which to choose.

Bach left several manuscripts and versions of the original text, resulting in differences from one edition to the next, and hence we hear this in recordings and live performances—from one interpretation to the next. In fact, it is often difficult to choose a favorite Bach pianist, because we may like one prelude and fugue according to András Schiff, and yet prefer a suite as performed by Glenn Gould.

I feel that, as pianists, it is a privilege and a joy to make these artistic decisions for ourselves, before we ever listen to another pianist's interpretation, and to try to present them convincingly. For piano students, I believe that a teacher's guidance, as well as the myriad recordings available, may lend valuable ideas and possibilities about ornamentation, articulation, dynamics, and so on. But the most organic performances stem from the convictions of each pianist.

In 1744, twenty-two years after he presented the world with his first remarkable volume of twenty-four preludes and fugues in every key, Bach brought out an even more highly evolved and varied volume of another twenty-four sets, Book 2, never once repeating himself and taking his inspiration mostly from his spiritual life. Once we realize to what extent Bach's religious devotion drove his composition, we find many examples of symbolism and metaphors.

I made the decision to perform a group of the preludes and fugues from both books out of the consecutive sequence in which they are usually heard, as unconventional as that may seem. I love each one for itself, outside of its place in the parade of keys in half steps, both major and minor, in both volumes, and I also have to remark to myself how wonderful they are in interaction with each other in key relationships other than being a half step apart; I also enjoy juxtaposing two sets of preludes and fugues in the same key from each of the two volumes alongside each other—yet another perspective for these pieces, which are already so varied.

Bach apparently had the idea of a second volume in mind over the course of many years, according to the dates on some of the manuscripts. The preludes range from the exalted, as in the C Major Prelude from Book 2, with its initial proclamation that seems to herald his monumental achievement while conjuring up an organ; to the more tactile harpsichordlike preludes, like the G Major (Book 2), D Minor (Book

1), or the C-sharp Major (Book 2)—each a kind of toccata (from the Italian verb *toccare*, "to touch"), with its delight in the fingerwork and inner voices. The modern piano has the range to do both: therein lies the best argument against musical fundamentalists who favor period instruments.

The fugues vary as much as the preludes: the C Major Fugue (Book 2) has a remarkably merry dance quality, considering the genre, and the G Major Fugue (Book 2), whether or not one shares Bach's religious fervor, is an undeniably "joyful noise." The F-sharp Minor Prelude (Book 2) might be considered a *Lachrymosa*, with its lamenting melodic lines, and its Fugue is as romantic as any work—one of the longest and most wondrously complex of all forty-eight. The A Minor Prelude and Fugue (Book 2) are both so Handelian, with echoes of the Hallelujah Chorus and "And with his stripes," that one has to wonder whether Bach had heard the *Messiah* before composing this set. And the A Major Fugue from Book 2 is positively jazzy! (I have been describing preludes and fugues that are included on my "Composer's Landscape" series of CDs, but the same diversity exists throughout both volumes of the forty-eight.)

Recently I was working on a very dense and difficult fugue from Book 2 with a student who has deep and sensitive responses to Bach. Before the end of the fugue, there are two bars of intensifying phrases, and at each cadence it felt appropriate to use an agogic pause as a kind of respite and then proceed with the next, even more intensely emotional phrase, pause, and go forward again. I commented that it felt to me like the Stations of the Cross. My student immediately concurred with excitement, but then carried it a step deeper by remarking that it was a metaphor for life—that we all had crosses to bear, and that informed the way we could understand this spiritual music.

This is not the place for a musicological diagnosis of the forms. I am much more interested and fascinated by the spirit of each piece and how best to technically achieve the artistic decisions we make. Even though the many genres within Bach's enormous keyboard oeuvre are so varied, the spirit of dance is present in most of his compositions, if not all. The Suites (both English and French) and the Partitas are composed of actual dance movements from the French court and, according to Bach's own words, were meant for "pure pleasure." (I have never read a good explanation of why one set is called "English" and the other "French," as they have almost identical movements.) One hopes to hear the unique character of each dance in all the movements. It is a prime goal for myself and one of the characteristics I listen for in others' readings.

The Preludes and Fugues, I believe, are the most exalted of his genres for keyboard—deeply intellectual, but at the same time highly emotional, lyrical, and extremely demanding. The Two- and Three-Part Inventions (also called Sinfonias) are arranged in order of keys, and although they were meant for instructional purposes, they are beautiful gems when played with an appreciation for their lyricism, as well as a quite wonderful primer in counterpoint. (Bach wrote his thoughts about cantabile playing in the preface.) The seven toccatas are gloriously challenging, not only in matters of touch—they also contain some tricky fugues and recitatives that require a lot of imagination. Then there are the organ works transcribed for piano and some individual works such as the Chromatic Fantasy and Fugue, the Italian Concerto, and the C Minor Fantasia, which are written in a more virtuosic style.

So many of the great composers such as Chopin and Schumann described their Bach regimens as their "daily bread" and urged their students to practice Bach diligently. Beethoven, who acquired the manuscripts of the preludes and fugues before they were even published, played all forty-eight from memory when he was still a boy and shared those hallowed pages with his students. The study of Bach serves to elevate—both spiritually and technically, at whatever the level of accomplishment, making all other music more accessible. I have seen that phenomenon clearly in my students and in my own work.

I have brought some of my students to Bach grumbling, but they learned not only to play his music, but to love and respect it, while acknowledging the benefits.

The touching accounts of Chopin bringing only one musical work with him to his retreat in Majorca—both volumes of the *WTC*—attest to its healing properties. And, of course, these pieces triggered Chopin's inspiration for many of his own Preludes, also composed in consecutive keys, and as varied as the Bach Preludes. Chopin had such a high regard for Bach that to prepare for his own concerts, he practiced the music of Bach, rather than his own works.

It is quite possible that Chopin, Schumann, and the other Romantics played Bach more indulgently and freely than we do now. We will never know, just as we will really never know how Bach himself played his own music, because he wrote precious little about the indications and demands of his works, and there are no written firsthand accounts of his playing from his contemporaries, as we have with almost every other great composer.

To try to play with that oft-repeated word *authenticity*, after all this time, is an almost futile pursuit. We must be guided, rather, by inherent taste and intuition, informed by what we do know about Baroque performance practices, and grateful, at least, that his music was kept alive by performance through the ages, because it would have died on the page without the composers and pianists who revered and resurrected his music.

Through the centuries there have been many stylistic shifts in performance practices of Bach from one generation to the next, some favoring Bach played with strict rhythmic interpretations, some preferring rubato. Some, including Glenn Gould and Rosalyn Tureck, use a decided staccato, detached touch, while Wilhelm Kempf and later Schiff favored cantabile and legato; and so on. But with all the varied views about performance practices in Bach, there has been one consensus: that Bach's keyboard music stands as the template and the insurmountable

Everest for all who came afterward. It has been called the most difficult of all keyboard music, and preparatory for any and all challenges in later music.

Bach's music transcends the instrument (it can be made to sound interesting even on an electronic keyboard or a xylophone!); but in order to play his music really well, one must understand the possibilities of the modern piano. Glenn Gould called Bach's music "instrumentally indifferent," but he was a pianist, nevertheless, and he understood his instrument intimately.

Anton Rubinstein once stated about the piano, "You think it is ONE instrument? It is one hundred instruments!!" And so, when we play Bach's music on a piano, contrast is an essential element (as it is in all forms of art). It is interesting to note that the same language is used to describe both visual art and music—composition, color, tonal palette, shading, and so on.

Czerny, in his dry, methodological way, also mentioned "one hundred different levels of tone." Perhaps we cannot put a finite number on the variations of sound a good pianist can achieve, but we can try to simulate harpsichords, clavichords, organs, lutes, guitars, flutes—all of which enhances all our playing, not just that of Bach's music. A whole palette of colors is available to us. When we talk about color, it is not just a question of quantity—*pppp* to *ffff*—but, rather, one of quality and timbre (what makes an oboe's A sound different from a violin's? or a clarinetist's?). For that kind of nuance, the pianist has to learn to use the hands in a myriad of ways, and to manipulate the pedals (all three of them).

Yes, I believe one can and should use pedal in Bach, even though there are pianists I very much respect who disagree. The left (*una corda*) pedal changes the timbre as well as the volume by shifting the action from three strings to only one; the right (damper) pedal can help to produce agogic effects and enhance resonance with overtones to help create legato, a connected line, from a percussion instrument—one of the hugest challenges of our instrument; and the middle (sostenuto) pedal can be used to sustain pedal points, lengthy held bass notes that were played on the organ with the foot.

Harpsichords have no dampers; the strings continue to vibrate, and they are often described as having "a wonderful silvery rustling sound." The harpsichord's strings actually vibrate much longer than a piano's would without the damper pedal sustaining the vibration. And so, in order to reproduce that sustained "silvery, rustling sound" on the piano, *we need the pedal.* Bach's beloved clavichord, with its extremely intimate tone, was capable of producing a vibrato—and to try to get close to that tremulous quality, *we need the pedal.* Many of Bach's huge keyboard works were performed in chapels on organs—in other words, huge resonating chambers—and for those grand effects on the piano, *we need the pedal.* Of course, in Bach, we must use the pedal discreetly—half pedals, even quarter pedals, barely grazing the pedal with our foot—but we must keep those strings in action!

The great composers, whether Bach, Mozart, Beethoven, or Brahms, were all at times frustrated with the limitations of their instruments and often wrote music with the conceptions of a larger, grander instrument in mind. Bach was anxious to have improvements made on the harpsichord, just as Beethoven became enraged about the limits of his pianos, just as Brahms wrote to Steinway, Streicher, and other piano makers for improvements. So the early-music mavens who advocate sticking to early instruments are in fact reducing Bach to what Rosalyn Tureck called, in her treatise about performing Bach, "a period piece." Yes, of course, a harpsichord comes closer to what Bach himself heard from his fingers. But what single instrument realizes the full breadth and depth of his concepts?

As good pianists, we must use all our body's possibilities and parts of ourselves. I cannot stress strongly enough how sitting correctly at the piano affects not only the way we play Bach, but also the way we approach all music at the keyboard. With nearly all students who have come into my studio, I have had to spend some time standing them up and then sitting them down again in the optimum way, for balance and freedom of movement, from the smallest, least joints and muscles to their whole fingers, hands, forearms, and shoulders—in fact, their whole upper bodies. Every part of us must be balanced, starting with sitting in such a way that we are not locked into the back of our seat, but with the very minimum of our bottoms on the bench, with the weight and energy of our bodies leaning forward into our legs. Our arms must be able to swing free of our torsos, and our elbows must be higher than our hands. It may take a while before the habit of sitting differently takes hold, but the payoff comes from the ultimate comfort and range of freedom.

And when we are physically at ease, then come the more refined decisions and choices: will we strike with the sensuous pad of the finger or the boney fingertip? And to effect differentiations in the articulation: will we cling to the keys deeply, or dance lightly on the surface? Will we use a legato (linked) touch, which even sometimes implies an overlapping of the tones? And with what speed will we strike the keys? (After all, the speed of the thrust affects the depth of the tone.)

The question of balance can be applied to every facet of Bach playing. For example, there is the anomaly of balancing the unerring pulse of the music with agogic effects and rubatos (to be discussed later). There is the balance between the various articulations, as they best express the phrasings and meanings; and of course, there are the balances between the many voices. Balance is particularly important in Bach because of the "slippery" nature of the music. The voices are so entwined, even entangled, and the spirit and pulse so dogged and unflagging, that one false move can utterly and completely derail the whole thing. It is as if we were on a precarious tightrope, and often there is the feeling of what I have sometimes described as a "flickering light bulb syndrome," as though we were in danger of losing the thread. So unless we have established secure fingering, are (again) sitting correctly, have our arms and hands at the optimum positions (unencumbered by our torso), are sitting far enough away from the keyboard to allow for complete freedom of movement (including the right weights of the various touches we desire), have decided upon *le tempo juste*, have practiced adequately to have a dependable muscle memory, and have a deep understanding of each horizontal line even before it is combined with all the other horizontal lines (because this is *all* horizontal music), then we should not, and cannot, count on security or success.

This is pure rocket science, and the balances between all our systems—intellectual, auditory, visual, muscular, emotional—lie at the core. A student I teach once told me that someone had tried to insult her by saying she had "a musician's brain." The musician's brain is, as much scientific research has shown, more evolved and developed than most others and is prepared well, after the work we do (especially in Bach), for any and all other endeavors.

Many pianists practice Bach mechanically until each hand is entirely independent. This makes sense, perhaps, in Bach's Two-Part Inventions, where there are only two voices (although Bach's treatise on cantabile playing in the preface of the Inventions would be reason enough *not* ever to play them mechanically). But there are two other reasons I believe that is not the best way to practice. First, most of Bach is more than two voices, with each line passing between the left and right hands. But the main reason is that I believe that practicing purely mechanically, without the expressive juices flowing, is missing the opportunity to practice the expressive elements as well.

Not all pianists would agree with me. In an interview with Claude Frank (*Clavier*, January 1983), I asked him about his practice routine.

There are several types of practicing. First . . . there is abstract technical work to keep up the "apparatus." Many pianists look down on this but I love it. It feels so workmanlike: much the same as a fisherman or a shoemaker getting his equipment into shape;

and it is nice to feel like an artisan. I really feel good when I practice technique for its own sake because I have no expectation for results, per se; I simply want to get the work done. Also I don't feel guilty if my mind wanders, as it does quite often, although no one likes to admit it. Although I like technical practice, I do a limited amount of it, a half-hour at most.

A brief account of a recording session of one particular Prelude from the *WTC* will underscore just how critical the sense of balance is for successful execution. Half of the Preludes and Fugues on my recent Bach CD were recorded in live concert, and half at home. I had all the components I needed—*save one*. I had my beautiful Steinway A in perfect tune, I had my own (usually reliable) "personal" equipment: a musical mind and soul anxious to make music, a quite good recording device, a husband who agreed to get the phone during recording sessions. But sometimes I ran up against my own quirky and ornery ear and mind, which are very nearly *never* satisfied. Many times, even when I got a quite good take, still the voice in my head said, "I can do it better."

Sometimes, of course, a piece ran smoothly and balanced the first time, and that was sheer happiness. I simply saved it and added it to my project. When problems occurred, they lay mostly in the challenges of sound (ambience) and that elusive feeling of being physically balanced. The sound at home is very different from the luster of halls in live performance. So elements such as the placement of the microphones and the recording levels can be tricky; even trickier than that are the touch, articulation, dynamics, and all the variables of playing.

The plan was to open with two Preludes and Fugues in C Major and G Major from Book 2, which would be followed by the E-flat Major Prelude and Fugue from Book 2, with several others recorded at home. But the key relationship between G major and E-flat major did not sit well, so I decided to insert the C Minor Prelude and Fugue from Book

1 before the E-flat. (The C major set was the subdominant tone of G, and C minor, as the relative minor key to E-flat, would lead neatly to the E-flat Major Prelude and Fugue, which, in turn, became the dominant chord to the A-flat Major Prelude, and so on.)

Well, the C Minor Prelude is a very difficult prelude to play exactly as one would wish, and the *balance is nowhere more essential.* András Schiff, in his first complete Bach *WTC* collection (he has since rerecorded all forty-eight and has even performed all of them in concert, an awe-inspiring feat), plays that C Minor Prelude quite deliberately, moderato, and *forte*, with almost no melodic line brought out in the tops of each half bar. Others play it faster, or lighter.

My own *tempo juste* felt right at a rapid pace, with more tonal accents on the first sixteenths of each half bar. (There is a beautiful melodic line hidden in there that I wanted and needed to bring out.) I had not listened to all the wonderful CDs available from great pianists such as Angela Hewitt and Glenn Gould, because after I checked in on Schiff's and found I did not agree with it, I realized how fascinating it is, how many choices there are that *could* be valid in the performance of this piece, and I wanted no further input from anyone else's interpretation—I wanted to feel entirely free of influence. (I should add that, in most of Bach, Schiff would be my pianist of choice. And it is probable, because he plays these pieces so often, that he does it differently each time.) And therefore I will pause to include some excerpts from my interview with Schiff (*Clavier*, October 1995) when he discussed the differences between his Bach and that of other interpreters.

Bach is the only composer who sounds good no matter what the instrument; this nonsense about harpsichord versus piano, and having to play on authentic instruments is silly. How one approached the music is what matters. Legato should not be played in the 19th century sense, but simply as not playing everything detached. Gould was not really playing the piano, but playing the piano in a manner as to imitate earlier keyboard instruments. What Bach needs, indeed, what all music needs, in a variety of touch and articulation . . . Bach requires lines with declamation. . . . Bach is very vocal. He is a singing composer. I find that as marvelous as Gould's playing is, it is not singing: he is singing, but not the piano.

Schiff, who was recently knighted by Queen Elizabeth for his services to the world of music, has recorded Bach's complete works, which are distinguished both by joy and melancholy. He plays with clarity, independence of voices, and a strong pulse, without ever being brittle. Even without pedal, he manages a resonant, singing line.

Most pianists keep pumping the gas pedal from beginning to end, and we miss the textures and the polyphony.

Bach is not just abstract music; much of it is religious. It is important to keep in mind that this is not the music of an atheist. The artist has to search for the spiritual message, regardless of whether he shares Bach's beliefs.

The Prelude and Fugue in E-flat minor from Book One is straight from the Passions.

He added that for Bach, nature held little of the importance it did for Beethoven and Schubert.

Schiff attributes much of his inspiration in Bach to Edwin Fischer's recordings and their gorgeous tone quality, and to the English pianist and harpsichordist George Malcolm, who he says taught him a lot about the Baroque period and Bach. And although he does not agree with many of Glenn Gould's stylistic practices, he credits him with "bringing Bach from being thought of in a dry, academic way, to being regarded as music full of energy and dance."

Even though Schiff plays the entire Bach oeuvre from memory, he laments the listeners who come to him after a concert and mention nothing more than the amazing feat of his memory: "Look, I don't use the music, but that is a personal choice. I happen to have a very good memory, but that is not a matter of merit. I was born with it, and it is a matter of luck."

Schiff told me he practices six or eight Preludes and Fugues a day to keep them memorized, but that memorization does not determine the quality of a performance. I asked Schiff about the differences between playing Scarlatti and Bach (who were born the same year—1685):

> It is not that different, except that Scarlatti is a Latin as opposed to Bach, the German, who managed to collect all the elements of French and Italian music while never leaving Germany. Bach is the towering figure of his time, but not necessarily the most original composer. When Scarlatti moved to Spain, at 50 years old, the Spanish flamencan and folk elements made all the difference in his writing.

Schiff reads anything about the composers that would cast a light on his understanding—not necessarily biographies, but letters, although he jested that reading other people's letters makes him feel a little guilty. (For this writer, letters are a favorite genre.)

I vividly recall a concert at Carnegie Hall that Schiff gave twenty-five years ago. He juxtaposed the music of Bartók and Bach because he understood Bach's daring chromaticisms and frequent atonalities, and in the alternation between the two composers an amazing phenomenon occurred: he played the Chromatic Fantasy of Bach and, without pause, went on to Bartók's Suite, Opus 14. The audience was shocked to hear and acknowledge the striking relationships between the two pieces, and the concert became an ever-intensifying and visceral correspondence, with Schiff in the middle as conjuror. Bach is a composer with endless possibilities, and it takes an artist and thinker as interesting as Schiff to find new angles for programming. The Bach-Bartók experiment is yet another balancing act.

To return to the process of finding one's *own* perfect balance in a recording session of Bach Preludes and Fugues: deciding upon the relative contrasts between the voices, which means the regulation of finger weight, the placement of the mics—all the myriad considerations discussed previously, not to mention that factor of how one hears oneself, which, in itself, can be very subjective, I think I played that C Minor Prelude at least thirty or forty times, in different takes, before I found one I could (almost) love altogether. Oddly, the take I chose one day was not necessarily my favorite the next. And many days I discarded all, in favor of starting again from square one, and rerecording it. Such are the exigencies of this process.

I read an article in *International Piano* quoting Peter Donohoe, a quite successful British pianist, who plays Stravinsky, Prokofiev, Shostakovich, Rachmaninoff, and every "big-handed" composer but is now recording "the forty-eight" and says, "There is no more difficult music than this." The bottom line is that each composer has his challenges, and each of us has our own fortes and limitations. Bach has always felt comfortably within my territory, but this was my first in-depth experience with the process of recording and getting it as right as I could for posterity. (*Posterity* is a fancy word for permanence, in this case. In concert, any irregularities that might haunt a pianist would have wafted away into the ether.)

The recording process of preserving one's efforts involves listening so intently to oneself that all of Bach's enormous challenges are intensified and even the tiniest irregularities are magnified. It makes one wonder about Glenn Gould's choice to quit the stage and limit himself to recording: but of course he believed in cutting and pasting, as he described to me at great length on the telephone at four o'clock one morning. He was known to be a night owl, calling people with educated ears and sort of talking *at* them; at that wee hour of the night for about a half hour, Gould described the process he went through making the video of the Goldberg Variations with Bruno Monsaingeon, yes, cutting and pasting away . . . this half of the variation from take 3, the next part from take 10, and so on and on.

On the other hand, it makes it easy to understand Radu Lupu's decision to quit recording and stick to live performance, which, of course, has its own set of exigencies. Other pianists, such as Krystian Zimerman, spoke to me about their excitement when playing before live audiences, a thrill altogether missing in the recording process. It's how we hear ourselves that makes it so difficult. Chances are that the minute flaws we might pick up in our own playing, if recorded on a CD, will serve to haunt us forevermore, while an ardent listener might never notice it.

A musician whom I respect greatly lamented a recent recording of his own that I had found superlative. I asked what made him reject the resulting disc, and his answer was that he knew he could play it much more closely to his ideal "in the middle of the night, for himself." My response to that is, "Of course! so can we all," without the pressures of a live mic, a live audience, the interruptions of thoughts and phones and other people. But at one point, we have to stop all the self-criticism and accept and *like* the human product that comes from us, through hard work, well-trained hands and mind, and a balanced body.

A few words about tone production. We may say that Bach's music transcends the instrument upon which it is played, but the sounds that are drawn from that instrument can range from strident and unpleasant to sublimely nuanced and beautiful, no matter who the composer is.

If we touch the piano too lightly, we could get nothing if the note doesn't "speak." If we touch it too fast and too heavily, we get a strident noise—one that can no longer be considered *tone*. That's one of the wonderful challenges we pianists face, and ideally we need a responsive instrument and the clear sense of the role played by each tone we produce: it is part of a phrase within its hierarchy of importance in the shaping of that phrase, and that phrase is, in turn, part of the organic whole of the piece. So each tone is precious. The great Heinrich Neuhaus, teacher of Radu Lupu, Josef Fidelman (one of my teachers), and many other fine pianists, wrote, "Tone must be clothed in silence, enshrined in silence like a jewel in a velvet case." And then, when we release it from that jewel box, how do we produce it?

In a rare essay that preceded his volume of Inventions, Bach describes one of his intentions as being "a guide for acquiring a cantabile style of playing." This may come as a shock to those who associate the Italian word indicating a singing style, with the Romantic era: the bel canto style that inspired Chopin, or the operatic composers such as Bellini and Puccini.

Bach was as Romantic as any composer! He expressed, in his music, all the human emotions that any Romantic composer did; and his music demands three basic touches: for cantabile, a singing legato (if not as lush as one used for Schumann, Brahms. and Chopin); a non-legato, portamento, detached touch: and shorter staccatos. There are no generalizations about the use of these touches, and certainly there are gradations of each, but usually the slower movements are better expressed with legato, and the faster, with non-legato. But a combination of all these touches, within even one phrase, is the most appropriate and beautiful choice.

The most surprising fact about playing Bach is that it requires more imagination than any other composer. The unfortunate misconception is that the requirements for Bach performance stop at good coordination, a strict sense of rhythm, and strong, even fingers. I have had several students who were excellent technicians but lacked imagination. They could not decide for themselves how to color or phrase the music, even though their fingers were even and clear and accurate; they were dependent upon me to demonstrate several choices (and there are *always* choices; there is never just one "correct" way). Once I did so, they were

astonished at how the music they thought they had been playing accept-
ably came alive! Often a demonstration spurs students to the realization
of what possibilities are open to them, and then they find the code that
opens their own creativity. Polyphonic music requires, above all, the
ability to produce many different varieties of sound to distinguish between the character and relative importance of the voices.

Imagination is an asset that separates the good, even fine pianists
from the artists. (A digression: *artist* being the highest designation,
I believe one should never refer to oneself as one; it is for others to
decide. Yet we hear the word being bandied about, with rock stars
and rappers calling themselves artists.) Radu Lupu (who is suspicious
of verbal language, any of his several, to define the elements of
music) humored me in an interview and tried to define "imagination"
(*Clavier*, July 1992):

> It is richness of experience and fantasy, and the ability to trans-
> port. The artist should have his own voice. Everyone tells a story
> differently, and that story should be told compellingly and sponta-
> neously. If it is not compelling and convincing, it is without value,
> no matter whether all the notes are there or not!

Imagination is required for bringing Bach's scores to life, as they are
almost bare except for the notes. There are exceptions, of course—for
example, in the Italian Concerto, where he indicates *forte* or *piano*, or in
some of the Echo movements in the suites.

The early instruments had narrow ranges of volume and tonal
possibilities, and emphasis could only be made by embellishments and
agogic devices (such as rubato). Yes, rubato in the Baroque era—freedom
of timing! I learned this relatively late in my music education after
having slavishly adhered to Glenn Gould-ish strict rhythmic impulses
for years, without allowing myself, and therefore the music, to breathe
adequately between phrases. It was during a privileged session in my

home, playing Bach cello and piano sonatas with the great cellist János Starker, that he most delicately suggested to me to "breathe more"—that it was "O.K. to take small rubatos." It was a revelation.

The more I study and play, the more I realize to what great extent tone and timing are interdependent.

What about the tempo? What we know about tempo indications during the Baroque period is that a term such as *largo* was more of an instruction regarding the character or mood of the movement than an indication of speed—wide (as in "largesse"—expansive, leisurely) rather than slow. *Allegro* indicated a happy or lively spirit, rather than an instruction to play fast. So then it remains for us, the performers, to determine just the right tempo, based not on speed itself, but on the spirit and, again, the element of dance wherever we can apply it.

In the Suites, we have only the names of the dances to guide us, but most of us have never danced a Gavotte or a Bourrée, and the metronome had not yet been invented. If we think of all the famous Menuets we have known, whether it be Mozart's Menuet from *Don Giovanni*, or Paderewski's Menuet, immediately we can find that even within one dance form the tempo can vary. In fact, in the Baroque period, the Menuet was more lively, and it became more noble and stately in the next century. The Sarabande, too, was more of a spirited dance in Bach's time, but became more reverent and slower with time. These are just more proofs of how nothing, neither the tempo nor the character, about Bach's music is etched in stone two and a half centuries later; the pianist must learn to make judgments about what "feels right" and accommodate and weigh all the factors without any definite precedents.

That being said, we do have some frame of reference from the nature of the dances. Bach wrote seven Partitas, six French Suites, six English Suites, three smaller suites, "and other Galanteries composed for the mental recreation of art lovers."

In the English Suites there is often a Praeludium to start—the only movement that is not a dance. Most of the movements are common to both the Suites and the Partitas. In the English Suite in A Minor, the Praeludium is like a perpetual motion of sixteenth notes, with two-voiced polyphony precariously balanced between the hands and many choices to make between the voices.

The Allemande—literally, "German dance," although it is probably not German but rather of French origin—starts with an upbeat, which is then repeated in the next bar as the downbeat (sometimes referred to as a "double knock"). The character is stately and the tempo moderate.

The Courante—literally, means "running dance"—is from the French courts around Louis XIV. This dance is in three, in rapid tempo, with deviations in meter in the last bars.

The Sarabande is an ancient dance from Spain, also in three, sober, steady, and according to some sources, seductive; in fact, it was banned from the early courts as "arousing evil and bad emotions in even decent people." The dance was actually repressed in Spain. The fun of this movement comes with the heavily embellished repeated sections, but the main melodic lines contain some of the most deeply sublime expressions.

The Bourrée (rhythmically almost indistinguishable from the Gavotte and Musette), has bouncy movements, often accompanied by bagpipes, and often followed by another Bourrée.

The Gigue is a very lively dance often in 6/8 time, originating in British Isles, where, of course, it was called a Jig. In the A Minor English Suite, this movement is full of ebullience and gladness in spite of the minor key, and like most of the movements, it is more heavily embellished upon the repeats.

One of the joys of playing Bach is the choosing of embellishments for important notes, another test of our imagination and inventiveness. And that was one mark of the artist's originality in Baroque times; in fact, in his day, embellishments were highly regarded and executed in an improvisatory way, and our modern educations have been woefully lacking in preparation for these challenges.

I have spent many a happy hour fooling around with "improvised" ornaments until I find the right turns to make it my own. I also encourage my students to invent embellishments, all the while guiding them to stay within reason if they get too elaborate, or to engage in a flight of fancy if they are still too restrained and pedantic. Students can be shy, and it is interesting to note how reticent they sometimes are to try inventing or improvising embellishments. I start by giving a few basic examples that they can copy, then isolating a passage that cries out for "trimmings." Hopefully, through trial and error, the student gets the hang of it, overcoming embarrassment when first attempts fall short.

I do not like to leave what comes out in the end to a game of Russian roulette; I prefer to plan, in advance, at least an outline of the shape and size of each ornament, according to the relative importance of the note in the melodic line. Then I have also been known to get carried away in a kind of joyful celebration (as I believe I did in the repeated sections of the Sarabande of the G Major French Suite).

Bach's scores were relatively uncluttered, compared to those of French Baroque composers such as Couperin, who was quite picky about the exactitude of the embellishments and therefore wrote more into the score. The Italians notated the fewest, encouraging the performer to improvise as desired. (I am certain that neither Bach, nor Chopin nor Mozart, for that matter, ever embellished their music in the exact same way in any two performances.) Just as the score could look too busy, a performer's version of the same mistake would be to clutter the music with too many embellishments. Someone, probably Alfred Brendel, likened that to a woman with too much makeup on!

The last point I will make about ornaments is that according to Otto von Irmer, who wrote the preface to the Henle edition of *The Well-Tempered Clavier*, even in Bach's "Table of Ornaments" he used the word *andeuten*, indicating that these were suggestions, rather than exact instructions as to the execution of his embellishments. What we do know for certain is that most were played on the beat and should never take away from the basic melodic flow of the music.

When we first open a page to study a new work by Bach, we should feel like a child with crayons, confronted with a fresh page of a coloring book. That's provided one is a pianist who has crayons, that is, the means to produce different colors. So much is left to the pianist to decide! Coloring it in and making all the other artistic decisions after we accomplish the nitty-gritties of coordination and accuracy are the most pleasurable and creative work of all. The miracle is that even though we must adhere to all the details in the score, the recreative process of performance leaves us a bounty of creative decisions with which to distinguish ourselves as individual interpreters.

But often, when we open that first new page of a work by Bach, especially a fugue from *The Well-Tempered Clavier*, what we may see, instead of an inviting page of great music to color in, is a thicket of notes, albeit starting with a single line (the subject, or *motif*) that seems to gain in density until it looks daunting, if not off-putting. This music, as in all great music, has cadences at the ends of episodes, which I call "breathing places."

As we already know that this music, *all music*, breathes (as it is *of* us, and is a human expression)—and that we are allowed a discreet rubato, these are the perfect and appropriate places to breathe and recharge. And I don't just mean figuratively speaking—I mean truly inhaling and taking a deep breath. No one ever tells us pianists to do that! We see and hear cellists breathing deeply as they draw a long bow, or flutists and other wind players inhaling a deep breath of air before a long phrase, and of course singers are taught breathing as an essential element in their art.

To breathe along with the music, to measure our own rhythms according to, and in sync with phrases, is to attune ourselves fully to the music.

So after we identify the episodes, where one ends and the next one begins, we can isolate our work areas and get to know all the voices within that segment, even as we are discovering the "connective tissue" between the episodes. The music becomes a series of meaningful statements within the whole. The piece is made of building blocks, and in between them is a moment, even a nanosecond, at which we can reconfigure and *breathe*. Now the score becomes less of a formidable single organism that must be conceived of in its entirety from start to finish, without error or pause, by some kind of automaton who doesn't breathe.

Ralph Kirkpatrick, in his excellent book *Interpreting Bach's "Well-Tempered Clavier,"* likened the fugues in their contrived perfection to the clipped boxwoods in a formal eighteenth-century garden. He shares many original ideas for study—for example, that a student "walk" the relative widths and depths of the melodic intervals in order to comprehend them fully.

Strange as it may seem, there are more differences between any two recordings of the same work of Bach than any other music. Those differences are among the most cherishable reasons to celebrate a performance, provided the pianist's choices are within the strictures of validity for that composer's landscape.

When a good pianist comes into contact with a good piano, there should be a completely symbiotic relationship between hand and keyboard. For Bach, in particular, we have to strive for a multiplanar tonal texture—like a painting with many shades of color, or a bas-relief in a frieze. Sometimes the music continues on like a kind of perpetual motion (the last movement of the Italian Concerto, or the Praeludium of the A Minor English Suite come to mind), with a nonstop stream of notes; only upon close examination and prioritization in the artistic process of making decisions can we distinguish our own understanding and interpretation from the next pianist's. We have to listen and hear, even look at the score: sometimes there are repeated patterns that are actually visible when one peruses the landscape of the score—pickups of two eighth notes before the following bar, or slurred bunches of sixteenth-note phrases, all of which help to determine phrasing. And then comes the work of presenting each musical idea, the varying degrees of volume and shades of tone that we choose to define and fully express each phrase. And as part of this process, one can never overstate the value and importance of the bass line, the foundation for all that is written above it. There are hidden or implied phrases within the continuous stream that can suddenly pop out at us like a hologram. And finally, there are those "resting places."

One of the great things about playing Bach is that his music combines the practical benefits of technical studies (which can otherwise be so dry and miserable, except for those relatively few pianists who seem to enjoy these mechanical pursuits) with beautiful great music, so that the pianist and piano student can grow technically and artistically, simultaneously, and with pleasure. That is probably the main reason so many of the great composers urged their students to practice Bach diligently and themselves practiced what they preached. Unless Bach is delivered with pleasure, and played with pleasure, it can, indeed, sound mechanical, which might be why some people don't care for Bach.

And the converse is true as well. The way one listens to Bach is critical. András Schiff's quip, "If you don't like Bach, perhaps it is best not to admit it," is priceless.

Some further comments about phrasing. In Bach, where phrase marks are missing, it helps to actually sing the melodic lines (and some have even suggested dancing the melodic line—and leaping the intervals). This can help to determine where one might take a breath and help delineate the phrases. In fact, as mentioned earlier, Bach's treatises about cantabile show how deeply he was influenced by the human voice, as were Mozart and Chopin. And because Bach's music is contrapuntal, it helps to play each voice straight through from beginning to end, determining the phrasing for each. If it is four-part writing, as in a chorale or a four-voice fugue, then soprano, alto, tenor, and bass will each have its own phrases, and these phrases are rarely parallel to each one another.

Then we will have to make decisions about which voice we choose to bring out. We have two hands, but we often have to transcend that basic fact of anatomy, because each hand might be covering two or more horizontal voices at once, and different fingers will have to use different touches and relative volumes. Sometimes a voice will traverse from left hand to right, and we have to effect that change without a discernible shift. Most often, the phrases will transcend the bar line, and we have to shape those phrases without accenting the downbeat while maintaining the heartbeat of the music throughout.

And in the end, when we have understood and mastered all these organic elements, we have to see the whole grand architecture, created voice upon voice (as steeple upon steeple in a great cathedral) in a Bach fugue, and wonder at the miraculous musical structure that was ultimately built from all its components. In a Bach fugue, sometimes the climax—the highest steeple—is in the middle, at the densest writing, and we come down the other side of the spire and close quietly, reverently, at the end; and sometimes the texture and tension build straight through to the end.

At times when I consider our anatomy and realize, in a Bach fugue for example, how all ten fingers take on the integrated meshing and distribution of voices, each with contrasting touches and dynamics, then I wonder at the marvel of that greatest tool, the human hand, and at the miraculous masterworks of Bach. I am grateful to be a pianist who can experience both.

Schumann described his disappointment in the people of Leipzig when he tried to search out and worship at the gravesite of J. S. Bach, only to be told by a gravedigger, "There are many Bachs." But then he concluded on the way home, "I would prefer to picture him seated upright at his organ in the prime of life, the music swelling out from under his feet and fingers, the congregation looking up at him raptly, and possibly a few angels among them."

Wolfgang Amadeus Mozart, Rondo in D Major, K. 485 (Jan. 10, 1786), page 1.
The Pierpont Morgan Library, New York, Heineman MS 154.

2

MOZART (1756–1791)

There is one essential point to be made about Mozart's piano music before any other, because I believe that we should listen and play his music with this in mind: Mozart once said, "Opera comes to me before anything else." And it follows that whatever he wrote had a sense of opera in it—perhaps especially his writing for the piano.

For example, consider the Sonata in C Major, K. 309, which begins with a declarative statement of authority. We might think of the Commendatore from *Don Giovanni*. And then, in some gentler treble passages, we can imagine and try to reenact the operatic soprano roles such as Zerlina in *Don Giovanni* or Susanna in *The Marriage of Figaro*; and then there are the comic figures, like Papageno in *The Magic Flute*, that appear here and there in the piano sonatas—and even in the shorter works.

And, then somehow, all these "characters" who make their appearances in different phrases of a piano work come together organically into a whole, just as they do in opera. The themes are not the same as the ones he used in his operas, although there are parallels; but the writing is vocal, and there are dialogues between the contrasting voices. Someone once called Mozart's operatic piano music "enlightened dialogue."

The great keyboard artist Wanda Landowska once noted:

The great Mozart players know how to spin out a tale in those few notes, to reflect every emotion in the spectrum of human feelings, to play a fluid scale in a singing way. There are many, many pianists who can play Mozart cleanly and creditably, but very few who do it artistically. Technical mastery is often the main focus, and imagination is under-valued.

This point is, of course, applicable to all music: imagination is the spark that transforms mere technique into artistry. In Mozart, taking on the roles of the characters, in every gesture of our bodies and souls, brings the music to life.

Great pianists such as Artur Schnabel, Arthur Rubinstein, and many others have quipped that "Mozart is easy for children and too hard for adults." Children are still "pure" and naive, and purity is an essential element of Mozart's music. Yet even though Mozart has a smaller *quantity* of notes, only fully mature artists can know about the great *quality* of those notes. And this is why it is very easy to give a poor performance of Mozart and hard to give a good one.

It is also much easier to be technically and emotionally convincing while playing a huge Romantic work than a transparent classical one. A "complete" musical performance of Mozart not only demands an understanding of the form and the genre, but also the context of the piece within the period of his short life, and—to the best of our ability— the sense and character behind the notes. Mozart often omitted dynamic markings, phrasing, and articulation, so we have to make many artistic decisions and judgments about interpretation. This is, for me, the most delightful and fulfilling work of all. But many students buy editions that are loaded with editorial suggestions, not at all those of the composer, and they are taken as gospel by the pianist. I cannot say how often I have disagreed vehemently with the editors of some of these publications on phrasing and even fingering.

Some pianists think that Mozart requires less physicality than other composers. But in fact, the opposite is true. As pianists, we must use *all* of our faculties—fingers and arms and entire bodies; ears, eyes, brain, and heart—to achieve the perfect balance that one needs to perform his music. As a matter of fact, some of the worst Mozart players are pianists who have been praised for having excellent fingers, but for whom playing Mozart stops at their fingers.

And speaking of the whole body, in Mozart, in fact, the gestures at the start and completion of each phrase become almost like a subtle, graceful dance when you are playing. The scales and passagework have to sound as natural and fluid as speech. I taught an eight-year-old student named Julie who could be the exemplar for all of us—a lithesome and responsive little person at the piano. When she "entered" a piece of music, or even a new phrase, just as she began the opening bar, she gathered up her entire small body and, with a very subtle arabesque-like gesture, gracefully swung into the music. No one taught her that. It was her own intuitive way of anticipating and participating physically, fully, with the music. And it was beautiful to witness, because it was genuine. Trying to get an adult student freed up like that is a real challenge. You want to get their bodies flexible and responsive while preserving the crisp energy in the hands and fingers.

I have many fine and musical adult students, but an excellent Mozart player is rare. One in particular, Chris, has been able to preserve the purity of a child while playing with great depth of understanding and the ability to stay free of physical tension and self-consciousness; he plays Mozart with his whole self.

For excellent Mozart playing, a complete technical mastery of the full range of color and possibilities of the piano itself is necessary. And the spectrum is a universe! At the same time, we must be considering the possibilities of the piano Mozart himself was writing for so that we don't get carried away with the possibilities of the modern piano.

Mozart composed just at the moment when the pianos were developing: Bartolomeo Cristofori invented the pianoforte around 1710. The fact that this piano could produce *piano*s and *forte*s and express a much wider range of emotions was a major historic event in the history of piano composition and performance. But it still had its limitations. In his private moments, Mozart used a clavichord that was capable of vibrato—he loved that kind of oscillating effect (called a *Bebung*), just as he loved the glass harmonica, with its unique resonating effects. All of these factors figure into how one uses the modern piano for Mozart.

One of the most important truths I have discovered for myself (in *all* music), is that the clearer our musical goals are, the clearer the technical means become to achieving those goals. What I mean is that Mozart conceived his artistic ideas simultaneously with the technical aspects. Picture the composer at his piano at the moment of conception of a lovely Rondo movement as he plays it for himself. His hands shape themselves in a natural expressive way around the notes of his phrases. And there is an uncanny way that the music can be *hand*led in rational groups of fingers, just as it was composed. Mozart was a great pianist, and thus his music was extremely pianistic, which basically means comfortable and rational for the hands on the keyboard. What we must do is cup our hands over the composer's and tread the same paths.

The technique has no meaning independent of the music, yet many pianists work independently on technique—speed, evenness, virtuosity—without trying to reveal deeper meanings. A fine technique is a prerequisite, to be sure, but as someone once said, it is merely the handmaiden to the music and at the service of the imagination. As mentioned earlier, without imagination there is just facility.

You need imagination, for example, in a Rondo, where the melody returns several times and you have to find a different inflection, a different coloration, a different philosophical take each time. Just the very fact that it has occurred before makes it different. The Rondo in D Major K. 485 is a bright and energetic work, very Haydnesque and a bit different from most Rondos, which have the returning main theme in the same key as its first statement. In this piece, Mozart's main theme is presented in many keys, in both hands. It is not at all a student piece, as it requires equal facility in both hands. I love the genre of the Rondo, with its happy returns, a certain kind of reassurance and comfort in the reappearance of the theme, and the challenge of changing the theme in various subtle ways to justify the repetition; and I love the jolly spirit behind this composition.

Haydn, who was not at all the pianist that Mozart was, wept when he heard the refinement and beauty of Mozart's playing, and Clementi, who *was* a great pianist, felt that Mozart had achieved the highest level of perfection in his playing. And thus it follows that a great pianist-composer would write beautifully for the pianist's hands on the keys and create music that is a pleasure to play.

When we are dealing with a Mozart masterpiece, we have to first realize that we are dealing with the thoughts, feelings, and ideas of the highest level of human spirit and creativity. It is a form of literature—*music* literature. Playing the notes correctly is just scratching the surface, even though the pressure is considerable to play "perfectly" in Mozart, as each note is so inevitable and exposed that even a child could discern an error. It may sound simple and pure, but it is highly complex and precious, and it demands the greatest efforts from us in return.

The painter Paul Klee, who was also a violinist, called Mozart's "Jupiter" Symphony "the highest attainment in all of Art."

In Europe classical music is part of the culture, and every artist from any European country I have ever spoken to grew up hearing it around them. One of the great tragedies to me is an insidiously increasing loss of culture in our schools. I think we all have to be trained and nurtured, from the earliest years, in the perception of greatness. For that reason, when I teach young musicians, I believe in using only great works, albeit smaller ones, of Bach, Mozart, Beethoven, Schumann, and so on, instead of second-rate stuff or simply technical studies, because these smaller works are microcosms, containing the same elements that make the larger works great.

Rudolf Firkušný, the great Czech pianist, had a special affinity for Mozart. In an interview (*Clavier*, February 1984), he told me that his instincts and love for Mozart evolved from what he referred to as a Middle European tradition.

> My great idol is Mozart. In Czechoslovakia, there was always a cult devoted to Mozart, and I was nursed on it along with Czech music. The Czechs adored Mozart, and Mozart, in turn, loved Prague. He used Czech motifs here and there in his music. . . . I think Mozart was happiest in Prague, because there he felt that the appreciation of his music was genuine. He was understood not only in musical circles, but by the people.

On the subject of Mozart on authentic versus modern instruments, Firkušný told me that he concluded that Mozart would have loved our modern piano.

> Both ways are right, but Mozart didn't really like the harpsichord, even though he composed for it in his early years. He was so delighted when he started to use the Stein piano, that he wrote enthusiastic letters about the piano's "new possibilities."

Sight-reading Mozart, for some, is quite easy. Excellent sight-readers used to be called "past masters," implying preknowledge and intuition, even anticipation. And even though these readings might be clean and accurate and fluent, they are often bereft of meaning. In order to get close to the meaning of music, we have to play it many times and slowly but surely peel off layers, like an onion, until we get to the core of truth at the center. Sometimes new revelations might occur in the eleventh hour right before a concert!

I learned a most valuable lesson from the great pianist Radu Lupu in a phone conversation about the Mozart Piano Concerto in A Major, K. 488. We were discussing phrasings when out of the blue he asked me whether I was practicing the second movement. I am embarrassed to admit that I told him I was not practicing it often, because I didn't want to "deflower" the beauty and run out of inspiration.

Lupu responded with a scolding voice, "But you must practice being inspired!" And now I realize that his words were a million-dollar admonition: inspiration is like another muscle that has to be exercised. I always took it for granted in myself, but I now realize that one cannot always just turn on the juices of inspiration and imagination. Those faculties come from a special, different source within ourselves that we need to know how to activate. This is a lesson I share frequently with my students.

We have to work to develop imagination in our students—by use of metaphor, and by relating musical episodes in the music to life experience. We must also demonstrate—not just one single way a phrase can be interpreted, as though we would clone our students, but by offering several alternatives, to illustrate the wide swath of possibilities.

Mozart actually makes this process rather accessible in his piano music—because as I mentioned before, his piano music is operatic. It is theater. He gives us characters, characterizations, even caricatures. And we have to put on stage makeup, so to speak, and project those personae.

There have been times when I have spontaneously "staged" a miniature one-person opera, taking on various roles represented by the different themes and even fitting in appropriate verbal dialogue to the music in order to accentuate a point—in a piano sonata, or in a set of variations. Amazingly, no student has ever run out of my studio after such a demonstration!

Mozart's letters reflect that he was a great observer of human nature. But how do we bring these characterizations to life? Many people think that the artist or performer has to be self*less*—self-negating in the service of the music. But the opposite is true! Only by unlocking or unfolding oneself to find our own inner grace—or passion, or fire, or humor, or buffoonery, or melancholy, or tenderness—can we do the masterwork justice. The freshest and best performances are created from the marriage between the artist's own vision and that of the master.

Striving for a rich cantabile has to be one of our highest goals for playing Mozart, just as it has to be for Romantic composers such as Chopin. In many ways Chopin was the inheritor of Mozart's fluid writing and vocal melodies on the piano, just as he was an inheritor of Bach's contrapuntal style. And cantabile is essential to all three composers.

One of the ways we can tell Mozart from Haydn is that all Mozart's lines are vocal—highly singable. Someone once described cantabile as the cartilage connecting two tones. We create this largely by using a finger legato—a sort of overlapping of the fingers for a continuity of sound, with sparing use of the pedal. In this case, the pedal is actually used more to create different colors than it is to sustain. But it should be used in Mozart, despite beliefs to the contrary. Mozart's piano had a pedal. Some of those instruments had the pedal near the right knee, like an old-fashioned treadle sewing machine. But many pianos of Mozart's day did not have dampers to shut the strings off from vibrating.

Without the pedal, we would deprive ourselves of the resonance of the old salons and halls. But we have to learn how to use shallower pedaling—demi, even quarter pedaling. It is like an amputation to play without the pedals. But discretion is the key word.

Alfred Brendel told me (*Clavier*, April 1989):

> In Mozart, I use the pedal as it comes into my mind in order to produce certain effects, but I certainly do not sit down like Gieseking did, and try to avoid the pedal entirely in Mozart. Mozart had knee-pedals on his pianos that worked very well: also, in those pianos, there was sometimes a different kind of resonance than in ours.

In a very interesting exchange with András Schiff (*Clavier*, October 1995), he described a chance to play Mozart's piano and even to make

some recordings on authentic instruments. Generally he is not an
advocate of playing fortepianos, but these were "different."

I jumped at the opportunity to play Mozart's instrument because
the idea was so moving. If the piano had not been in such beautiful
condition, I would not have recorded with it. It is difficult to play on
a fortepiano, but my relatively small hands helped; that which dis-
qualifies me from playing the Rachmaninoff Third Piano Concerto,
or the Liszt pieces, gave me an advantage here. A Rachmaninoff
pianist could not play on the keys of a fortepiano, which are narrow
and short, with a light, even action, which exposes every inequality.
The artist has to be careful, and the adjustment is delicate; at first
the instrument seems to have a very small sound, but after becoming attuned to it, you realize its fantastic range. Mozart was a practical composer who wrote exactly for the expressive and physical
range of this instrument. (For Beethoven nothing was big enough;
for Mozart, it was plenty.) Possibly the sound would not have been
enough for the concertos, but I did not try that. We recorded in a
small room; for the quartets and trios, we used a tiny concert hall
that seated about 100 people, and it was a wonderful experience.

For the Fantasy in c minor that precedes the sonata, I had the
distinct sensation of going from the bottom of the keyboard with
the bass C, to the top of the keyboard, which is F, the last note,
whereas the modern piano still has the remaining two and a half
octaves above the F. It is impossible to use the full range of the
modern piano; the performer has to hold back, especially with a
violinist, because the modern piano is always too loud.

Schiff added an important last point:

You cannot please everyone. If you play Mozart on a Bösendorfer
or a Steinway, some will criticize you for playing it on the wrong

instrument. Then if you play on Mozart's own pianos, others will say, "Well that's all very well, but he is not someone who should be playing that early instrument. He is not a specialist." Of course the [fortepianist is] not a specialist. He needs a different touch than on a modern piano; but you either have a sense of touch, or you don't. I have heard some strange things from those so-called fortepianists, including terribly mannered and chopped up performances. The artist has to have clear articulation along with a sense of tempo and flow and rhythm, especially in Mozart.

About Rubinstein's oft-quoted quip about Mozart being best played by the very young or very old—well, in between, it is very hard. Children play his music most beautifully with their innocence. Let's not forget that Mozart never got to be very old. He was a little supernatural in the sense of his maturity. He achieved the maturity at age 30, that others do not achieve at age 100.

Speaking with a fortepianist, as I did, shed important light on the instrument for which Mozart wrote and was very informative for a pianist who wants to fully understand the realities of playing Mozart on the modern piano.

Steven Lubin is well-known as a fortepiano specialist who has also combined Romantic piano repertoire on one program along with Classical on the fortepiano. Other early instrumentalists, such as Igor Kipnis, chose to stay with the fortepiano because the physical differences between the instruments made switching back and forth too difficult. A pianist's first encounter with the fortepiano can certainly be disorienting. Visually, the reversal of black and white keys is the most immediate; tactilely, the dip or depth of each key is much shallower. The key widths, and hence the octave lengths, are several millimeters shorter. The keyboard has five octaves instead of eight, so that centering on middle C takes a bit of consideration. In addition, the pianist might have to prop his leg in order to reach the treadle-like pedal with his knee.

The treble notes of clotted chords are not nearly as penetrating, yet the instrument gives more volume than a pianist would expect.

Said Lubin (*Clavier*, November 1988):

> The fortepiano also offers much more tonal control than a modern pianist might think, albeit within a smaller range. You learn to think a little smaller, but your approach is basically the same except that you create the illusion of continuity through rhythm, accents, and agogic devices. Because the fortepiano has less sustaining power, legato is more difficult. On the other hand, more silences suffuse the sound and give refreshing relief.

Among the myths we have to shatter, like the very porcelain of the metaphor itself, is that Mozart was a "porcelainlike" composer of delicate, music box–type music. His music is as expressive, sensuous, and varied in emotional content as any, and we have to pull out all the stops to play it as dramatically as it requires. He was a musical dramatist.

Leon Fleisher (*Clavier*, October 1986) spoke about the subject of ego and self-doubts in our students in playing the great composers:

> Very often the teacher has to remind the student that although Mozart and Beethoven were great composers, they were also human beings. What they experienced, all of us are capable of experiencing and communicating. I have to remind students not to be so much in awe—the great composers were people who got angry, crazy, wild—and their humanity ought to be allowed to come out.

It is also very important to teach our students that there is never one right way or one style of interpreting Mozart (or any other composer). Some say Mozart is purely Apollonian—classical in nature, elegant, reserved, symmetrical; others consider him more Dionysian—romantic, colorful, ecstatic. But all of art has to contain both sides of the coin to be balanced, and it is always fascinating to compare one artist's interpretation to another. That's what brings a performance to life: that dynamic between the artist and the composer—so long as it all falls within tasteful bounds. Mozart's music is flexible enough to allow for many different inflections and readings.

Another myth we have to dismantle is the sense of Mozart as pure graciousness and goodness—all sweetness, joy, and light. Mozart's music can express bitterness; he can be raucous, disturbing, even defiant. Mozart liked to gamble; he was known to say and write scatological words and thoughts, to be silly, and to try to break down conventions with nonsense and banal actions. So his music is filled with sudden surprises, patter, subtle humor, bawdy humor. If we want to define an overriding value or quality of Mozart, maybe it is not sweetness so much as purity, combined with cordiality, refinement, and balance.

Radu Lupu once said that when he studies great works by Mozart or Beethoven, in order to fully understand them he first *de*composes the music—in order to then *re*compose it. He looks for the various details—the polyphonic elements (the thematic material), the harmonies, the transitions, the phrase lengths, the accompanying figures (wherein there are often much more than just accompaniment)—he picks it apart to see what it's made of. In Mozart every detail has a reason—no note is redundant or superfluous, and so we must leave no tone unturned! It is the most economical of all music.

A few words on the subject of tone quality. Tone is produced by a combination of perception and a complete understanding and intuition about the use of one's hands in different ways. A pianist cannot achieve a beautiful tone unless his or her ear can perceive the whole available range of tonal continuity—all the shades of colors between ff and pp— all the timbres (which are orchestral and imitate different instruments as well as the human voice), and the multiple ways of using the hand to achieve these sounds through touch—non-legato, staccato, portato (that is, separated and detached, which reveals the hammer quality of this percussion instrument)—never a dry or banging touch, but a certain refined particularity of the notes that enhance certain meanings, all the way to super-legato—produced by clinging to the keys.

Again, the pianist must be especially cautious about the *forte*s in Mozart. We always must keep in mind the small size and limitations of Mozart's piano, the halls, and the thinner textures of his music when compared to Brahms or Tschaikovsky. On the other hand, his conceptions were often huge—and the classical composers often dreamed of bigger instruments that could more fully express their ideas. So it is a balancing act, a test of judgment, and a matter of listening to oneself.

The pad of the finger is animate flesh—and the piano key is an obdurate, hard, inanimate object. The finger's strike has to permeate ivory and wood and felt and metal to connect with the source of sound—the vibrating string. That is perhaps the hardest thing about playing the piano: trying to stay connected to the source of the sound—not just for Mozart, but for everything we play.

The hand and wrist must be both pliant and firm—firm to transmit and accomplish the unerring heartbeat, pulse, and intention of the music, pliant to play cantabile and to shape the phrases. Again, in so many ways Mozart is the forerunner of Chopin—particularly in his surpassing melodiousness. We have to keep in mind, though, that most of those Mozart melodies are written in the second octave above middle C, and those tones from the thinner strings decay much more rapidly than the bass tones of the accompaniment. Another balancing act.

In recent years, reading as much material about Mozart as I could find, including his letters, I came across a rather silly one that boasted of how he reproduced a tone by bending over the keys and playing it with his nose! Well, as a matter of fact, Anton Rubinstein (and one of my teachers) once said, "I don't care *what* you use to produce it, but in the end it is the *sound* that counts." I mention this because there is a school of thought that one must never divide a passage between two hands if it is notated in one hand. This is another "musical fundamentalist" view.

It's the end result that is the ideal. And yes, fingering is essential! One of my teachers, Josef Fidelman (whose teacher was Heinrich Neuhaus), elevated fingering to an art. He was, and now I am, a stickler for putting fingering into the music, because fingering *consistently*— that is, practicing it each time with the very same fingers—is the only route to fluency, evenness, and security. Using random fingers every time you sit down to play is not practicing—and it leaves everything to chance.

Peter Frankl is a superb Mozart player: expressive and not in the least self-conscious. His Mozart is energetic without being brittle, lyrical and playful without being precious. To watch him play a chamber work is to know that he is to the genre born. One evening he performed three Mozart concerti on the same program. Afterward, in an interview (*Clavier*, December 1991), Frankl said:

> Mozart is always demanding, not physically, but in concentrating to find the right character and atmosphere. The three concertos differ from each other and a lot has to do with their keys. The F major (K. 413) and the A major (K. 414) are much more gentle, while the C major (K. 415) is a majestic key for Mozart. He uses it in the "Jupiter" Symphony, the Concerto (K. 503), the triumphant ending of *Seraglio*, and *Così fan Tutte*.
>
> To interpret Mozart well, you have to be familiar with his entire output, particularly the operas: the characterizations, the dark side of the drama, the singers' breathing, which for pianists becomes the phrasing. I agree with the observation Horowitz made, shortly before his death—that practically all music since Bach, is romantic, because it expresses feelings.

But I would include Bach.

Frankl continued:

> Horowitz may often have been too free in his interpretations, but
> he had a genuinely likeable and innocent approach. I wouldn't
> model my Mozart on his, but I prefer the freedom of his approach
> to, for example, the rigidity of Richter's Mozart. Usually I am
> rather outgoing in Mozart.

I heard Frankl play the Mozart Concerto in C Major, K. 415, with a
string quartet. One problem for the pianist in this project was creating
the sense of fullness and majesty of this concerto without the orchestra.

> Mozart often played these concertos with a quartet, and he wrote
> in the words "ad libitum winds." You really cannot do without
> some of those magical wind entrances. The vast majority of the
> time when the pianist is playing, the orchestral accompaniment is
> only strings; in K. 415, timpani and brass play only in the *tutti*. In
> Mozart's day and sometimes today, in *f* passages the soloist adds
> support and even imitates the trumpet, the two oboes, or other
> winds. I [will] do that too.

Frankl's recipe produced an entirely satisfying sound.

There is a dangerous opportunity and temptation—and a wonderful,
seductive challenge—for the more creative pianist to try to improvise
a cadenza at the points where Mozart writes a fermata and everything
is on hold so that the soloist (whether in a sonata or in a concerto) can
show off a certain virtuosity and inventiveness in passages that are
derived from the text but are altered, embellished and varied in any way
the artist chooses. And I have heard some really way-out cadenzas!

Alfred Brendel, whose Mozart playing has a wonderful propulsive
energy, cautions against trying to be spontaneous as Mozart could
be on the spot. Rather, he suggests planning ahead and writing down

ideas to avoid spoiling the perfection of the music. Most of the time Mozart wrote in his exact embellishments and cadenzas, because he didn't trust any other pianist to embellish his music. But some of his later works he left unfinished, unadorned, and many pianists overdo the embellishments. Brendel laments those types of pianists, calling them "villains" and likening the resulting music to "overcluttered" rooms. He reminds us that Mozart has restraint, and that's one of the reasons his music is so elegant. It's great advice.

This is the anomaly: the pianist has to approach Mozart with both confidence (to produce the sound of ego and the certainty that commands the ear of the listener) and self-questioning and humility.

Some of my greatest joys in music have been the opportunities I have had to perform concertos, especially when I can feel a chamber-music rapport with the orchestral musicians. That kind of deep pleasure reaches its pinnacle in Mozart, and I felt like a child in a gumdrop shop while considering all my wonderful concerto choices. I selected K. 488, rolled up my sleeves, and set to the task of making the concerto my own. Having taught this piece many times, I was intimately familiar with the score and fully confident technically; but there is an elevated state that transcends mere excellence of execution, a state that evolves from one's own life experience and synthesizes with the music, along with a sense of humility and wonder that any mortal should have left us such a legacy.

I have heard some exceptional young musicians play this same concerto with every note and detail in place, and even with grace and a natural sense of phrasing. But this is a late work (at least in the context of Mozart's tragically short life), and I believe it benefits from the perspective of having lived a long life. Perhaps I never will achieve the enviably carefree and unpolluted purity exhibited in a gifted youngster's playing, but I found that the longer I spent with this masterpiece and the deeper I probed, the closer I felt I was coming to the core of the work—and myself.

Despite the many strictures and conventions associated with Mozart performance, from the moment of the piano's first entrance there are many ways the pianist can personalize the performance. Mozart was somewhat lax here in notating details, and so through phrasing, nuances of articulation and touch, gradations of dynamics, even a few added embellishments, the pianist enters the high realm of creativity. Of utmost importance is the *heartbeat*—the energy and living spirit of the music conveying the basic message, which, in the case of K. 488, seems to be joy's triumph over sorrow.

Mozart's piano music can best be understood through his operatic writing. In fact he was at work on *The Marriage of Figaro* while writing this concerto. The elements of comedy and tragedy, characters, and above all singing and speaking lines are evident in the voicing and phrasing of the solo piano part.

Yet it is in the cadenza that the soloist may take the reins and fly off into fancy, alighting into a realm of unabashed and full-hearted self-expression. Cadenzas are made of "flourishes, inventions, and the execution of spontaneous and elaborately decorative passages," according to *The Oxford Companion to Music.*

Mozart wrote a perfectly fine cadenza for this work. Mozart and Beethoven, who were two of the greatest improvisers of all time, did their best to quell others' attempts to improvise cadenzas to their concertos because they didn't trust anyone else with their own music; hence, they wrote their own cadenzas, often offering several choices to the pianist to ensure their high quality.

One day while working on the cadenza that Mozart wrote right into the score, I came to the trill in bar 25 and, I suppose being thoroughly infected by the high spirits of the work, proceeded to improvise an extension to the cadenza to prolong the unbridled joy of it all, which is so short-lived and then gone forever. At that moment I grabbed a pen and started jotting down some of my ideas on paper. Composing has never been one of my primal urges; in fact, the only writing I have ever done was for composition courses as a music major in college. Suddenly all these references to the thematic material presented by Mozart in the body of the work were occurring to me and recorded in fragments— some harmonically skewed, some playful, some reverential—and I began to piece them together. In the end I had a page of writing that seemed to jell. I thought I would like to append it to the Mozart cadenza at the right-hand trill in bar 25. So I began to practice the composite cadenza, and although it pleased me, I was plagued with my historic self-doubts: God forbid that it be interpreted as an arrogant suggestion that my own humble efforts deserved to be hyphenated onto the master's own. Did the fact that Mozart wrote out the entire cadenza within the movement itself suggest his intention that it remain inviolable?

Yet, I reminded myself to consider the violinist Nigel Kennedy's cadenza to the Beethoven Violin Concerto, which starts off conventionally enough and soon takes off on a trip into the twilight zone. When I heard it many years ago, I applauded its originality and the notion that the cadenza be an expression of the artist's own impulses and responses to the work.

Does the fact that Mozart wrote his own cadenza mean we are duty bound to play it centuries later? I did not think so. Improvisation is a corollary of imagination, and after the conventions and strictures to which we reverentially adhere during the work itself, I felt a strong urge to allow my imagination to "fly the coop."

These were my spontaneous responses, and so I took one step closer to a decision and taped my page into the music. Several weeks before the concert I decided to play the cadenza for musicians I respect. Their overwhelming consensus was, "Do it!"

Because of my work at *Clavier*, I felt comfortable to send copies of the page I was adding on to André Watts and Radu Lupu. Watts encouraged me to do my own thing, and when Lupu called from Switzerland we had a protracted discussion on details of phrasing and dynamics. Finally we got to the cadenza. His take was that I either play the Mozart cadenza as is or write one entirely my own instead of appending my writing to Mozart's. I continued to consider the matter, grateful for the rare and wonderful coaching and advice.

In addition to my quandaries about the cadenza, I was presented with another challenge: the music director of the concert series informed me that they would not be hiring a conductor; I would be conducting from the piano, in the manner of Mozart and Beethoven, something I had never done. She assured me that the musicians would be highly professional. Although my initial response ranged from panic to fascination, after acquiring the orchestral score and trying to analyze Mozart's decisions about orchestration, along with the operatic interplay between all the instruments, I was brought into a new realm of study that cast further light upon my interpretation of the solo piano part.

I had already memorized the three movements, but when I found out that I would have to conduct, I made the decision to use the score— perhaps a miniature score, so that I could highlight with a red marker the important cues I would have to give to the orchestra. I practiced the nodding and prodding to imaginary musicians, and I hoped the live ones would be as responsive as those I fantasized were.

But the issue of which cadenza to play continued to confound me. I definitely felt the original Mozart cadenza to be too short but was deeply affected by Radu Lupu's advice and ruled out adding my page onto the Mozart.

Another choice might have been to play the Busoni cadenza, which was sent to me by a friend; but I found it to be too florid and out of character. In fact, I ruled out playing *anyone* else's cadenza: once I decided that it would be permissible to substitute another cadenza for Mozart's, I decided to expand on my own sections. After some good hard work, I came up with two good pages that were not only longer, but more fun to play than the existing single Mozart page. I had the overwhelming sense of paying my own homage to the score all the time I was working on it.

No sooner had I written my cadenza and begun to feel comfortable about using it (not without the considerable inner struggle of ego versus repression of ego), I bumped into a friend who is quite a famous pianist backstage at Carnegie Hall. He chanced to ask me whether I had any concerts coming up, and I mentioned the Mozart concerto engagement, which was a couple of weeks away. Then I decided to ask him what he thought of my decision to substitute my own cadenza for the Mozart. He stepped away from me in abject horror, as though I had suddenly come down with the plague, exclaiming, "You can't do that! It is written right into the score! I'm sorry you told me you were going to do that!"

A few more days filled with self-questioning followed until I related the incident to my friend Jerry Lowenthal. "Nonsense!" he assured me. "You can play any cadenza you want. That remark is the voice of musical fundamentalism, a purist faction that adheres strictly to the rules. Play your own!"

David Dubal cautioned me against becoming too awestruck, also encouraging me to follow my instinct and inspiration. And so I played my own cadenza, happily, but with a twinge of regret for the lost Mozart bars: my own ideal would have been to add my own page to the existing cadenza.

Several weeks after the concert, I was speaking to another pianist friend, Paul Schenly, the director of the Cleveland Institute of Music's piano department. I thought he would get a kick out of the discussions about the Mozart cadenza, and out of curiosity, I asked him his opinion.

> Since you are asking me my opinion on a subject where my good friends and colleagues have differing opinions, let me say (with an ear for politics) that of course you are *all* correct. Seriously, let me say that I think I could imagine Mozart viewing the situation in the following way: he would have wanted a cadenza to reflect the context of a performance (technical resources, number of

players, and so on), and I am sure those considerations still hold true two hundred years later. Coincidentally, earlier this year I met Charles Rosen at a flea market, and we went over to a piano and spent the morning together talking about Mozart and Beethoven. He mentioned that he was performing the A major concerto K. 488 himself, and asked me if I didn't think the cadenza was too short—that he was thinking of adding some measures of his own! So there is yet another vote for your point of view.

Rosen was adding his own bars to Mozart's cadenza! How I wished that I had had that conversation with Paul before my concert. Charles Rosen, the distinguished pianist and scholar, corroborating my own instincts, would have given me just the fodder and courage I needed, to do what I had truly wanted to do.

If this tale proves that there is there really is no right and wrong to matters of cadenzas, that same rule might be applied to the kinds of trills we must use. I have many recordings of the same sonatas on which one can hear a variety of world-famous pianists embellishing the same notes in different ways. So I have come to feel that this is one of the ways the pianist can and should express individuality without fear of breaking with the conventions of the times. There is, however, a vague boundary between the eighteenth and nineteenth centuries, and a weak rule that trills were started on the upper note before the turn of the nineteenth century and on the main note thereafter. This rule has been broken as often as adhered to.

I will add that Mozart was very critical of inaccuracies and a lack of good taste in ornamentation. It falls to us to determine what is good or bad taste.

Yet another myth about playing Mozart concerns the tempo. It is definitely true that the best Mozart players can feel and project that unerring inner beat in the music, which yields a driving energetic force that really engages the listener and is very infectious. However, Mozart used rubato in his own playing—he even wrote a letter about it to his father. Rubato, of course, means an ebb and flow, literally "robbing" time—speeding up a bit if the music intensifies, pulling back to equalize it. It is usually achieved by having a stable steady left hand, with a more expressive and meandering right hand. It has to be very, very subtle, but it is definitely a part of Mozart's Andante and Adagio movements.

Mozart cautioned the pianist not to play too fast, which would end in sloppiness, and he was unhappy with audiences who listened for velocity and virtuosity rather than musical value. He advised the pianist to have what he called "quiet hands—supple and light for fluidity." He was insistent on evenness, even in rubato. (I read the curious fact that Mozart, when at rest and not at the piano, constantly drummed his fingers—anything *but* "quiet hands." Perhaps he was in the process of composing his next piano piece.)

I have mentioned the operatic nature of Mozart's writing; but it is also sometimes symphonic, conceived with the orchestra in mind. For example, the Piano Sonata K. 309 is a composition that reflects both operatic and symphonic influences. It was written when he was in Mannheim in 1777, and there are strong orchestral elements and instrumental phrasings. While there Mozart met with the piano builder Johann Andreas Stein, with whom he enthusiastically discussed greater possibilities for the range of the pianoforte. So this sonata has several influences—orchestral influences along with his usual operatic effects, resulting in quite stark mood changes from the very beginning of the work. The opening theme is very heroic and is followed by a sweet and tender response, with stark contrasts in dynamics. There is also an intensification of texture and passages that seems to imitate instrumental effects, with rolled octaves and reinforcing chords.

Mozart warned that the Andante should be played full of expression, as it was a "portrait" of one of his pupils, Rosa, the daughter of Mannheim's *Kapellmeister*, Christian Cannabich. The Rondo is one of the purest expressions in this genre. It combines its simple and delightful theme with undulating and extended florid triplet passages and some of his rare *fortissimo* tremolo passages, all quite strangely juxtaposed between the returning Rondo theme. But in the end, the movement winds down with a coda disappearing into the ether.

The Sonata in B-flat Major, K. 570, is in many ways like a string quartet. You can hear the cello's eighth notes bumping along, and the upper voice like the first violin part, and then the two inner voices. It was written in 1789 and was entered into his journal as "a sonata for keyboard alone," but as I suggested, it seems to me more like chamber music. There are the four string voices, with some puzzling questions about phrasing and articulation; also there are differences between the several editions and the bits of the original manuscript that have survived. And there are no dynamic markings in the last two movements, which, of course, gives more artistic freedom to the pianist while at the same time presenting one of the challenges: to be discreet and tasteful with all artistic decisions. The second movement is one of the few Adagio movements within his sonatas; most of his second movements were Andantes. This movement has long, legato melodic lines that form a strong contrast with the final Rondo movement, with its crisp and lively rhythmic figures.

The Sonata in D Major, K. 576, also written in 1789, was Mozart's last contribution to keyboard music. His difficult contrapuntal writing, using the bouncy opening "hunt" motif, keeps the unrelenting pace and spirit of the movement in 6/8 time throughout. This may be his most difficult piano sonata, but the pleasures of this sparkling writing far outweigh the challenges.

Mozart's latest works contained an obvious shift from the music he wrote and admitted were written for the pleasure of the listener to an introspection and wish to write for himself.

One of the two remaining works I included in the "Composer's Landscape" series is the Six Variations on an Allegretto Theme in F Major, K. 547, with its elegant and circuitous theme, taken from a violin sonata; there is an added variation for the piano solo version, the last one, which is like a piano obbligato—very florid, and enormously satisfying to play. This is my own favorite set of variations by Mozart (included on the CD accompanying this volume). Some of the sets of variations were written for his students; others, often improvised, were for himself. Whereas they do not exhibit Mozart's wonderful talent for inventing themes (they have only one theme, after all!), they do demonstrate his limitless creative ideas on how to embellish or vary the theme.

The Theme and Variations on a Menuet by Duport in D, K. 573, is probably one of his two most famous of sets of variations (along with the Variations on "Ah, vous dirai-je maman"). The Duport set was also written in 1789, apparently while Mozart was in Potsdam, and possibly first improvised in front of King Wilhelm Friedrich II. Earliest accounts had Mozart playing only six variations and adding three more later, and apparently there was some sort of rivalry between Mozart and Duport, from whose sonata for cello and bass the theme was taken. (In Duport's work there were only four simple variations on a menuet theme.) This is a charming work and one I have never tired of teaching, as each variation is like a little etude with various pianistic challenges.

Different techniques are required for different kinds of music. Many concert pianists can tackle and accomplish a huge Liszt paraphrase, but they cannot fully and convincingly interpret a Mozart sonata. I agree with Alfred Brendel (who can do both) that the technique needed to control Mozart's transparent textures actually demands greater mastery, and the sonatas are much more difficult than the concertos.

Mozart wrote lots of letters to his father from the road, but not so much is known about the inspiration and ideas behind Mozart's latest works, as Leopold Mozart, who had been the chronicler of Mozart's career and work, died in 1787, four years before Mozart's own death at the age of thirty-five. Mozart once wrote his father that not a day went by that he didn't think about his own death, and that he had come to a point where he was not at all terrified by the notion, but rather, calmed by it—that he was not at all morose, but contented and blissful. How prophetic of him to write that, when we think how abbreviated his life was.

The great conductor Bruno Walter explains that these thoughts prove how close Mozart's heart was to eternity—that it explains the unearthly beauty of his harmonies and melodies. It may also explain the fact that Mozart composed entire symphonies in his head without jotting a single note down on paper—and then out it all came, perfectly, like a printing machine on delay. He hardly ever had to change a note. You see the scribbled manuscripts of other great composers like Beethoven, with angry crossings-out and blots. Not so the manuscripts of Mozart; they are pure and pristine and perfect. That fact is one of the reasons some scholars and musicians have mused that he might have had a straight connective wire from Heaven.

Mozart has moved all those who love his music to find ways of expressing the extent of their admiration. A dear old Hungarian friend of mine, confined to bed in the last year of his long life, had a pile of CDs next to his bed. During a visit I asked him what he was listening to, and his reply was, "I do not have time for anything else but Mozart."

The painter Renoir said that two "proofs" of true art are (1) that it is inimitable and (2) that it is ineffable. Yet in spite of its being indescribable in words, sometimes we try, as I am doing, to understand what we feel by writing about it; when we play, our goal is to get *beyond* words.

But the greatest difficulty in playing Mozart comes from the awareness that we can never get to the level of greatness as the music itself, no matter how hard we try.

Ludwig van Beethoven, Piano Sonata in A-flat Major, Opus 110; autograph manuscript, first page of the last movement, Adagio ma non troppo. Beethoven-Haus, Bonn, Germany, Collection H. C. Bodmer.

3

BEETHOVEN (1770–1827)

Beethoven is, for me, the most *human* of all the composers, which should make him the most accessible to write about; and yet, again, as it is with any music of genius, words are rendered nearly inadequate.

Alfred Brendel once wrote me in a letter that if he felt, as I obviously did, that writing about music is almost a folly, he would never have written as much as he has about it. But, he continued, some of us write to examine what the music means to us, personally, what it seems to express, how best to find the means within us to express it; and others like him—more scholarly and intellectual (although he did not put it that way)—analyze the form and the methods of composition to try thereby to gain insights into the meaning.

But then there was Schumann, the music journalist, playing the devil's advocate in his reviews: "The music critic's [journalist's] noblest destiny is to make himself superfluous! The best way to talk about music is to be quiet about it!"

For whatever purpose, however the means, and for anyone who ever contemplated Beethoven's legacy, it is like contemplating the universe; the gratitude his music arouses makes one want to try to embrace and explain the phenomenon by writing about it, from any angle—however fruitless it might prove to be.

The best way to perform his music is to try to *become* him: experience his joys and sorrows, his utter pastoral peace, and his sudden explosive rages; wonder at his humanitarianism, his good and benevolent nature, his earthy humor; and at the same time understand his isolation and despair from his increasing deafness, read his heartbreaking Heiligenstadt Testament, feel his pain and misery, and forgive his occasional misanthropy—he once wrote, "I love a tree more than a man"—and just love him.

I have admitted before that once, in an outpouring of gratitude I experienced while overwhelmed and moved by his music, I wrote a letter to Beethoven. (I didn't mail it.) I know that it is not always a good idea to know too much about the personal life of a composer lest our response to the music become skewed. And yet we do want all the facts. It is strange that with certain composers—Wagner, for example—I am unwilling to forgive the mean nature and cannot help but subjectively project it onto my listening experience with the music.

With Beethoven we can forgive everything, because his abiding character traits, soaring above all the struggle and rage, are optimism and determination, generosity and an abundance of love; and that in itself explains Beethoven's eternal appeal. His anguish and triumph over such adversity as his deafness, and learning to draw from his inner ear to produce music that may have been even deeper than what he might have written had he not lost his hearing, is part of the inspiration. We all need those uplifting emotions in our own lives, and they stream to us directly from the music.

This is the same spirit in which we need to approach the performance of Beethoven: we need courage and fortitude when exploring his complex music. Even world-renowned artists have admitted to being confounded as to "the actual meaning" of Beethoven's late sonatas. It is the process of the search for meanings, the pilgrimage, that becomes the joyful work. It is not always possible, nor even necessary, to know what it "means." We must only know what the score "says," and do it. Every little mark is there for a reason.

Above all I love and am motivated by Beethoven's spiritual triumph over such hardship—not just what we know about the facts of his life, but what we hear and feel in his music. The more despondent and ill he became, the more defiantly productive he was. It is so moving to see it all recorded onto his manuscript paper—all those visceral signs and gestures, the soil, blots, and tears from frustrated crossings-out. The passion and temperament are so palpable, especially when viewed alongside the pristine manuscripts of Mozart and the almost obsessive neatness of Chopin's scores. The latter two composers seem to live in a more orderly world; at least, it all comes out that way. Beethoven's music feels as though he has created order out of the chaos of the world, something so valuable, philosophically and emotionally, for us all.

Alfred Brendel (*Clavier*, April 1989) once asserted:

Of course I am interested on the side: what kind of person was this composer? But I refuse to acknowledge that the music will, necessarily, give away the personality of the composer. Often it is not the case at all. It may be a completely different side of his nature that comes out in the work of art, maybe the opposite of how he appeared as a man, maybe something he needed in order to survive. Beethoven, for instance, seemed so chaotic in his handwriting and was surrounded by such squalor. Well, there is no squalor in his music. Sometimes there is the odd, careless, note; but an enormous sense of order was achieved, perhaps with a great deal of hardship and energy, but this is the most durable order one can imagine. It justifies itself all the time, and is just the opposite of certain personal problems the man might have had.

Looking at the manuscript pages of great composers and seeing the style of their notations can sometimes lend insights into their personalities and intentions, but these are extremely superficial conclusions. After viewing an exhibit of manuscripts, including some of Beethoven's, at the J. P. Morgan Library in New York City, I could only speculate about the parallels between the end product and the style of notation.

William S. Newman, in his fascinating book *Beethoven on Beethoven*, describes some deeper revelations: passages scribbled by Beethoven that reflect the intensity and the drive of the music—the stems slanting forward as the music intensifies and straightening up as the music diminishes, notes leaning left or right depending on dynamics or agogics. In other words, Beethoven, as Newman says, "not only recorded, but *experienced* his music as he wrote it down" (italics mine). This can absolutely be seen in the excerpts from the score that he offers in his text ("Appassionata," Opus 57, first movement, bars 9–10). A serious student of manuscripts might deduce much in matters of interpretation of this music, but who of us has the time or access to the archives to view these hallowed pages?

Mozart's pristine scores, with not a single blemish, might relate more to the manner of his initial conception of musical ideas, the unalterable and economical results, and his basic aesthetic. But such was not the case with Beethoven. Mozart always had in the back of his mind that he should never alarm or disgust his listeners with ugly sounds that offended the ear. This may or may not relate to the neatness of his scores. But Beethoven, the messy, impulsive, almost wild recorder of fragments of ideas for several works at once seemed to want to disturb, stir up, create controversy. Therefore, as pianists we should never shy away from his dissonances, nor should we try to smooth over the unconventional or perplexing elements of his music. (I recall that Radu Lupu once asked me ironically, "Why do you want to play the Beethoven 'beautifully'? Maybe the music requires an ugly sound, not always 'beautiful.' In fairness to myself, I think I used "beautiful" to mean "well-played.")

Mozart and Beethoven were different species of genius—one with a direct connection to what has been referred to as divine inspiration, the other towering as a monument to humanness, with all its frailties and possibilities.

Beethoven was supremely aware of the music and art of his contemporaries, even competitive; but he strove to surpass what was being
written by others, even telling an unruly negative audience, "I write
not for you, but for those who come after." Lucky for us, we came
after. There is an irony here, though: audiences in Beethoven's time
listened much more to contemporary music than to that of old masters,
far more so than audiences today. But Beethoven seems to have eventually grown past their understanding, and his late work perplexes us
even today.

Peter Serkin, who has always balanced his programs between
the modern and the classical literature and understands Beethoven's
relationship to his public, said to me (*Clavier*, November 1989):

> I think some of the Beethoven I play is much more difficult to
> listen to and get to the heart of than the new music I do. . . . Our
> relationship with classical music can become quite ossified; we
> can easily take it for granted. Everything has been recorded, and
> we can always hear a piece played somewhere before we work on
> it. With contemporary music, a work is delivered without any ref-
> erence point. You are on your own and are forced to work within
> yourself to get what the composer is after. That process can help
> you understand what it might have been like in Beethoven's time
> to encounter the score of Opus 106. Even his younger works were
> bold. That aspect of outrageousness was right there in the music
> and the mentality of Bach, Mozart, and Beethoven.
>
> I try to approach the classics with an open mind: without a ref-
> erence point, and at least initially, without much interest in how
> others have done it; just trying to relate to the notes and rhythms
> as I see them on the page. I try to be more casual and less com-
> pulsive about the practicing. I don't even like to use the word
> "practice" because it implies investing for the future . . . practic-
> ing *for* something. So I talk about playing some every day, and

I try to guard against the self-indulgence of saying, "I don't feel like playing today."

That week, for example, Serkin was performing the Beethoven Piano Concerto No. 2, which he had not done for twenty years.

So I try to start with scales, arpeggios, and trills, which I do quite dutifully: scales with different rhythms, articulations, fingerings, and so on. I don't even think of scales as purely technical; I try to make music with my scales. Then I get to the Beethoven concerto.

Radu Lupu is a great pianist who, however, never thinks of himself as a piano virtuoso. His ideas on preparing for a Beethoven concerto performance differ from Serkin's. He has eschewed practicing technique per se and has his own unusual methods of preparation—insisting, for example, that he may not necessarily practice the Beethoven concerto he is engaged to play, but rather Mozart.

It relaxes me and distracts me to play something I don't have to play, and it prevents me from getting stuck inside the music I do have to play.

The piano is a means by which I express the music that is inside of me. The important thing is to play. "Enjoy" is not the word, but to feel that I give something genuine of myself. Then I might be satisfied.

Lupu talks about conducting himself, about overseeing and balancing voices, and about listening. He has remained his own most critical listener and is severe in his self-assessment as a pianist, despite the respect and admiration of his peers and audiences worldwide.

It is cruelly ironic that Beethoven, as a great pianist and composer, did not experience some of the greatest innovations in piano construction in the nineteenth century. He was always asking piano manufacturers for sturdier instruments with a stronger action and tone. The most obvious explanation would be because of his deafness; but it is equally true that he required an instrument capable of withstanding his herculean energies and projecting his intense feelings.

Fortepianos were clearly inadequate for Beethoven's conceptions. The earlier instrument's sixty-three notes (five octaves + one whole step) were expanded to include especially more bass, which Beethoven utilized to the fullest, reveling in contrasts in registers and creating dramatic effects. The earlier instruments had certain advantages over the modern piano, however: much softer, sweeter *pianissimo*s, for one thing, resulting in greater dynamic contrast, a quality that I believe should be kept in mind at all times.

Beethoven got the Streicher company to produce a triple-strung piano with a shifting-action *una corda* pedal that became his favorite instrument; but still he was never entirely satisfied. Beethoven was, in fact, more experimental on the piano than any other classical composer, trying to squeeze superhuman effects out of it and exploiting its limits. Mozart's goal was to use the piano in an operatic sense, both dramatically and to imitate the human voice, whereas Beethoven tried to make of the piano an entire orchestra. And truly, we should try to utilize every last bit of possibility—the entire range—that a big, beautiful grand piano offers in playing Beethoven.

(Haydn and Schubert were always perfectly happy with their pianos, since they were not great pianists. They used the piano to express musical ideas that might have been just as well expressed on other instruments.)

Therefore eternal questions persist between musical fundamentalists (a term that describes those who refer back to old instruments and styles to remain faithful to the composer's realities) and those of us who wish to express and realize the master's visions and hopes and dreams on our modern instruments. But sometimes we run up against such issues as the shorter keyboard, which forced Beethoven to clip off an ascending octave passage into single notes, or to suddenly dip down an octave in the progression, rather than continuing upward, as we now can do. Each artist makes his or her own decision in those cases.

There are also technical matters, such as the octave glissando in the last movement of the "Waldstein" Sonata, which was quite possible on the shallower action of a fortepiano and utterly impossible on our modern pianos (unless we have indestructible cuticles).

Beethoven could play all the forty-eight Preludes and Fugues of Bach from the age of twelve; as strange as it may seem, Bach was not known, for the most part, so he must have borrowed manuscripts in order to learn them. Beethoven was becoming one of the finest pianists of his time. In Vienna of the 1790s Haydn and Mozart were practically national heroes, and young Beethoven distinguished himself with his unique and unconventional ways and self-assured performance style. The composer's first sortie before the public was in Prague in 1798 (when he was twenty-eight), with his virtuosic and grand Concerto in C Major, Opus 15 (which was, in actuality, the *third* concerto he had penned, after an early E-flat work and the B-flat Concerto, usually called No. 2).

Beethoven's debut was before an audience filled with the illustrious musicians of the time, including another great pianist named Václav Jan Tomášek, who recalled, "Beethoven's magnificent playing stirred me to the very depths of my soul; indeed, I found myself so profoundly bowed down that I did not touch my pianoforte for several days."

Beethoven was soon considered to be *the* premier pianist of his generation.

In those days, even the greatest pianist-composers used the scores in performance, even when playing their own works. I have written treatises about memorizing, and the fact that these great musicians played from the written music speaks to one of the most oft-repeated and self-righteous of criticisms: that anyone who uses the score in performance is not fully prepared or doesn't understand the music thoroughly. Sometimes, if these composer-pianists were conducting as well, they sat with their backs to the audience, facing the orchestra.

The pianoforte itself continued undergoing many changes and innovations so that Beethoven's chronic frustrations with the limitations of his earlier instruments were lessening. Although his favored piano in the earlier days was a Streicher (though about even that he had reservations), he praised the company for the fact that its instruments allowed him "to sing." He also had several other instruments: a smaller piano built by Érard and given to him as a gift, and a Steiner on which he composed. He kept demanding a new instrument from Streicher after determining that the French instruments had become "certainly quite useless" to him. In 1781 Broadwood produced a piano that equalized the tone quality and extended the keyboard to six octaves. In 1818 Beethoven received one with his name inscribed on it as a gift from the company.

Moscheles criticized the sound of the Broadwood as "broad, full, but muffled," but there was a sort of nationalistic competition between Viennese and English piano makers that may have played a role in pianists' reactions. Nevertheless, Beethoven's Broadwood piano had a prominent place in his last Viennese apartment.

(All of the lithographs and pictures of Beethoven's various instruments strike me as delicate and fragile when imagined beside the huge Steinway Ds or Bs or As on which we now play his music. This realization serves to remind me of the balance between knowing Beethoven's own reality and knowing what he envisioned and desired for future keyboard sonorities.)

The descriptions (mostly from Czerny, his most devoted pupil) of Beethoven's appearance and bearing when he played are touching and wonderful to read: "noble, quiet, beautiful, without grimace or affectation, instead increasingly beautiful the deafer he became. His fingers were powerful, not long, but broadened at the tips, and he apparently used more pedal than were indicated in his scores!"

Witnesses said that no one could play slow passages with more sustained beauty than Beethoven, nor did any pianist have better trills, double thirds, leaps, or smooth rapid passagework. Reports are that he had a magical effect upon his listeners. Legato was an all-important element in Beethoven's own playing, and he was critical of Mozart as having a "choppy, crisply disconnected style" of playing. It was just at the end of the eighteenth century, in fact, that the "touch of choice" shifted from the Baroque and Rococo detached touch to the new preferred touch of legato.

Staccato was reserved for particularly "spirited" musical passages. The shift to a more legato touch, of course, was largely related to the shift from harpsichord to piano, when words such as *cantabile* and *tenuto* started to appear as indications in piano music, especially in Beethoven's compositions. He had become the indisputable master of legato playing, quoted by Anton Schindler, a friend, as instructing that the hands be placed "over the keyboard in such a position that the fingers need not be raised any more than necessary. This is the only method by which the player can learn to generate tone . . . and to make the instrument sing."

The use of pedal and legato playing are very much linked, and Beethoven was the first composer to be quite concerned with the pedal as an integral element of piano playing. He indicated pedal marks liberally, but perhaps never so much so as in the Rondo movement of the "Waldstein" Sonata, in an eight-bar passage in which tonic and dominant harmonies are clashed together into a surprising blur of sound—another example of innovative effects initiated by the master with complete, unabashed clarity of intention. He risked the danger of being misunderstood by copyists as having made a careless oversight and omitting a pedal change—but there were no errors of notation here. Now, centuries later, we can marvel at the astonishing effect this long pedal creates.

Beethoven did also have an *una corda* pedal, which shifts the hammers to strike only one of three strings, thus, the common name "soft pedal." So he often wrote in the score *una corda, tre corde* (three strings), or *tutte le corde* (all strings).

But when he wrote *senza sordino* he did not mean without pedal—he meant without dampers (literally, without the mute), which meant *with* the right damper pedal, which raises the dampers off the strings and thus allows the strings to vibrate. Conversely, *con sordino* means with dampers—in other words, without pedal. This was all very confusing to me when I was young and learning the Third Piano Concerto in C Minor, with its frequent sordino markings.

With Beethoven's strange and lush sonorities on the piano, there was a new element of fullness that became almost Brahmsian even before there was a Brahms! It was a new dimension of depth in piano writing. And his music became more and more like a massive stone sculpture of Henry Moore than a delicate Alexander Calder wire sculpture.

Just as Beethoven's playing was becoming more powerful than the fragile pianos could endure, some accounts are that his public began to prefer the more *leggiero* playing of Johann Nepomuk Hummel; Schumann wrote that Hummel "adapted Mozart's style to the purpose and pleasures of the piano virtuoso." Schubert, in fact, dedicated his last three piano sonatas to Hummel, but as they were not published within his lifetime, the publishers ultimately changed the dedication to Schumann.

Beethoven was friends with Hummel, and they respected each other's playing. But with all his great success as a pianist, Beethoven's performing career ended in 1809 at around thirty-nine, not just because of his increasing deafness, but because of the near-loss of a finger from an accident; yet he continued to improvise on the piano and played occasional concerts, to mixed reviews. It is curious to note that when both Beethoven and Schumann had to stop their performing careers because of injuries to their hands, as much as a loss as that was, it was a blessing in disguise, because of all the resulting great piano music that subsequently came pouring from them.

Much great music can be considered musical chronicles of the composers' lives: Schumann's *Kreisleriana, Davidsbündlertänze, Carnaval,* and others, were autobiographical; Mozart's concertos and Beethoven's string quartets and piano sonatas were perhaps the most intimate and imaginative musical chronicles, not only for their personal travails and evolution but also for new and innovative musical ideas. Unfortunately, only fifteen out of the original thirty-two scores to Beethoven's piano sonatas survive.

Comparing the music of Mozart and Beethoven, one might conclude that you have to tread a narrower path in Mozart, with much more freedom in playing Beethoven—even though Beethoven was the first composer to give us exact instructions. For example, in Beethoven's time there were certain standard tempo indications (*tempi ordinari*)—Allegro, Andante, Presto, Adagio—that were closely related to the spirit of the piece and even which city you were performing in according to tradition and practice. But for Beethoven, matters of timing were of utmost importance. He wrote to a publisher about the restrictions of the *tempi ordinari*, complaining that "one must be free to respond to the call of unrestrained genius." "Adagio" was often not enough; he had to add "ma non troppo e molto espressivo." And it is very important to know the exact Italian translations, because, for example, there are many ways to say "slow" (Largo, Lento, Adagio, etc.) that are nonetheless philosophically different from one another. In Beethoven we read such directives as "espressivo," "un poco più adagio," "allegro ma non troppo," "Largo appassionata," or "Largo con gran espressione, sempre tenuto, sempre staccato," and so on. Beethoven eventually became frustrated using the Italian language and turned in his later works to his native German, in which he felt he could express himself more exactly and intimately. But whatever the language, you always know what he is thinking and feeling. He makes it known to us; he *wants* us to know.

(It is interesting that the indication Adagio was much more frequently indicated by Beethoven in his sonatas than by Mozart, who rarely varied the indication in his slow movements from Andante; there are far more Andante movements in Mozart than there are Adagios.)

For Beethoven, not only the timing was important, but also the ways in which the tempo related to the mood and spirit of the piece. Timing was important for Mozart as well; as he wrote to his father, "Time is the most essential, the most difficult and the chief requisite in music." But Beethoven was aware of how matters of timing related closely to expressive elements such as tone and articulation.

Claude Frank, the noted Beethoven interpreter and teacher, whom I had the privilege of talking to and ultimately being coached by, shared some views about tempo in Beethoven (*Clavier*, January 1983):

> Tempo is probably written and talked about more than any other aspect of music-making. When something goes wrong, the tempo is usually blamed. And this seems like over-simplification to me. Too many other things could be wrong, and tempo can often be more flexible than we are willing to admit. What further proof is needed, than the many composers who do not follow their own metronome markings?
>
> Speaking of metronomes, of the 32 Beethoven sonatas, only the Hammerklavier has original tempo markings. Even then, the story goes that Rubinstein was once taken to task for not following them, and someone asked, "Haven't you ever seen Beethoven's metronome markings?"
>
> Rubinstein answered, "Yes, but I have also seen his metronome!"
>
> Brahms was reproached for playing the same piece at an appreciably different tempo on different occasions, and he replied, "So my heart beats faster today."
>
> Too many elements figure into the choice of tempo; there can be no absolute. In teaching I try to stay away from dictating a

tempo. Again, this is where theory and practice part. With demonstration, naturally comes an involuntary imposing of tempo, along with other ideas.

Even though Beethoven and his contemporaries all had the use of the newfangled device built by Johann Nepomuk Maelzel called the metronome (from 1813), more questions have arisen because of the indications on his sonatas, than have been resolved. There are some doubts as to whether his metronome was calibrated the same as the modern one, as too many of the sonata movements are nearly unplayable, or at least unplayable *musically*, at the indicated tempos; also, the master often changed his mind about interpretive matters, including tempo. Perhaps most important, no piece at the level of greatness of Beethoven sonatas or concertos can or should be played at only one set tempo marking. There are also suggestions that the longer Beethoven was away from the keyboard as a performer, the more he might have lost touch with the realities and exigencies of the technical aspects of realizing his tempo markings.

But Beethoven expanded the range of keys he utilized in his piano compositions. His first sonata was in F minor—four flats; Mozart had never written in that key. The indication *fortissimo* rarely if ever appeared in Mozart or Haydn; each stops at *forte*. In Beethoven we now have crushing dissonances, enormous contrasts, sudden volatile shifts in emotion, subito *piano*s and *forte*s.

For many years it was thought that Beethoven was greatly removed from the world around him, writing abstract compositions of absolute music (which means without a program or references to the world). Of course, we know that one of his greatest sources of inspiration was nature. He said, "You ask me where I get my ideas? They come to me out of nowhere, from the air, when I am walking in the woods. The woods, the trees, the rocks, they speak to me!" The more one reads from his notes, letters, and sketchbooks, the clearer it becomes that

Beethoven was also very concerned with narrative and description, poetry, and philosophy.

And nature was ever-present. The master's rooms were right by the city gates in Vienna, through which he could pass quickly into the meadows and woods that he synthesized into musical language. The opening of his "Pastoral" Symphony bore the inscription "Awakening of cheerful feelings upon arrival in the countryside." Who among us cannot hear the inhalation of fresh air in that opening F major phrase?

András Schiff is, for me, one of the greatest of today's pianists and musical minds. His lecture-demonstrations on Beethoven sonatas are among the most treasurable of musical events. They are never dry, methodological, musicological discourses; he brings the composer's humanness to us directly through his words and readings. Schiff told me that it was for that precise reason that he lived in Austria for a few years: "to breathe the air that these giants breathed." But both he and Alfred Brendel have also said that there is very little of the essence of old Vienna or Salzburg in those cities anymore.

The great pianist Richard Goode told me (*Clavier*, January 1994):

> I think that Beethoven's language is such that all his natural resources are transformed but not necessarily recognizable; Beethoven was nourished by nature and therefore the tree gives forth fruit. But the fruit does not tell you what Beethoven felt to bring the music forth. The Pastoral Sonata and Symphony have long stretches where nothing happens harmonically, as the major chords distill stillness and peace. Then there are the rustic sounds and shepherd's pipes.

Goode cautions against reading too much into every bit of Beethoven's music: "I never feel the strong connection between Beethoven and Nature from his music. With someone like Debussy, I feel it, and the music says it to me."

There are synthesized sounds of nature in Beethoven's music, but for me, more important than listening for birdsong and such effects is to get into the same state of communion with one's natural surroundings, to reproduce the transformation of energy from what Beethoven experienced into musical language.

The music that was written in Beethoven's earlier years reflects joyful and youthful exuberance and love of life, as it was conceived before the tragic onset of his deafness and his ongoing struggle to come to terms with the loss of his most precious faculty. However, in any of his periods, the wonderful and touching thing about Beethoven, again and again, is his humanness. Whereas Mozart's conceptions seemed to pass *through* him, all ready to be set down in manuscript, Beethoven, in contrast, struggled with every musical idea, writing it down, wrestling with each phrase, as evidenced by the anguished marks and drips and blots on his manuscripts, until he felt he got it right. He wore his heart on his sleeve, from every gentle dolce to each powerful utterance; and so we feel we know the man through the music. (Every time I play the *Andante favori* in F, the opening bars seem to speak and sing "I love you"—even the cadence of the phrase, with the emphasis on the first C major chord after the pickup: the word "love." For me, it is unmistakable.)

The pianists who are fortunate to truly experience these human expressions will invest their performances with a boundless gratitude and generosity of spirit that elevates the music as it deserves. The longer we live and the more we experience, the more deeply the music speaks to us. But of course it is that way with all of art.

This leads to the question of whether or when to introduce the later sonatas to younger piano students.

Claudio Arrau, on the occasion of his eightieth birthday, granted me an interview (*Clavier*, March 1983) in which he addresses this issue:

> For a young person to think that he understands Opus 111, is absurd. There are those who have spent 50 years on this work,

before daring to think they understand. Young artists can occupy themselves with late Beethoven sonatas, but certainly ought not to have the lack of modesty to perform them.

To understand the cosmic transcendental world of late Beethoven, an artist must have traveled far in experience and suffering. On the other hand, too much awe can be unhealthy too. Either extreme is no good. Furtwängler used to ask, "Why is it that some young pianists who come to play for me, do Chopin and Tschaikovsky so well, and when they come to Beethoven, they become paralyzed with awe?"

The main thing with interpretation is to have patience—with one's own self, to wait until things come shaped out of your own subconscious. Too many young artists lack the patience to wait for their maturity.

Arrau then admitted that in his later years, he had more patience than ever with "let[ting] things happen." He said he had more technical ease, needed less practice, and experienced more impetuosity.

Arrau's views are similar to those of András Schiff, who cautioned a young audience at a conservatory that if they must study the late sonatas, they must also wait to perform them before the public in order to show the proper respect and reverence.

But this view is in strong contrast with that of Claude Frank (*Clavier*, January 1983). We discussed both the reviewing of pieces learned in the past and the introduction of Beethoven works to students:

Younger pianists study a program for a few weeks or months, and play it anywhere. We "grownups" don't. We think we can't. Yes, if called at the last moment to fill in, we do: and the performance usually goes as well as if we prepared, but we wouldn't choose to do it that way.

Reviewing already-learned repertoire may result in additional or altered musical ideas, or it may not; but each time these great pieces are played, they must be approached as if they were new— with fresh ears and eyes. Every time I program one of the great sonatas, the Waldstein, Appassionata, or Opus 111, the greatness of the work is so overwhelming that I never cease to marvel.

Having studied Beethoven and the masters with Artur Schnabel from the age of 15, I knew that the teacher played it best, but never questioned my own spiritual readiness. It never occurred to me that young people should not play that music, and I haven't changed my mind. A young person's musical diet must include pieces that are spiritually, as well as physically, taxing. In master classes, I prefer to deal with the more spiritually taxing litera- ture. Beethoven sonatas are ideal for these classes because they incorporate a good balance between the notes themselves, and the meaning behind the notes.

I asked Frank whether the same process of teaching interpretation as there is for acting and understanding Shakespeare could be applied to Beethoven. Can interpretation be taught?

This is where theory and practice part. In theory, the good teacher does not superimpose ideas, but in practice, it often happens that way. We try to do two things in a lesson: show the "what" and help with the "how." In master classes I do more of the "what" especially when the audience includes non-pianists or non-musi- cians. In private lessons I work on the "how" whenever possible, keeping the "what" as top priority.

I suppose this means I do teach Interpretation.

There are many elements of interpretation, and Frank distinguished between them:

Certain elements are more personal and subject to debate. If I feel suddenly that a passage ought to be *semplice, senza espressione*, for example, that might suit my own personal feelings only; it's the same with bringing out inner voices, or the choice of a certain sound, or the use of coloring, pedal, and tempo.

In thinking, always, about the complexities of the human condition, Beethoven pushes us to the limits of our own physical, emotional and psychological possibilities. For example, when Beethoven puts a crescendo marking over a long held note, there is of course no way we can actually do that on the piano (as a string instrument could). And yet, by *thinking* crescendo and willing it to happen, sometimes we can create the illusion of that intensification—crescendo! With the pedal and by pure dint of will I often feel we can, if we want to, rise to any challenge that Beethoven sets before us. His legacy is so great that we owe it to him.

The phrase marks in Beethoven are also sometimes very difficult to interpret. If a series of phrase marks seem erratic and Beethoven puts the slurs in different places over the same sets of notes, we must not presume that it is an error or careless editing, because the variant phrasing may simply mean that Beethoven *meant* to impart a different meaning or character to each group of similar notes. The slurs in Beethoven's piano music can be cause for distress, as they are often irregular, and one wonders whether they surround a group of notes that belong together (as a phrase)—that is, encompassing a musical idea—or are more closely related to technical matters, such as a group of notes belonging together for the sake of ease and natural execution by the performer.

Sometimes Beethoven drew a slur over three notes to indicate that they should be played as triplets, and that could easily be misinterpreted as a legato marking. His energetic pen reflected the originality and speed of his thoughts, but it frequently resulted in enigmas. The truth is that Beethoven was extremely exacting about the starts and finishes of his phrase marks and even berated his publisher, "For God's sake, please impress on the copyist to copy everything as it stands!!" And even though most often he tried to mark it all clearly, at times it was very *un*clear. And even more often, over the same repeated phrases, he intentionally changed the phrasing, so that these erratic marks were taken to be carelessness on the master's part and subsequently changed by well-meaning copyists.

It should be added that Beethoven was, in fact, known sometimes to notate carelessly, and sometimes the copyists were careless. But to me, the worst offenders are the editors who try to interpret for us what *they* think Beethoven meant. I would always rather see the original and judge for myself.

The trouble is that there are so many editions! Beethoven had to deal with the pirating of his first editions, so often inaccurate, resulting in many foreign publications. Furthermore, there were no protective copyright laws, nor payment for subsequent editions, and Beethoven was forever furious at the inaccuracies. Ironically, however, he was frequently caught straying from his own texts in performance.

A long time ago, when I was the senior editor of *Clavier* magazine, I was sent five volumes of the facsimiles (mostly from the Hoboken Collections of the Austrian National Library) of the first and early editions of all the Beethoven sonatas, complete with the florid title pages, with their dedications. The volumes from Tecla Editions (London) are in a "landscape" (wide) format, the way the manuscripts first appeared, rather than "portrait" (tall) printing we are now used to. It is fascinating and beautiful to see the handwritten, slightly erratic, but almost perfect copyists' strokes and markings, and quite a special feeling to read and play from these pages, which seemed to bring me closer to the original manuscripts (which would be nearly indecipherable even if I had access to them).

Beethoven used several kinds of strokes to indicate different articulations in his piano music—dots for short staccatos, vertical strokes for weighted portamenti—and when you see a legato phrase with staccatos underneath, it may sometimes imply an imperceptible slowing down. In Opus 110 there are little staccato marks after every group of four thirty-second notes; these are meant to indicate a melodic stress—lyrical, tender harmonies—without any big dramatic conflicts. And all those seemingly insignificant details that figure into the physical part of the work are just the beginning stages, of interpreting the great mystery and miracle of Beethoven.

Another element of interpretation, with built-in challenges regarding irregularities, is embellishments. A trill is an expressive device. It may be an elongation of an appoggiatura (which is like a suspension), or it may have the function of prolonging a sonority in order to sustain a note. In the eighteenth century (until about 1775), trills were generally started on the upper note, but most scholars advise that in music composed after that, the trill be started on the main note. This, of course, includes nineteenth-century compositions. The important thing to note here is that, according to witnesses, Beethoven was not always sure how to play his own trills. And he was said to do them differently from one performance to another. (What a comfort to know that!)

Of course, there are important exceptions to the functions of the trill, especially when used as creatively as it was by Beethoven in Opus 109, where, in the last variation in the last movement, Beethoven increases the accompanying inner notes from eighths to sixteenths, to thirty-seconds, and finally to earth-shattering trills, bringing the intensity into the explosive range—only then to be followed by his heavenly theme, bringing the movement around full circle.

So the bottom line is that we have to make an artistic and more educated decision based on what we decide is the function of a trill, and we may never have an assurance that Beethoven played it exactly that way. This fact probably stems from the fact that for Beethoven, improvisation was the central mode of his work. He sat for long hours at the piano contemplating and trying new ideas, and as Lewis Lockwood describes in his excellent book *Beethoven: The Music and the Life*, the master "sat in a kind of rêverie—that he would have called a *raptus* that we associate with fantasy and daydreaming, in order to let his hands release and spread his musical imagination." He would also often interrupt these reveries to jot down fragments of ideas or concepts in his sketchbook for future use, sometimes working on several pieces at once.

As Lockwood suggests, we "would do well to imagine what Beethoven's improvisations were like." However, many pianists are locked into the black-and-white exactitude of the score and its strictures and have difficulty going beyond that reference.

Of course we should not allow ourselves the same spontaneous impulses and last-minute improvisations of embellishments wherever we wish, but the mere image of Beethoven's freedom of process should free up something in our own playing as well.

The frustration anyone would experience in writing a book of this nature stems from the choices that have to be made as to which sonatas would be discussed in detail and which ones omitted. The several compositions I chose to perform for the "Composer's Landscape" series of audiobooks are from different periods of Beethoven's life, as described briefly here. Beethoven's thirty-two piano sonatas are like a lifeline traced through his music, and these are some of the sonatas that I want to keep with me throughout my whole life. Whatever I have lived through since my last performance or even practice session reflects itself in the music, changing my view. Wilhelm Furtwängler once said, "Music is about the state of becoming." I believe he meant that music evolves from what came before it: the opening phrase of a sonata came from the silence before it, and entering a sonata is a poignant moment.

The Piano Sonata in F-sharp, Opus 78 (included on the CD), one of Beethoven's own favorites, foreshadows later sonatas with its unconventionality in form and key. Beethoven knew, with this sonata, he had written his greatest to date. For me, it is the most lyrical and good-natured, and probably a declaration of love, dedicated to Countess Therese von Brunsvik, one candidate in the perennial game of conjecture "Who Was Beethoven's Immortal Beloved?" Beethoven had a lifelong yearning to establish a permanent loving relationship with a woman who could lift him out of his miseries. He never succeeded. Yet, according to a friend of his, Franz Wegeler, "Beethoven was never out of love."

This was Vienna, and the countess was a noblewoman—which ruled out marriage to Beethoven, a commoner. Besides, Beethoven was always in conflict: he wanted a relationship, but he dreaded any commitment that would prevent him from having the time and energy for his work. And then there was his deafness and a perception of him as "ugly and half-crazy."

The amiable melodies of the Sonata Opus 78 are like a love song; and that amiability is all the more astonishing given that it was composed in 1809, when he was already quite deaf and utterly miserable about his fate. The very key of F-sharp, with six sharps, was extraordinarily complicated, and the publisher even expressed concern about its accessibility to amateurs. But Beethoven conceived it in F-sharp and, of course, would not compromise. (Schubert resisted the same request. His publisher, however, waited for him to die and then disrespectfully took the beautiful G-flat Impromptu, Opus 90 No. 3, and transposed it into G major, to make it more accessible to dilettantes.)

This F-sharp Sonata is the shortest of the thirty-two, but even so, it is totally complete. It is compressed, as are the later sonatas: it has only two movements, with a short Adagio introduction that is almost like an abbreviated, displaced slow movement placed at the beginning. In only eight bars, with an F-sharp pedal point, and the tonic chord at the beginning of each bar, Beethoven says so much, so eloquently, and so completely. He then proceeds into the movement marked Allegro ma non troppo, with that admonishment of "not too fast."

The main theme is one of the most intimate, affectionate, and beautiful melodies. Beethoven was just as capable of tender feelings as he was of heroics. The difficult, meandering, contoured, and highly chromatic sixteenth-note passages could seduce a pianist with virtuoso inclinations into showmanship, but good nature and suppleness should be the goals.

The opportunity for fast playing comes soon enough in the last movement, Allegro vivace, where Beethoven is more playful and giddy than perhaps anywhere else in all of his sonatas. Here are downright eccentric and wacky galloping couplets—and he makes no attempt to explain the irregularities. Could this mean that he was head over heels in love?

But again, our challenge is not so much to figure out his intentions as it is to play the erratic little phrases. There is no way around the necessity of analyzing the phrase lengths, the groupings of tiny couplets, the sequences, and surprising harmonies and then just throwing our hands and selves into it, hoping for the best! There are questions and answers, shifts from major to minor, *forte* to *piano*, unexpected dissonances; and a fragment of a theme is reminiscent of "Rule, Britannia! Britannia, rule the waves" (a theme upon which Beethoven also wrote a set of variations).

Donald Tovey describes the Piano Sonata in A, Opus 101, as the most difficult—technically and intellectually (and, I would add, emotionally)—of all of Beethoven's later works for piano and warned that the pianist's most sincere and earnest intentions would never feel equal to Beethoven's . . . and that is certainly true. The self-doubts prevail, no matter how accurately or deeply we perform this sonata. *Have we done justice to Beethoven?* is the prevailing mantra that races through the mind. It is an irony worth mentioning here that Beethoven once said, "My music comprehends mankind; but mankind does not comprehend my music." We may never know exactly what the master had in his mind, but maybe we don't have to. Simply studying and working on this masterpiece is a privileged and pleasurable pursuit; the work itself is the best part.

Opus 101 signifies a shift from the agitation and depression of his middle years to the later years of resignation, acceptance, and peace.

Opus 101 opens as though from nowhere. We tiptoe into his reverie, which extends throughout the first movement except for one short dissonant passage. I recall a lecture by Daniel Barenboim in which he described the feeling that this sonata not only *will* go on forever, but *has* gone on forever.

The second movement is a jerky and quirky March, energetic and difficult, with a gentle interlude in the form of a Trio. The slow third movement is filled with yearning, with references back to the first movement. The sudden fury of the Finale, with its almost perpetual motion and brambly fugato, is an unrelenting challenge, full of dangerous curveballs, and thoroughly fatiguing, even as it is bracing and exciting. Again, it is more about experiencing it than understanding it—the journey is in itself the truth.

Beethoven's illness disturbed his writing of the trilogy of his three last sonatas, Opus 109, Opus 110, and Opus 111. When he could write again, he apparently recovered his amiability of the Opus 78 (present in the opening theme of Opus 110) and his sense of humor in the Scherzo. He then went on to depict, in musical language, his illness—telling it in the recitatives and in the Arioso dolente, whose breathless sobbing helps make it one of the saddest movements ever written by anybody. Whoever attempts to play Beethoven's late sonatas has to endeavor to take on his burdens, to close oneself into his soul and experience his beautiful, multifaceted character. Richard Goode called the master "the gate-keeper of Paradise."

Another interesting fact about the late sonatas is that they utilize the extreme ends of the keyboard while reducing the use of the center. Barenboim, in his Beethoven lectures, suggested that the energy and strife from these extremes make one feel as though discomfort is part of the intention, part of the expression itself, and that there is a balance between both ends that creates a sort of equilibrium. András Schiff likens the two extremes in Beethoven to Dante's Inferno and Paradise—heaven and hell.

I came across a strange book with a cumbersome title—*A Tour in Germany, and Some of the Southern Provinces of the Austrian Empire*—written in 1821 by a Sir John Russell, in which he describes Beethoven mostly in terms of his unruly and antisocial behavior among others in society. I almost put it away in dismay (because it seemed disrespectful, with a lack of understanding for Beethoven's struggles) until I came upon a description of Beethoven at the piano: "The moment he is seated at the piano, he is evidently unconscious that there is anything in existence but himself and his instrument . . . the music of the man's soul passed over his countenance."

The Rondo in G, Opus 51 No. 2, made itself known to me and lifted me out of months of lamentation after the terrible events of September 11, 2001, in New York City. It is pure, human, restorative, and reconfirming as only Beethoven can be. It is written in the same key and is the same vintage as his great Fourth Piano Concerto, Opus 58, and in some ways I find it a miniature version of that monumental work. *Rondo* means "around": the main theme comes around several times with more varied and fanciful ornamentation, and each time we hear it, we are reminded that some things are elemental and permanent, a notion that is in itself comforting.

The Sonata in E-flat, Opus 27 No. 1, "Quasi una fantasia," is an early work, but Beethoven was already a renegade, breaking the rules of the conventional sonata-allegro form. This sonata has no sonata-allegro form at all! It is through-composed, which means one movement runs into the next, with hardly a pause. In this way, as its name implies, it is more a fantasy than a sonata.

Almost as a penance for nonconformity, Beethoven begins in a simple, square 4/4 rhythm, with a plain and good-natured theme, including the suggestion of gentle laughter, interrupted briefly by a rousing frolic. The second movement takes us on a ride over hills and valleys through the master's beloved landscape, including a galloping section that plunges us into a gully—but only for a second, until we are uplifted by the heavenly Adagio. The last movement is an energetic Rondo that is almost a breathless perpetual motion; and then, once again, we are rescued by the serene Adagio theme—but even then only for a moment, until we are caught up in the giddy and spirited coda.

Richard Goode, one of the great Beethoven interpreters, offered some interesting ideas to me about this sonata (*Clavier*, January 1994):

> The sonata is all one big experience. The opening is often played too seriously and solemnly. A pianist must capture the open-eyed naïveté of the opening theme. This became clear to me one day when I was to perform the sonata in New York . . . and a doctor-friend, who studied with Emil von Sauer, learned that I was to play this sonata later the same day as my visit. He started singing the theme, and cautioned me not to play it too slowly—"You know, it's a popular tune of the time—'Margaretha, Girl Without Compare.'" I was so convinced by the Viennese lilt in his voice, that I played it somewhat differently as a result.
>
> I take it in 2, which often makes a big difference in Mozart and Beethoven.

Goode does not change the fingering to two hands in the C major Allegro immediately following the opening Andante:

> I avoid that if I can. If I feel that I cannot do it as well and convincingly with one hand, then I might. It's a risky place, but I think it is important to take risks . . . there is something daring about those musical gestures that you want to capture. (Rudolf Serkin was absolutely against any kind of creative fingering. If I am not mistaken, he never played Opus 2, No. 2, because of a perilous passage in the first movement, where Beethoven wrote a fingering that almost no one else could do. Most people use two hands there, but Serkin felt that

if you could not do it the way Beethoven indicated, you shouldn't do
it. That far I wouldn't go.)

The c minor Allegro molto of opus 27, No. 1, is really a scherzo
with a trio, and I think we are really meant to feel the energy and
the hammering of those quarter-notes.

I think that is Beethoven's invention, and one of the things that
makes him so modern. So much of modern music depends on this
kind of rhythmic impulse, and Beethoven may have invented that.
(When I say "hammering" I mean the excitement and driving force
of equal impulses—perhaps this is the manic side of Beethoven.)

The three movements of the Sonata Opus 81A, "Les adieux," are
marked "Das Lebewohl" (Farewell), "Abwesenheit" (Absence),
and "Das Wiedersehen" (The Return)—in French, "Les adieux,"
"L'absence," and "Le retour." Both languages appear on Beethoven's
original manuscript, with more detailed instructions in German in the
last movement to describe the very lively (actually, in Beethoven's
words, the liveliest) tempo.

So whose departure and return was Beethoven referring to? The
sonata was written in 1809 and 1810, concurrent with the French attack
on Vienna led by Napoleon, which forced the upper classes to leave.
Archduke Rudolph (who was said to be a very good pianist) had not
only been Beethoven's patron, but a close friend—indeed, Beethoven
dedicated this sonata "On the departure of His Imperial Highness" to the
archduke as well as a number of his other important works, including
the "Emperor" Concerto, from which he borrowed several ideas for this
sonata, especially in the last movement (the E-flat arpeggiated passages
are very similar in both works).

Linguists tell me that the German word *Lebewohl* has a much more
intimate and endearing connotation than *adieu*. In fact Beethoven wrote
the syllables—*Le-be-wohl*—over the first three chords of the opening
to the sonata. But the third chord is a deceptive cadence. We expect

the hornlike reveille to end in E-flat, but instead the sadness is already apparent right in that surprising C minor chord, for which we must try to find a darker timbre.

This was not at all a case of deferential dedication to a benefactor. Beethoven felt he was losing a dear friend, and that sadness was worn on his sleeve and woven throughout the first and second movements. That second movement, "L'absence," is filled with melancholy and restlessness, with many recitatives, with questions—"Where are you?"—and the movement leads right into the furiously galloping horses that bring the returning beloved friend back to a joyful reunion. That last movement is technically very demanding, but one is buoyed up by the blithe spirits and brilliance of the writing.

One of the most touching passages written about Beethoven is from a phantasmagorical set of musings from Schumann's journal. He imagined climbing the steps of No. 200 Schwarzpanierstrasse (the house where Beethoven died): "Not a breath is stirring. I step into his room. He raises himself up, a lion, a crown upon his head, a splinter in his paw. He speaks of his sufferings . . . he complains that he is left so much alone."

It is said that Beethoven believed and stated, "I will hear again in Heaven." Yet he also uttered, on his deathbed, "It doesn't matter—I have done what I was meant to do on earth."

Almost two centuries after his death, Beethoven remains the titan of music. His legacy is so basic a part of our culture that it has even begun to be vulgarized by use in advertisements, for example, excerpting the three "knocks of Fate" from the Fifth Symphony for the most mundane associations; yet I try to think of this kind of abuse of his writing as a positive sign, a kind of embrace, however late, even by the uninitiated and uncultivated among us.

I find my own gratitude to Beethoven expressed so much more powerfully in Schumann's words: "BEETHOVEN! What a word! The deep sound of the mere syllables has the ring of eternity."

Franz Schubert, Four Impromptus for piano, D.935 (Opus 142 No.1);
autograph manuscript (December 1827), page 1. The Pierpont Morgan
Library, New York, Cary 341.

4

SCHUBERT (1797–1828)

Someone once said that the only thing that really matters about music is the part that cannot be explained; and here I am engaged in the process of writing with hopes of getting closer to the inexplicable Schubert.

Until I was in my forties I held Schubert's music on such a high plane that I chose to play it only in the quiet and solitude of my own home rather than play it publicly and risk not doing him justice. Schubert's piano music has neither the wild chromaticism and virtuosity of Chopin (although it is filled with harmonic surprises and many technical challenges) nor the sudden huge passions of Beethoven or Brahms (although it contains enormous emotional ranges). Because any type of display was alien to Schubert's retiring disposition, a Schubert performance is not an exhibit of technical prowess, but rather an invitation for the listener to enter into a private musical world.

The music is fragile, like a flower that might wilt upon being picked and therefore resists—like "Heidenröslein," the little heath rose in one of Schubert's beautiful lieder. It has to be handled with utmost delicacy and approached with a pure heart, in a state of grace. As the words *Impromptu* and *Moment musical* suggest, there is a quality of spontaneity along with a songfulness for which we must attempt to imitate the human voice. And these qualities hold true for all his compositions.

Schubert was one of the most guileless of composers. He writes a tune, and then asks us, "Isn't that a nice tune? Here, I give it to you." It may come to us from nowhere, weightless, transparent—and indeed, one of the greatest challenges in playing Schubert is to become as close as possible to weightless and selfless, maybe invisible, because it is not at all about us.

The first interview I ever did was with André Watts, who is a most wonderful Schubert pianist. He grew up in a house where his mother played Schubert lieder recordings all the time. We spoke about the guilelessness, and the ambiguities and constant shifts between major and minor that run all through Schubert, and he related the tale about Schubert having a dream in which the composer lamented, "Every time I tried to speak of sadness, it turned to joy, and every time I tried to speak of joy, it turned to sorrow."

By *speak*, of course, he meant *compose*; and that dichotomy of joy and sorrow that defines his music results in passages in major keys that are bittersweet and heartrending, and sections in minor keys that are positively jolly. In fact it is possible that Schubert is at his saddest in major keys. The lied "Lachen und Weinen" (Laughing and Crying) epitomizes these sudden shifts between major and minor modes.

What is all that ambiguity about? It speaks to Schubert's own nature. People who knew him describe two contrasting sides of his character. There was modesty and ego, peasant coarseness and aristocratic sensibility, naïveté and sophistication, mysteriousness and candor, sociability and melancholy. The moods are so ephemeral, they defy being captured; one almost doesn't want to.

Schubert was quoted as saying, "Happy moments brighten this gloomy life; and happier ones give glimpses of happier worlds." (Were those meant to be presentiments about life after death or prophecies of untimely death?) He was only twenty when he learned of his terminal illness, and he set himself to the task of writing an incredible number of the most poignant compositions for the next twelve years before he died at thirty-one, four years younger than Mozart.

Schubert was rather lonely, even at parties, where he was generally at the piano, improvising *Ländler* for others to dance to. There is, perhaps, nothing more Viennese than the Schubert waltzes and *Ländler*. Haydn, Mozart, and Beethoven wrote dance music on commission for the court or for noble families. But Schubert's waltzes were not written for any commercial gain: he simply wanted to give pleasure to his friends and to society.

Indeed, rarely did any genius struggle as Schubert did, with so little material reward. He wrote twenty-one piano sonatas, more than a dozen string quartets, seven completed symphonies, and others left "unfinished," and yet there were very few public concerts of his music within his lifetime.

Still, there he was, gladly seated at the keyboard at parties, preferring not to dance, as he was shy and awkward. He was described as a rather unattractive fellow; but as earthbound as he was in body, his imagination soared in these improvisations, out of which, amazingly, came hundreds of short dances. There are thirty published sets of dances—sometimes called *Ländler*, sometimes *Walzer*, and sometimes *Deutschertänze*. Some of them are quite heroic, and sublime, others bawdy and slight; and many are of moderate difficulty, providing excellent teaching material. Every one of them is lyrical.

There are questions as to whether the dances were written to be played together as they appear in the sets. They came out randomly in collections for piano under various opus numbers and were never orchestrated. These little gems are as listenable as they are danceable. It is a great pleasure for the pianist to go on a safari through these volumes, finding favorites and stringing a group of them together for performance, sorting them either by contrasting mood or key relationships.

After a brief love affair with Therese Grob, a soprano, Schubert became a sort of loner, almost a misfit . . . except with his friends and admirers who got together for those famous Schubertiades—frequent gatherings with instrumental ensembles, singing, solo performances, and dancing. He had a close family life—even a family string quartet in which he played the viola, later learning violin and piano. And he worked as an early-education teacher in his family's school, which gave him a half day off to compose.

Of all the major composers, Schubert was most closely associated with Vienna (as Mozart is with Salzburg); but his parents had come there from Moravia and Silesia, which became Czechoslovakia. (Musicians who truly know Vienna, however, have argued that whatever the Viennese elements that contributed to his music, they have not been present in Vienna for many years since Schubert lived there.)

The only teacher he ever acknowledged was Antonio Salieri, whom Beethoven had consulted about opera, but Salieri did not share Schubert's love for lieder. Schubert, like Mozart, was led by the qualities of the human voice, and he preceded Chopin as one of the great melodists. Not just his songs, but everything he wrote, are characterized by his beautiful melodic lines with their naïveté and purity. It falls to us to try to find those same qualities in our hearts and spirits to do his music justice.

Some of Schubert's sonata movements are of inordinate length, often referred to as "heavenly length." I asked Radu Lupu, whom I got to know during the period when I interviewed him several times for *Clavier*, about how he makes his decisions regarding the repeats in those exceedingly long movements. His droll, half-serious reply, delivered in his deep baritone with its Romanian accent, which I am certain was *not* meant to be inscribed in stone, no less in print, bears repeating—if only for the reader's amusement.

> I will tell you . . . I have my own rules of repeats! If I play the first time, and it does not go as well as I wished, of course, I repeat it!
>
> If I play it so beautifully that I think I could never again play it so beautifully, I do NOT repeat!
>
> Or, sometimes, if I play it well, but I love it so much that I cannot let it go, then I also repeat it!

Of course, Lupu had his tongue firmly in cheek, but certain truths are uttered in jest, and there is in this tale a good lesson, which is that we pianists have more license than we think.

The great pianist Alfred Brendel is very direct about his views on the repeats, mentioning many variables that would determine whether to take the repeat or not. If the first ending of the exposition has bars that are not included in the second ending, most pianists would agree to honor the repeat, instead of leaving out unplayed material. However, Brendel argues that if those few bars that exist only at the first ending do not add anything of great importance to the movement, they ought not to count as reason enough to repeat. His advice is: "Repeat marks should not be taken as a command and obeyed unquestioningly as if the composer had written it all out in full."

One of the differences between Beethoven and Schubert is that Schubert's recapitulations are almost always identical to his expositions (that is, they are in very strict sonata-allegro form)—which presents another argument against repeating the exposition. It also seems to create a better symmetry without the repeated exposition.

Apparently Schumann deemed Schubert's length ("as if without end") his greatest shortcoming, and when Mendelssohn conducted Schubert's C Major Symphony, "The Great," he made cuts. Harold Bauer, a great pianist at the beginning of the twentieth century, recorded an abridged version of the Sonata in B-flat. But as Alfred Brendel points out, Mahler and Bruckner, with their own endless symphonies, as well as other epic artworks since Schubert (enormous paintings, lengthy novels, six-hour *Hamlet* productions, Wagner's operas), have all helped to alter and relax audience perception and tolerance of what he calls "musical space," to the point where now, as Brendel puts it, "Schubert's music, which used to appear as too lengthy, is suddenly not long enough!"

Nowadays we are used to all-Schubert programs; Brendel was one of the earliest pianists to venture into that format. In fact, even at the outset of these endeavors, Brendel managed what seemed impossible: to play all-Schubert programs to sold-out houses. I asked the pianist (*Clavier*, April 1989), whose Schubert manifests cohesiveness, intensity, a driving force, and some good jokes alongside the deeply serious moments, whether the fact that there is so much repose in Schubert's music added to the composer's appeal. His answer was more general, addressing two more of Schubert's qualities—its purity and its naïveté:

> Naïveté is not the recipe for a good Schubert performance. Schubert is much less naïve than people think. It depends on what the music is like: if the music has a childish side, then bring out the childishness. It may be the only way to make the music alive. To ennoble it or sprinkle perfume over it, would probably spoil the whole thing.

While Schubert contributed to the acceptance of longer works, he also strongly influenced the future literature of the nineteenth century, giving great stature to smaller forms. The other day I was practicing an Impromptu several times in a row (and it is rather repetitive even in one playing), and I thought to myself as I was purposely overdosing on the music, "It can never be repetitive enough."

That same moment my husband, a nonmusician who is nonetheless highly musical, commented, "I want that music to go on forever—I want to reside inside the music!" First of all, how does one get so lucky to have a husband who is so responsive? And secondly, if a person yields himself sufficiently to be enfolded by this music, it can be a balm for the spirits, a meditation, and a great gift. That is the genius of Schubert: that he can, with such sweetness, always stop short of being saccharine.

To most pianists, Schubert does not feel as pianistic as Beethoven or Mozart (although some do find his music pianistic). He himself was not a great pianist—he was a violist and violinist—and his music is sometimes not too comfortable under the hands. In addition, there are so many surprising turns of phrase and unexpected modulations that we cannot predict or anticipate what will follow, and so, for me at least, it takes longer to learn than Beethoven or Mozart. The best way to approach his music (and perhaps any music) is to venture into the score without first listening to other interpretations.

András Schiff, who has produced beautiful recordings of all of the Schubert sonatas and has played them often in series, told me in an interview (*Clavier*, October 1995):

> It is easier to play a work without such imposing figures before you. We already have and know so many wonderful performances . . . that are difficult to forget. I enjoyed learning the early Schubert sonatas that I had never heard anyone play before me. What I had was an idea of Schubert's music in general, and I worked it out for myself without the echoes of previous performances in my head, like huge mountains before me.

For any of us who cross the barrier of hesitation before approaching these great masterpieces, ultimately there is a wonderful moment, after you work and work, that you suddenly "get it." And then you are in what Richard Goode calls "Schubertland."

Goode has also recorded the Schubert sonatas with great depth of understanding and sense of line and continuity, making of the lengthy sonatas a fresh and riveting experience. In a discussion about Schubert (*Clavier*, January 1994), Goode quoted Karl Ulrich's description of the great Sonata in B-flat, Opus Posthumous, as being "halfway between heaven and earth." When performing Schubert, Goode is conscious of the need to enter into the music even before starting to play.

> Only by thinking about it beforehand, can one get into the mood. There's something about Schubert sonatas. Maybe it's the length

and the beauty, the sense of traveling that you do, the feeling of a journey by the way they are written, that makes me feel particularly like performing them. There is also the feeling of having a great deal of time. . . . Maybe one reason that Schubert is becoming more popular is that, in an age when everything is compressed and too fast, his music requires patience. He creates a different time scale, one with time to breathe and meditate.

Schubert had to suffer from the feeling that he had a giant sitting on his head: Beethoven. For a long time his sonatas were considered inferior to Beethoven's in form and structure; Schubert dedicated a set of variations to Beethoven, which were published in 1822 and signed "by his admirer and worshipper, Franz Schubert"; and he served as one of Beethoven's pallbearers. But while he deeply admired, even adored Beethoven, he followed his own course, in form, harmony, and ideas. And time has proven that his sonatas have great originality and uniqueness: first, there are those astonishing sudden modulations and new textures (such as parallel octaves and repeated, hypnotic accompanying figures over which he writes long, lyrical melodic lines), all requiring exquisite tonal control and a certain Mozartean lightness of touch—one might say, a "lightness of being."

Radu Lupu, whose Schubert recordings I love and admire, said of the composer (*Clavier*, May–June 1981):

Schubert is, perhaps, the most natural of the composers. But at the same time one of the most disturbing. He struggled to write, to find the form, the shape in which he could express himself. He is the composer for whom I am really most sorry that he died so young. . . . Mozart was Mozart, and he didn't struggle one bit. He was the most instinctive genius . . . but Schubert, except in his lieder, had to experiment all the time. Just before he died, he wrote his beautiful Quintet for two cellos, and he said very modestly that he was trying to learn a little more about counterpoint, and he was perfectly right. We'll never know what direction he was going or would have gone. The melodies and harmonic turns and motifs came naturally to him, but for a long time, not the big form . . . but finally in the end, he did find the means of expressing himself in the big form as in the string quintet and the G major piano sonata, for example.

The G Major Sonata opens with G major chords that come from nowhere (not unlike the heavenly G major opening of Beethoven's Fourth Piano Concerto). Lupu discussed the question of tone production.

Basically everything in music comes from the head. Honestly, if you have any concept of sound, you hear it in your inner ear. All you have to work for is to match that sound on the instrument. The whole balance, the line, the tone, is perceived and controlled by the head, determined by the color or timbre you hear, the piece you are playing, the phrase.

Obviously there is the touching of the instrument, but it is a very individual thing. Tone production is a matching process for which you practice. Why else, than to get the right sound? Just mechanical? Never!

Richard Goode's suggestion to place oneself in that atmosphere before playing would work just as well in the G Major Sonata as in the B-flat. Then it requires exquisite tonal control, not just for the *pp* passages, but for the budgeting of the incrementally increasing strength until it reaches *ff*; and the pianist should beware of the danger of falling faint with sheer bliss while playing the indescribably beautiful right-hand obbligato passages in the first movement. It is some form of ecstasy.

Goode noted that musicians are reluctant to admit to the use of visual imagery:

I believe that anything germane and appropriate that illuminates the experience and makes it more vivid is justifiable. A student playing a passage may say, for example, in the Schubert G Major sonata, "At this point I hear a hymn coming from a far-off church." If that makes him play that passage more appropriately and it works, I say, "Yes! Fine!"

Schubert's method of composition was quite different from that of Beethoven, who was always jotting down motivic themes in his notebooks upon which he would build architecturally—something he learned from Haydn. But Schubert wrote down complete melodies, more in the manner of Mozart or Chopin.

Richard Goode spoke of the element of time that makes Schubert so unique. Many refer to it as his "manipulation" of time. He can drive the lines forward with a galloping momentum, racing against time; and then, by use of repeated figures and patterns, he can arrest time and make us feel as though we are suspended in space, in limbo, marking time. At certain of his fermatas, we feel as though we are allowing the sound to wisp off into the ether; and then he resumes, as though nothing had disturbed the flow of the music.

He can make us feel as though we have entered into different realms of dreams and memories, as though we are in a strange, hostile environment, filled with unrest and other surprising emotional states.

The phrasing and articulations are very carefully marked by the composer, and closely connected to the emotional components of the music. He may have a series of four bars, repeated four times, with varying legatos, slurs, accents, and staccato marks, all of which very much alter the character and meaning of the music.

Schubert used a strange tempo indication, Molto moderato, which Brendel suggests indicates "a calm flow of a measured allegro." In fact, Schubert's music, if played with the right balance and control, can be mesmerizing or even create a feeling of instability. His music often rambles, traversing whole pages of unexpected harmonic progressions and tonalities, so that we feel as though we are utterly lost in a foreign land; and you wonder as you play how he will ever get us "home" again.

One of the essential traits in Beethoven's music, one that I particularly respond to and need, is his way of establishing order out of chaos. In Schubert, it seems sometimes that our biggest challenge is that we have to do that ourselves; the meandering through strange and exotic keys can leave the pianist at sea, and we have to find the connective tissue, the means, to make sense and peace out of it. In the end, Schubert does land on his feet, level, at rest. And we hardly know how we got there. Then there is an overwhelming sense of peace, reconciliation, and homecoming.

Leopold Mittman, once berated me, saying that if you do not see "something in particular to *do* [in a certain passage of music], then don't *do* anything! Let the music speak for itself."

Schubert's "Wanderer" Fantasy is an episodic one-movement work that later influenced Franz Liszt when he was composing his monumental one-movement Sonata in B Minor. The way Schubert ranges through one key and another, surprising us, and possibly himself, in the process, one might say (and Alfred Brendel did say) that he is himself a "wanderer"—possibly even a "sleepwalker."

Schubert left many of his works unfinished. This may possibly be due to his highly creative, prolific (but disorganized), and innovative energies and the constant outpouring of his melodies, causing him, after determining the basic melodic lines, to put certain works aside and go on to others, with every intention of coming back and completing the earlier works.

For that reason there is a lot of controversy, conjecture, and confusion about the chronology of Schubert sonatas. Some he started and then completed years later; some others he left incomplete.

In the crowning last year of his creativity, a year during which he was very ill (with typhoid and syphilis), he produced the great song cycle *Die Winterreise*, the wonderful *Fantasie* in F Minor for Piano Four-Hands, the Octet, and the String Quintet, and just as he was finally gaining recognition and respect, if not remuneration, he also wrote the Impromptus, Opus 142. Such an intensely productive period must surely have been instigated by the pressure of his increasing illness and the fear that it would all soon come to an end.

If discussions persist about the length and repetitive elements in Schubert's sonatas, then in his smaller works, such as the Impromptus and *Moments musicaux*, he was concise and amazingly varied in their emotional affect—and freed from the constraints of the sonata-allegro form. But they are long enough to be considered sonata movements. The Opus 142 Impromptus were numbered 5–8, making it clear that he meant them to be a sequel to the Opus 90 set. Actually, Schumann believed that Opus 142 was a sonata in disguise.

But Schubert himself was quite indifferent as to whether they were published or played separately or together. Nos. 1 and 4 (5 and 8) (Opus 142), which are included in the "Composer's Landscape" audiobooks, are both in F minor but are quite different in character. He spins webs of pure sound from mere arpeggios and scales. The Impromptu in B-flat Major, Opus 142 No. 3, is another example of how Schubert takes a captivating little melody, reminiscent of the theme from his ballet *Rosamunde*, and develops it with charming and diverse variations. A trip to YouTube reveals a dozen videos, in some of which the theme is taken at a lively clip by, for instance, Horowitz and in others at more leisurely tempos by equally famous pianists. The common trait among all the most successful interpretations is the element of spontaneity and improvisation, as though one were making it up on the spot. That is the most important quality for Schubert's short pieces, along with the touch and the lyricism. If the pianist is capable of understatement and the same guilelessness as the composer himself, these pieces speak for themselves, expressing sometimes unbearable beauty.

When death did finally come, ending Schubert's life of illness and poverty at age thirty-one, most of his works were unpublished; he died never having heard them performed. These included all his seven symphonies, operas, masses, chamber works, the music to the ballet *Rosamunde*, and hundreds of smaller pieces, some of which were discovered by Schumann, others by Sir Arthur Sullivan and George Grove, and some of them edited by no less a giant than Johannes Brahms. Many of the manuscripts had been treated with utter disrespect, as wastepaper, by the Viennese publishers.

It is heartbreaking to read what has been claimed as his last utterance: "Do I not deserve a place on the earth?"

Some of the deepest insights into Schubert, and the most satisfying and challenging works for the pianist, are in his more than six hundred lieder. These are among the most sublime and rarefied musical expressions, and as satisfying an experience as any solo Schubert piece. (I should say that for me, lieder playing and chamber music are pleasures at least equal to those of the solo repertoire.) Both the singer and the pianist must understand every word of the poetry of Goethe, Heine, Schiller, and others in order to create a complete and enriching musical experience. Schubert was particularly responsive to poetry about nature, which he viewed as a symbol of the human condition. Many of the accompaniments to the songs demand that the pianist portray the rippling effects of lakes and streams and transform them into musical language. Delicate imagery, such as that of hedge roses and quivering leaves, reminded Schubert of man's own fragility; poignant sunsets were metaphors for death.

I had the enormous privilege of having a correspondence with the great and peerless lieder pianist Gerald Moore. In his incisive and witty essays on accompaniment, *The Unashamed Accompanist*, *Am I Too Loud?*, and *Furthermoore*, Moore described the vitality and importance of the piano part in Schubert lieder in creating atmosphere, supporting the text with gesture and proper dynamics, and painting "watercolors in tones."

I also had the good fortune of working on an article with the great baritone Dietrich Fischer-Dieskau on the subject, from the singer's point of view, of the pianist in playing lieder (*Keynote*, April 1981). As he well knew, great performances of lieder presuppose a close partnership between the singer and the pianist. The word "accompaniment" in such collaborations is neither adequate nor applicable. What are the makings of a great lieder pianist, I asked him?

> For me, the main qualities required . . . would be real musician-ship and of course a very highly developed technical ability. Without trying to say anything against the professional accom-panist, many of them in former times were pale technicians who tried to duck behind the soloist. The whole difference lies in the word partnership, for which, perhaps, the best example would be Gerald Moore's artistry. The pianist should never be a mere shadow on stage.
>
> The poetry and meaning of the text are, of course, at the core of it all. While the pianist does not, necessarily, have to speak the language of the particular lied, an intimate understanding of the words of the poem is essential, because of the musical symbolism and the parallel musical expressive indications. Even more than that, the pianist, as well as the singer, must be an enthusiastic lover of lyric poetry in order to be a first-rate interpreter of poetry set to music.
>
> Schubert is, for me, the climax of the meeting between words and music, and this creates, at the same time, both the simplicity and the difficulties in his songs. It was he who once said, "There are no easy things in music."
>
> In his later songs, the piano becomes an energetic force that was not known before in the piano parts.

Schubert's lieder reflect all the states of the human experience and much of the composer's own struggle. He also recorded some of his own trials in his diary: "Suffering sharpens the mind and strengthens the heart." Several days later he wrote:

> No one understands somebody else's unhappiness or joy. People think they go toward each other, but they only walk next to each other. How sad for the man who realizes it! . . . MY work is created through my understanding of music and my suffering, but those works that were created mostly by suffering do not seem to please the world.

Despite Schubert's many self-doubts and struggles to make his music known, when publishers told him that people found some of his songs too difficult, his response manifested his strong belief in his work: "I cannot write differently. Anyone who cannot play my music should leave it alone. My music should either be performed well or not at all." (It might be interesting to note here that Schubert himself found it hard to play some of his own music.)

It has been suggested that in listening to Schubert, we can almost forget the instrument he was using, and only think of it as pure music. The pianist must overcome the technical challenges of our instrument so that we end up sounding like less of a pianist and more of a musician— in a realm unlike any other.

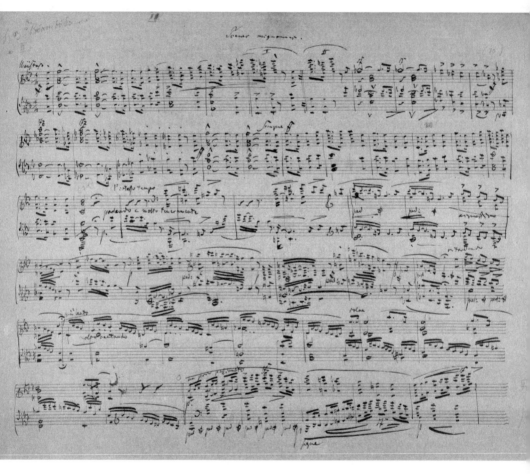

Robert Schumann, Préambule from *Carnaval*, and Variations on Schubert's
Sehnsuchtswalzer, Anhang F.24 (fragment); autograph manuscript
(1831–1834), page 1. The Pierpont Morgan Library, New York,
bequest of Alice Tully, 1995.

5

SCHUMANN (1810–1856)

I f the terrain of a specific composer can be identified by an experienced musician from one glance at the score, and if each composer's turf has its own look, Schumann's landscape would often appear to be a formidable and thorny wilderness with lots of underbrush and a jagged topography. The pianist becomes a trailblazer or an explorer trekking through the thicket, advancing with caution lest the hidden treasure of an inner melodic line, not readily apparent, be overlooked.

An added challenge lies in the fact that Schumann is not nearly as pianistic as Chopin, Mendelssohn, or Liszt. Indeed, he himself often complained about feeling constrained by the piano and its limits; yet he continued to compose at the piano, even his symphonic music. And that struggle against the limits of the instrument that he lamented is also felt by the pianist who plays the wealth of piano literature he left to us.

Like most pianists, I have lived with Schumann all my life since my earliest days when I jousted with "Knight Rupert," galloped with "The Wild Horseman," frolicked with "The Merry Farmer," or rode on a "Rocking Horse," sharing his nightmares, and his dreams; then up to the next notch with *Kinderscenen*, through *Carnaval*, *Fantasiestücke*, *Davidsbündlertänze*, *Faschingsschwank aus Wien*, *Kreisleriana*, and many shorter works; then on to the wonderful Piano Concerto in A Minor, which I had the great pleasure of performing; and finally I arrived at what I consider to be the pinnacle: the *Fantasie* in C, Opus 17.

I studied and performed the Schumann Piano Concerto at a time when I was experiencing major changes in my personal life; and perhaps because this is particularly subjective music, each movement seemed to represent a different emotion and phase of life: the first movement reflected the turbulent and passionate struggles, the second movement the questions and answers, and the third movement the final payoff of unbridled joy.

Some years later I had the good fortune to speak with Richard Goode, who was also deeply involved with the Schumann Concerto. During the interview in his apartment, the score was lying on the piano because Goode was restudying it for a performance with the New York Philharmonic under Kurt Masur. Although it was a work he had performed for many years, it is one of the few pieces he said he keeps with him all the time. His remarks (*Clavier*, January 1994) corroborated for me the deeply personal nature of this music for all pianists.

I don't have to restudy it very much, but if a year goes by and I haven't played it, I spend time with it. I am not sure I have a set way. I play it and see how it strikes me: I become aware of things that seem different to me.

Recently I became dissatisfied with the relationship between the various tempos in the concerto, and I figured out that all the tempos in the first movement are related. There is an organic relationship between the Andante and the Allegro. When the A-flat Andante comes right out of the end of the Allegro tutti, it's not dull if the tempo remains the same. It's rather like a marvelous variation, and I think it helps to draw the piece together.

The last time I played the concerto with the New York Philharmonic, a representative from Sotheby's came backstage and asked me if I would like to see the original manuscript, and of course I did. He was soon going to sell the score, so Marcia [Goode's wife] and I visited him the next day, and for two hours I had the opportunity to look it over in great detail. It was a particularly wonderful manuscript because it contained the original version of the first movement, with all the corrections, which I hope will be published soon. He made a lot of changes. I will play you the most obvious one.

Goode bounded over to the piano and plunged into the opening bars in their original form, quite different from what we are used to hearing. "I think both are wonderful, but would feel funny about going back to Schumann's first thoughts. It's more of an academic idea. . . . Schumann was constantly revising the orchestration."

Goode went into great detail about some of the changes:

The manuscript shows four attempts to write the bridge between the second and last movements. First, he had no 8-bar fanfare intro; he just went right into the A major theme. You can also detect the differences between Clara's, Robert's and the copyist's handwriting. I took notes on some of the small details, such as the metronome markings, and they turn out to be the same disastrous ones we have. Whose they are, I don't know. In the end, you have to find what's right for you, and what seems organic and comfortable. I think pianists sometimes play it a bit too slowly and sentimentally.

There are ambiguous hemiolas and counterrhythms in the third movement that confound even a seasoned conductor, and Goode prefers to think that

Schumann really wanted an alternation of the hemiola and the 3/4 meter, and didn't mean for us to feel that 3/4 all the time. Whether you feel the three large beats or the three small ones is very personal and open to question, I think.

There are Schumann pieces which have a strong dance element: some of the songs in *Carnaval*, and the coda of the concerto, which is like a waltz that never ends. It is abandoned and the momentum keeps building, careening into different keys. The difficulty for a pianist is that it is like a marathon. Sometimes the excitement is so great at the end, that I imagine a ballroom dance, swirling into the wee hours of the night. The emotional atmosphere of that work is so passionate and exuberant, it makes you have to identify with it subjectively.

To paraphrase the pianist, author, and commentator David Dubal, "The great geniuses of music can take the ephemeral, the confusion, the chaos of life, notate it, and convert it into some kind of order and beauty." Then, if we are lucky, with our own artistic sensibilities, we can recreate and experience what David calls "artistic rapture." This arduous process of sorting through his passionate outpourings is a similar challenge in all of his music. Yet this can only be done in music. If we tried to combine the disparate elements that come together in Schumann's music into speech, it would be sheer blather.

There are certain masterworks that we "save" and put on a back burner until the right moment comes; more recently in my musical life, the time came when I approached the great *Fantasie* in C.

I do not believe that this is a work for a young pianist, no matter how gifted; at least, I would not like to hear it. I did, in fact, hear a CD of this piece played by one of the rising stars of the keyboard, whose name I shall omit because I lamented this musician's lack of deep understanding. Yes, a young pianist's enthusiasm and ardor to play the piece, even though it may be premature, is something to love. Yes, I realize that Schumann himself was a young man when he wrote it. But we cannot compare ourselves to the geniuses who wrote their ideas down for future generations to fully grasp. And I always have felt that these geniuses who died young compressed their maturation into those shorter spans and lived more intensely than we mortals. And I will gladly listen again, some years from now, to this pianist's *evolved* version of the *Fantasie*.

Before we discuss this great work, let us meet the cast of characters: Robert Schumann himself along with all his multiple personalities; his (then) "distant beloved," Clara; her tyrannical father, Friedrich Wieck, who kept her cloistered from Robert; Beethoven, Schumann's revered master; and Brahms, the dear younger friend who worshipped both Robert and Clara.

Although much of the passion in the *Fantasie* was born of Robert's love for Clara, at least an equal source of inspiration was Beethoven. Robert and Clara shared a lifelong Beethoven bond; in fact, Robert's nickname for Clara was Leonora, Beethoven's heroine from his opera, *Fidelio*.

Clara was one of the foremost pianists of her day. (She also did some composing, and her songs are written as much for the pianist as the singer.) She became a Beethoven devotee and public-relations person, bringing his music to Berlin and Vienna. It is incredible that in the two decades after his death, Beethoven's piano music was not neglected—it was *unknown*. When Clara performed it from memory, she was called "intolerable," "ostentatious," "pretentious," and lacking in respect. (Not to mention how she ruined things for pianists for generations to come by setting the precedent of playing from memory!)

So before we can understand anything else about the *Fantasie*, it must be underscored that Schumann was among an impressive group of Romantic composers who all idolized Beethoven: Liszt had Beethoven's death mask and bust in his room, and Brahms, Wagner, Berlioz, Mendelssohn, and Chopin all revered the old master. But Schumann was the chief idolator of Beethoven worship. He wrote in one of his essays that "the magic influence of Beethoven's music moves us so deeply that, while immersed in it, we almost forget to think and hear."

Schumann was the most generous of all composers to his colleagues, and was responsible for presenting many young gifted composers, including Chopin, to the established music world. He referred to the twenty-year-old Brahms as a genius in an article he wrote; he used the same high praise about Chopin (his oft-quoted "Hats off, gentlemen, a genius!"). The Schumanns, immediately impressed with Brahms' talent, took the young composer under their wing and made him a regular member of their household, even having him babysit the Schumann children when Clara was on tour and Robert was ill. Brahms was utterly devoted to both Robert and Clara, eventually becoming a mediator between the couple and acting as head of the household while Robert was in the asylum.

In 1836 Schumann was asked to contribute something for a Beethoven memorial, a project that was realized many years later in 1845 in Bonn with a beautiful statue dedicated to him. The *Fantasie* became the vehicle through which he would honor his master, and it ultimately became the favorite of his many compositions.

As pianists, we form a friendship with a piece. We take it into our lives, and it becomes a deeper and deeper part of us; we develop a spiritual connection with a work over the months and years we live with it. We deal with solitude for hundreds of hours—but not loneliness, because we are with Schumann. We learn the landscape to discover what it's about, and then we have to believe we have something important to say about it.

There are a few important elements in the *Fantasie* through which Schumann expresses both his adoration of Beethoven and his grief over his enforced estrangement from Clara at the time he was composing the first movement.

At the heading of the music on top of the first page of the *Fantasie*, there is a poem by Schlegel, posing a sort of puzzle.

> Through all the varied sounds which fill the world's many-colored dreams
> One gentle tone may be heard by those who listen in secret!

Schumann seemed to love puzzles and mysteries and hidden meanings. There are many theories about his riddle. To the best of *my* ability to decipher the meaning of these lines, I think that "gentle tone" may refer to the many ways Schumann has embedded bits of material from Beethoven into the melodic tapestry of this composition. Also, though he calls it a *Fantasie in C*, he begins in D minor and then teases us with ghostlike appearances of C major until the end of the first movement. Then, at the end of the whole *Fantasie*, and only then, there is a sense of coming home to C major.

At the very end of the first movement Schumann quotes Beethoven's song "An die ferne geliebte" (To the distant beloved—a poem written by a Viennese physician, at Beethoven's request, as part of a song cycle); that theme enabled Schumann to pay tribute to Beethoven and at the same time to use his "distant beloved" theme to refer secretly to Clara, to whom he sends his love and sorrow. Most of the melodies in this movement are derived from that theme, and by saving it for the end of the first movement, it becomes a culmination. I would like to add here that I have found bits of Beethoven here and there in many of Schumann's works—little tributes that flicker almost subliminally, such as the B-flat theme in the middle of "Aufschwung" from the *Fantasiestücke*, the same theme Beethoven writes in his Adagio movement of the Ninth Symphony. It is almost as though Schumann could not help but allow his love for the master to shine through.

To return to the *Fantasie*: I love the instruction Schumann gives to the pianist at the outset—"Throughout the *Fantasie*, play with great pleasure, joy and positive energy!" (And I always obey this dictum!)

He originally entitled the first movement "Ruins" because he was in a desperate, "ruined" state of mind as a result of the separation between himself and Clara. Robert told her that this first movement was the most passionate thing he had ever written—"a deep lament for you"—and he told others that he felt that this composition represented his highest achievement.

Schumann went through a whole series of titles for his *Fantasie* and for the separate movements. He first decided to adapt the *Fantasie* into a "Sonata for Beethoven," then an "Obolus for Beethoven." He then added two more movements, calling the majestic second movement first "Trophies," then "Triumphal Arch," and the last movement "Palms," and then "Constellations." In his literary journal he lamented that no monument to Beethoven would be sufficient, and that a hundred century-old oaks should be replanted in a flat space in such a way as to spell out the name Beethoven in colossal letters.

Ultimately he deleted all of his titles, and we are left with only his indications and intentions as to how they each ought to be performed; but throughout the piece, the musical quotations, references, and strains from Beethoven are very much present. Even though everything Robert wrote for the piano was meant as a message or gift to Clara, yet, in these passionate declarations, as with any great work of art, there are many layers, and personal relevance for us all.

The greatest challenge in this very episodic music is finding the means to connect Schumann's mood swings, which range from fiercely passionate to utter silence. One has to become something of a character actor, taking on a variety of roles; but the greatest difficulty is weaving it all together into a tapestry. If we fail to do so, it all descends into chaos.

The first movement goes back and forth between the highly emotional episodes and exquisite tenderness. The second movement is basically a triumphal march that is so elating that I almost have to harness my excitement when I play it. There are playful scherzando passages and then that impossible coda at the end of the second movement, arguably one of the most challenging and terrifying passages in all of piano literature. When I played it for Peter Frankl, whose Schumann playing is wonderful, I asked him for any advice he might have, and his wry reply still makes me chuckle: "Are you asking me whether we can take out life insurance on that coda? The answer is No!"

Schumann's three personalities are present in everything he ever penned, and he acknowledged them with names: Florestan, the outgoing one; Eusebius, the inward, thoughtful one; and Raro, the mediator. He faceted himself so that he could speak in different tongues in his music journal, and in his compositions. And these conversations with himself are episodic, fragmented, volatile, mercurial, a phenomenon that was present in all his work long before the manic-depressive episodes that led to his eventual hospitalization for mental illness.

Schumann is one of the composers for whom it is helpful to know the facts about his personal life, because it is all clearly reflected in his music. Therefore, with all that we know about Schumann the man, we approach the *Fantasie* expecting an arduous and emotional journey during which we will experience his anguish, sadness, joy, triumph, and ultimate repose.

There are so many of Schumann's own indulgences—ritardandos, ritenutos, accents, fermatas, sudden demonic shifts—that if we added our own on top of his, the whole thing would fragment. He seems to want to hold the harness around us and control our rubatos to the last beat. To be sure, we will each hold a fermata according to our own inner rhythms and impulses; we will each strike a sforzando with our own speed and depth of thrust; we will express the momentum of each phrase our own way. His rhythms are often difficult to understand, because he purposely disguises them with offbeats and hemiolas. This is all part of Schumann's musical language.

We come across frequent indications for ritardandos in all of Schumann, sometimes in every other bar; and I have found that if we try to follow every single ritardando to the letter, we can end up with something sounding very forced and unnatural. I believe Schumann surely meant for us to use rubato, a liberal ebb and flow, give and take, of the tempo; and he seemed to want to control where and when and just how much. If we come across a patch overrun with these ritardandos, we must use discretion and intuition and not overdo it.

There is a curious anomaly in the *Fantasie* concerning the parts and the whole. Because each part presents unique challenges, I found that the best modus operandi, after reading through each movement in its entirety, was to approach and practice each episode as an entity unto itself, technically, while setting aside the grander task of relating each to the whole. I also found that in order to play each section to its full potential, it must be isolated, mentally and spatially, because there are diverse physical demands in each section. One must look until the melodic lines are found amidst all the dense material, because they *are* in there, though often not so easy to locate in the brambles of Schumann's landscape. Once found, though, they pop out like holograms, and there is great satisfaction in each discovery, however small.

When we are ready to string all the technically demanding episodes together in tempo, we must constantly recharge and reset both the hands and the mind at the outset of the section according to its special considerations and character, executing what was learned about that part in practicing, but without breaking the seamless flow of the whole. Yes, there are rests and fermatas, natural pauses, and tempo changes, but the most important thing to remember is that each phrase and musical statement either grows out of, reacts to, or works against what came before, philosophically. No note or phrase exists in a void. And that, as mentioned before, is the biggest challenge. Brendel said we have to both let go of ourselves and achieve complete freedom, while at the same time exercising complete control.

Brendel also wrote that if a pianist can play something slowly, he can play it fast. I counted on his wisdom and my patience as I worked in this leisurely way until the thing got under my fingers.

With this *Fantasie* I gently, slowly, allowed all the gestures and responses to enter my network of eye, ear, brain, fingers, hands, arms, and self. Once in a while, after working on it slowly, I allowed myself to go at it in tempo (for example, in the coda of the second movement) to see what I had accomplished. And lo! there it all was, magically, as some kind of reward for being "good" and diligent.

After working from the full score and learning about 90 percent of the *Fantasie* from memory, I reduced the pages to a mini-photostat. Then a strange thing happened. I felt as though I had googled Earth from high above, and I could see the terrain of the score from an birds-eye view—all the mountains and valleys, and highs and lows—what I like to call the topography of the music.

Just as I had experienced in the Schumann Piano Concerto at an earlier stage, each movement seemed to be a phase of life itself, made up of smaller events; the three movements together are a complete entity that connect uncannily for me to express the most deeply meaningful passages of my own life.

Nothing struck me more deeply than the discoveries I experienced while exploring the last movement—I was overcome with a sensation of déjà vu when playing Schumann's exquisite descending passages of three-against-two, which appear twice.

Schumann's *Fantasie* in C, Opus 17, third movement, mm. 15–19

Where had I heard this before? Finally I realized that they were reminiscent of the middle movement of Beethoven's *Emperor* Concerto.

Beethoven's Concerto No. 5 ("Emperor"), second movement, mm. 16–21

Yet another element haunted me until I finally identified those phrases as being from the second movement of Brahms' First Piano Concerto.

Brahms' Piano Concerto No. 1 in D Minor, second movement, mm. 29–30

What I found astonishing, and what deeply moved me, is that Schumann drew from Beethoven, his master; and then Brahms, writing his movement precisely at the time of Schumann's attempted suicide in the Rhine, paid homage to *his* master, Schumann.

Brahms penned an indication at the outset of the second movement of his First Piano Concerto: "Benedictus qui venit in nomine Domini" (Blessed is he who comes in the name of the Lord). That spiritual quotation has been thought to correlate with the chorale-like nature of the movement, but when I read that "Domine" was Brahms' nickname for Schumann (!), the dedication took on much deeper meaning. There are others who think that Brahms' second movement was meant as a portrait of Clara; but I believe it was more about Robert. And it was upon the death of his beloved friend and mentor that Brahms was inspired to write his great *German Requiem*.

Now when I play those profound measures in the *Fantasie*, I am imbued with the combined creative forces of all three geniuses. Not only do we have each composer's own inspirations in the context of his own life's work, but we also find the incredibly moving continuity of inspiration from Beethoven, to Schumann, then to the young Brahms. (And who was Beethoven's master? Johann Sebastian Bach. Beethoven paid homage in his last four sonatas with great fugues, his tribute to the old master.)

In a letter to Robert in 1853, Brahms, then twenty, wrote:

Revered Master,

You have made me so immensely happy that I cannot even try to thank you in words. God grant that my works soon give evidence of how much your affection and kindness have elated and inspired me. The praise that you openly bestowed upon me will arouse such extraordinary expectations of my achievements by the public that I don't know how I can begin to fulfill them even somewhat.

Similar adoration was expressed by Schumann toward Beethoven, as Schumann's master, guiding him in everything. Beethoven, for Schumann, was "the single vessel into which God put enough gifts to fill a thousand vessels." And so it goes, with so many touching examples of how one genius nourished the next, through musical history.

I have always felt that I want to play every last note that Schumann ever composed, so I went back to the great *Kreisleriana*, Opus 16, of which I had only studied three movements; it was like a *coup à foudre*, and I fell in love again.

The *Kreisleriana*, I once remarked to a pianist friend, is like a study of mental illness—shifting from mood to mood, mercurial, unpredictable. No, she replied, it is like life itself. And she was right, but so was I. In his madness, Schumann could see more clearly, feel more deeply, cover more territory, express more intensely everything we experience during the course of our lives. Moreover, Schumann manifested those episodic spasmodic shifts in *everything* he wrote.

Therefore, much of what I would like to say about the *Kreisleriana* applies to *all* of Schumann's early piano compositions: it is again, all about Robert and Clara: their tempestuous relationship, the self-revelations, and intimate reflections.

A bit of background will also help us to understand Schumann's state (or states) of mind. Schumann lost his father and sister within one year, in 1825–26. when he was fifteen. In 1833 he contracted malaria and was also drinking a lot from despair; he then, in the same year, lost his brother to tuberculosis and his sister-in-law to malaria. Then his mother died in 1836. All this added to his own weakened health.

To add to that, Friedrich Wieck was making Robert's life miserable by forbidding their relationship and sending Clara away. This nearly threw Robert over the edge with symptoms of deep depression, anxiety, fear of solitude, shortness of breath, even periodic loss of consciousness, and he began to fear he was going mad.

The last straw might have been his failure as a pianist, due to an injury to a finger on his right hand and a series of unmentionable "therapies," some self-inflicted, some quackery, all of which worsened his situation. The theories about the cause are also too unsavory to mention.

But we owe the treasury of beautiful music we have from him to his failure as a pianist, when he had no other outlet for his extraordinary musical gifts except composition. He was still able to pick himself up through writing and composing. He and some of his forward-thinking, progressive male friends formed a group and called it the Davidsbund

(Band of David), and he founded a literary journal called the *Neue Zeitschrift für Musik*, thereby becoming a music journalist and critic.

And in 1838 he also started writing a musical diary of his emotions—his high hopes and desperate loss, his mania and depression (personified, as ever, in the imaginary characters Florestan and Eusebius, whom we encounter throughout all his musical compositions)—all recorded in five days—and titled *Kreisleriana*.

The opening movement is a rush of spontaneous emotion, executed in brilliant but difficult passages that have to be well fingered, well practiced, and felt in subphrases in order to ensure accuracy and no derailments, but never compromised in terms of their passionate and impetuous progression. This is followed by the contrasting tenderness of the second movement. Then comes a restless, mercurial section, followed again by utter desolation. Such are the continuing mood shifts from segment to segment; if there is a wildly emotional outburst, you can count on a serene, sad, or deeply introspective section to follow. If the music is noble and stately, chances are the next one will be playful. And each movement presents its own pianistic challenges, from legato octave passages to fast, complicated, strange, finger-twisting configurations.

The young Clara, upon hearing the *Kreisleriana* for the first time, said to Robert, "Sometimes your music frightens me and I wonder, is it really true that the creator of such things is going to be my husband?" But Robert instructed Clara to "play my *Kreisleriana* often—a positively wild love is in some of the movements and your life and mine, and the way you look."

Clara continued to plead with him to be more lucid in his writing because it hurt her so much when people did not understand him. Schumann had said he would dedicate the work to Clara, but he ended up dedicating it to Chopin. I wonder whether that was related to her lack of sympathy with the score . . .

The fragmentation that defines Schumann's music consists of bits of memory that coalesce—puzzle pieces that come together, or, better, loose gemstones that are set into a single sparkling piece of jewelry.

In later collections such as the *Kinderscenen* and *Fantasiestücke*, the pieces stand alone and are often played as encores, but these *Kreisleriana* pieces are organically woven together into a whole. Most of these early works were written before Schumann was twenty-nine, and he revised them twelve years later when he didn't quite agree with his earlier frivolities.

Some pianists enjoy his original versions more, but in certain cases I have been grateful for his changes, which include some cuts of redundancies. Clara made some revisions according to her own preferences, and there is a Brahms edition that is better, because it is probably closer to Schumann's intentions. I would love to have seen his original score.

There are many idiosyncrasies in Schumann's piano music. Sometimes he writes on a third clef (the Romance in F-sharp, and the *Humoreske*, Opus 20), sometimes there are notes only to be imagined, not played but rather just pressed down quietly (the Sphinx in *Carnaval*); and sometimes he writes a chord, releasing one note at a time, so that only one tone is left at the end, sort of like the disappearing Cheshire cat with only the smile left at the end (*Papillons*).

But Schumann (unlike, say, Haydn, with his broad sense of humor and deliberate comedy) does not mean to be funny. Schumann takes us to the brink of the absurd with his seemingly bizarre ideas. He was very adventurous with the pedal effects, much more than Chopin, and when he writes in "pedal" I believe it is an indication to use the sostenuto pedal, because the bass could not otherwise be sustained while the rest of the music is played. Also, there are no indications for the damper pedal at all even where certainly one would naturally apply it quite liberally, another proof that by "pedal" he meant the sostenuto pedal.

Schumann experimented with cross-rhythms, concealed inner voices, and odd textures (such as the parallel octaves in the second movement of the *Kreisleriana*), and he knew how to create strange effects, auditory illusions, and even harmonics.

"Des Abends," from *Fantasiestücke*, Opus 12, has loving inscriptions in the margin by both Robert and Clara to their friend Becker, who was the best man at their wedding. This is possibly the single most sublime piece in all of Schumann's oeuvre; along with the beauty, the piece is an example of his experimentation with the way one holds one's hands on the keyboard, overlapping, with crossed thumbs on the keys, minimizing movement, and therefore increasing the legato—all commendable musical goals. And then, aside from all the ambiguous rhythms and hemiolas, there are his dissonances, which are based mainly on the small interval of a minor second and create gorgeous tensions to be resolved.

Jerome Lowenthal is one of the most interesting people I have ever met, and his great pianism can be heard on his eightieth-birthday CDs. Lowenthal transforms Liszt, one of his specialties, into sheer poetry, where others display their prowess. This attests to his superb imagination; but Lowenthal, the intellectual, has delved into interrelationships between literature and music, and in doing so has added historical and theoretical perspectives to musical elements. In an interview (*Clavier*, January 1992) we were discussing a poem by Robert Browning and how it was helpful in revealing the spiritual nuances of certain chords. The poem is "A Toccata at Galuppi's." This was the first time I had ever heard of the Venetian composer Baldassare Galuppi, and the line from the poem "sixths diminished, sigh on sigh" led Lowenthal to wonder whether Browning had erred in his definition of the interval, since diminished sixths would sound exactly like a fifth. And that musing led into further discussion of Schumann:

> I thought it was clearly that Browning meant diminished sevenths.
> My professor, although not a musician, was certain that Browning
> had not made a mistake. That made me wonder whether there, in

fact, were diminished sixths, and I then discovered that not only does Schumann use them, but it is one of the fingerprints of his style!

Lowenthal continued, with typical wit, "I am far from a Galuppist myself!" and then proceeded with a discourse on the diminished sixth as it functions pivotally in the Schumann *Fantasie* in C, moving on to that work's derivation—a typical Lowenthal digression, his thought in action, punctuated at the piano. And all this from a line of Browning poetry, as the proverbial pebble that had been thrown into the sea and produced waves in his mind for all these years.

> To understand one art, understanding others is basic. Literature, with its wide-ranging possibilities, is the art that casts the most direct light on other arts, in particular, music.
>
> Similarly, I think that music, by its purity, illuminates aspects of literature that often are ignored. The subtlety with which a great writer moves from phrase to phrase, building his structure, helps me understand the real structure—as opposed to the textbook structure—of a musical composition.

In these views, Lowenthal comes close to the thinking of Robert Schumann himself (but without the chaos!), who drew constantly from literature and poetry for his musical inspiration and ideas.

The *Kreisleriana*, for example, is a good example of the cross-pollination that occurs between the arts. It was based on a book by E. T. A. Hoffmann about an eccentric musician named Kreisler with whom Schumann identified. That, and the fact that it was written in a stream-of-consciousness style, is all we need to know about the book itself. Yet Schumann synthesized his experience of the literary work into his own descriptive musical experience. All *we* need to do is to relate this musical experience to our own lives.

I think that is what art does, or should do: stir us to activate and draw from our own life's experience. Schumann believed, as did many nineteenth-century poets and writers, that life was a series of fragments that were mysteriously related and could be united and transfigured only by the poet or musician. This is the key to understanding Schumann— and quite possibly, *Kreisleriana* exemplifies this philosophy the best with its quixotic shifts.

It is, of course, easier for an audience to understand this fragmented style in a literary work, where words describe each fragment. With music, the abstract expression is harder.

Schumann's musical allusions and style must truly have mystified his public by their unconventionality. (His almost obsessive dotted figures have turned away a few pianists of my acquaintance from loving his music.)

I had the good fortune to meet William Masselos, a quiet, unassuming, but great pianist and teacher, for whom words did not come easily. His recording of the *Davidsbündlertänze* is one of the greatest of that work and is in some ways a microcosm of the pianist. Masselos said that this piece was like a musical diary of his own life—that it gave him a voice. Moreover, he himself was like the music: gentle, refined, witty, and a bit inward due to an illness that kept him out of the public eye. He was a student of David Saperton, Carl Friedberg (a disciple of Brahms and Clara), and Nelly Reuschel (a disciple of Clara). I asked whether his lineage as well as his own temperament nurtured the personal identification with Schumann that gained him wide acclaim as a Schumann interpreter.

Absolutely—it all goes back to Papa Friedberg and Nelly Reuschel—with them to Clara Schumann—and with Clara, to Robert. Clara may be the key to it all; she was the world's greatest keeper of the flame. The further time takes us away from the tradition, the less authentic the interpretations are, I'm afraid. Schumann has to be played with intensity and passion, of course. But with the complete absence of exaggeration or undue liberty. We started on the *Davidsbündlertänze* when I was 14. Schumann is my mother tongue, so to speak.

I often have the feeling that Schumann may have been the noblest of all the Romantics—combining the most intimate with the heroic, the most innovative in form, and the direct heir of Beethoven. Even the smallest selection from any of his collections—*Kinderscenen*, *Album for the Young*, *Waldscenen*, *Fantasiestücke*—manifests his greatness, and I love it when I hear a young child playing these short works with a sense that these pieces are special in a way such a young person cannot yet define.

Schumann was very interested in the minds of children, perhaps ever since Clara, still a very young girl, called him "a moonstruck maker of charades." The *Kinderscenen* are an adult's recollection of childhood, for adults to play, but the *Album for the Young*, Opus 68 (containing forty-eight pieces!), was deliberately planned to put his music within the reach of very young players. It was written for his oldest child, seven-year-old Marie, who was born in 1841. He also wrote duets and *Klavier-sonaten für die Jugend*, Opus 118, for her and the Schumanns' next two daughters.

It is interesting that the pieces of Schumann's that depict childhood in retrospect, or that were composed for children to play, were written later in his short life (note the opus numbers) than some of his more difficult and favored concert pieces.

In one of his youthful works, *Carnaval*, Opus 9, subtitled *Scènes mignonnes sur quatre notes*, Schumann gathered together friends, family, an old flame named Ernestine von Fricken ("Estrella"), Clara ("Chiarina"), composers (Chopin and Paganini), and characters out of commedia dell'arte (Pierrot, Harlequin, Pantalon, and Colombine), along with his alter egos Florestan and Eusebius; these subjects are portrayed in miniature musical vignettes as they whirl around the carnival grounds in pieces based upon four notes: A, E-flat, C, and B-natural. These tones in German notation (which designates E-flat as "Es" ["S"] and B-natural as "H") spell out the town of Asch, Ernestine's birthplace, and are scrambled into various motifs. (Clara was said to omit "Estrella" whenever she performed this collection.) Those letters also appear in Schumann's own surname.

Carnaval also includes quotations from his *Papillons* and concludes with the "Marche des 'Davidsbündler' contre les Philistins"; Schumann often referred to, and derided, a certain unintellectual faction of the music world as Philistines, and here he drives them triumphantly away from the carnival gathering, with great musical fanfare.

Schumann's thorny landscape, from the outside looking in, even in his very short works, can be somewhat off-putting at first glance. I have had to urge reluctant students to enter his world when they first behold a page of the score . . . all sorts of dotted figures, hand crossings, and metrical changes, accompanied along the way by lengthy German indications to guide us onward. But after I remind them that the music is based upon same system of notes and rhythms that they have encountered before, we set to the task of exploration. (Clara herself had trouble performing the first of Schumann's piano compositions—*Papillons*—and spoke of how her audience became confused and fidgety when presented with the unrelated fragments.)

The abiding myth that in the performance of Romantic works such as Schumann's we have more freedom than we did in playing, say, Mozart is misleading. In fact, we don't. These Romantic composers wrote down everything they wanted from us, whereas Mozart had almost no markings in phrasing, tempo, dynamics, and so on. In other words: to perform Schumann, we have to read the music. And although it is not accessible as a Mozart sonata, we can at once acknowledge the whims and impulses of his creative unpredictable mind; and we might have to buy a German dictionary, or have, as I do, some kind German-speaking friends who don't mind a call at odd hours of the evening.

Incidentally, Beethoven started those long demands in German in his late sonatas, and Schumann just continued it; in fact, sometimes I feel that Schumann is, in many ways, a continuation of late Beethoven. Or maybe one could say that Beethoven, in his last works, was actually the dawning of the Romantic period. In the end, the greatest challenge in Schumann's music, besides the achievement of its technical demands, is, as mentioned before, making of all the episodes and fragments an organic, cohesive whole.

And that means we have to create what I call "connective tissue" between the sections. Sometimes there is a single tone that, if deepened or prolonged, will act as a harmonic pivot from one fragment to the next. Sometimes relative tempos will yield an answer. And often, there seems to be *no* answer. Schumann presents us with a non sequitur, and we have to just play it, and trust blindly, without a clear answer. But isn't life like that—a series of unexpected, unrelated events?

As to the fragments as bits of memorabilia, I think that to play this music well we have to abandon our reserve or even decorum, fish around in our own pasts and presents, and throw ourselves into it as though we, too, were a little bit mad, or at the very least mercurial and complex; and then we must try to define and express those emotional states according to our own experience.

Johannes Brahms, Sonata for Two Pianos in F Minor, Opus 34b; autograph manuscript (1864?), page 3. The Pierpont Morgan Library, New York, Cary 4.

6

BRAHMS (1833–1897)

When I was nineteen at Queens College, in New York, I entered a concerto competition on campus. My teacher, Leopold Mittman, tried to dissuade me from preparing the Brahms First Piano Concerto, but I was too passionate about it to give up the idea. I had listened ecstatically throughout my teens to Artur Rubinstein's recording with Fritz Reiner and had that "first fine careless rapture" of a young person for Brahms. But I now know that the rapture of Brahms is there for us at all ages.

My teacher had concerns about the technical difficulties in Brahms that require a large hand, but he showed me some tricks of the trade (for example, in those cataclysmic octave trills in the first movement). I'll never forget that he winked and said to me, "I defy any of the judges to discover how a little one like you is doing those trills!" (And that is still my secret!)

Moreover, he was concerned that Brahms' conception of the piano as an integral part of the orchestral score in this concerto, and at least an equal partner with the orchestra rather than a virtuosic piano solo with orchestral accompaniment, would make it less appropriate for a competition than, say, a Rachmaninoff Concerto.

I think my teacher also worried about whether I had the maturity to process and project the profound masterpiece. But it turned out that he needn't have worried. I was successful and got to play it with the orchestra two nights running. It was one of the highlights of my early musical life and the beginning of my long love affair with Brahms. For that reason, I would never want to discourage a student who passionately desired to play something I didn't think he or she was ready for—I would just try to help to achieve the goal, as my teacher did, because I think that with passion, anything is possible. (Except, perhaps, the late Beethoven sonatas and the Schumann *Fantasie*.)

In his music journals Schumann noted that Brahms' own playing was "full of genius" and that he "transformed the piano into an orchestra of lamenting and jubilant voices," and that although Brahms' music was clear in form, it was difficult to perform—it could be "insanely colossal and demonically wild, from ecstatic joy to longing for the grave." That may seem like one of Schumann's manic overstatements, but it isn't.

And with all of this adulation, the sad fact was that Brahms suffered much verbal abuse from critics and jealous peers. To think that the First Piano Concerto, which is so beloved by me and by millions of music lovers, was first described by a critic in 1859 in the Leipzig magazine *Signale für die musikalische Welt* as a "retching, plowing, jerking and yanking . . . patching and tearing of phrases—mostly clichéd—[that] has to be endured for over three-quarters of an hour."

Dvořák loved Brahms. Wagner did not. Tschaikovsky, who knew Brahms, called him a "self-inflated ungifted mediocrity." Benjamin Britten, Hugo Wolf, George Bernard Shaw, and even some American writers, including a recent *New York Times* critic, were equally malicious or at the very least indifferent toward his music.

How can they have missed the tenderness, the colossal sonorities, the brooding, the joy, the despair, the charm, the gentle heart, the massiveness? Is it any wonder that Brahms suffered so many self-doubts that he destroyed much of his music before it could be published? It is best not to dwell on these negative opinions, however, and just be grateful that Brahms kept on working until he became "Brahms."

The pianist and musicologist Charles Rosen once wrote that "the ideal virtuoso piece sounds a lot harder than it really is." In fact, Liszt, whose name is most associated with virtuosic piano writing, does in fact feel much more comfortable than it sounds. Rosen added, "The music of Johannes Brahms is actually much harder than it sounds." And with that I can agree as well. Gary Graffman once quipped, "A *great* performance of Brahms will make the audience responsive. But all it takes is a mediocre performance of Liszt to elicit the same response."

The piano music of Brahms requires a technique that is almost the antithesis of the virtuoso pieces of earlier Liszt in its avoidance of bravura for its own sake: instead, there is intimacy, introspection, multiple entwining melodic lines, luxuriant harmonies, extended arpeggios, and peculiar configurations that are rarely comfortable for the hand. The rewards lie in choosing between the voices and truffling out the intentions so deeply embedded by this very modest and solitary composer.

The elements that make Brahms difficult to play do not always meet the listener's ear. The main challenge, to my mind, and one of the few opportunities for individuality, is the aforementioned dense writing, which provides the pianist with choices regarding how we can bring out one voice without sacrificing the others. So not only do we have Brahms' sorrows to express, but we have the exquisite torture of prioritizing between his musical lines, each of which is always compelling.

Which one would we give one up? Neither! So how do we balance between them and bring both out?

Balancing contrapuntal lines applies as much to Brahms as it does to Bach or Chopin. Brahms declared that the bass line was just as important as the upper melodic line. They were the two polar boundaries and frames of the music, and the music, whatever its character—whether calm or explosive—would be a universe defined and confined within those boundaries.

Brahms' piano music is not two-hand music—it cannot be divided into left and right hands, as though "OK, the left hand has this, and the right hand has that." (The only exceptions to this may be the Hungarian Dances, which do have a kind of oom-pah bass accompaniment to the melodic right hand. And in many of his beautiful Opus 39 Waltzes there is also a clear division between the accompaniment and melodic lines.) But in his late works, the *Klavierstücke* from Opus 76 through Opus 119, there is a continuum of melodic and harmonic material that transcends two-handedness. (Arthur Rubinstein called the late piano works of Brahms "chamber music for the piano.") Each line is horizontal, and although they have to be synchronized vertically, each line must be seamless under the phrase lines that pertain to that voice. Listening to oneself is critical; then comes the mastering of the various touches, which often are simultaneous. Sometimes one hand is required to play two touches at once: the top fingers of the right hand may be legato, and the tenor or alto voice, played by the lower fingers, is staccato, or vice versa.

Currently I am in the process of relearning and recording almost all of Brahms' late piano works from Opus 116 through the last work, Opus 119; many of these pieces, which I studied when I was younger and think of in a whole new way. Brahms referred to these late works as "the lullabies of my sorrows" (other translations read "the lullabies of my old age"), and although I am not ready for any lullabies of my own later age, I do find deeper meanings: resignation, acceptance, sadness, but also joy and many light moments.

These are all supreme utterances; if they are like chamber music, they are also lieder without words, and they express every emotion from serenity to malaise. The complete set of Opus 116 (which are the least often played of all the late works) consists of seven fantasies subtitled either *Capriccio* or *Intermezzo*. They contain some of the loveliest conversational writing, as in the duet between soprano and tenor voices in the Intermezzo in E Major, Opus 116 No. 6, Andantino teneramente (included on the CD). (Brahms referred to his inner voices as his "tenor thumb," an apt description, as the thumbs do get many of the most sensual melodic lines.) The restless and impetuous outcries of the Capricci contrast dramatically with the tender and loving questionings of the Intermezzi; the Capricci are generally more energetic and powerful; the Intermezzi are more mysterious and often ineffably sad.

In Brahms, there is a lot of musical sighing, and so the tapering of the phrase ends to express *weltschmerz*, or world-weariness, is of great importance.

What is not immediately apparent to the listener is all the details that go into the creation of these moods—their coordination within the context of the big picture, the balancing, shaping, and weighting of each voice, establishing hierarchies of importance, creating a balance between the vertical pressure and speed of each note (the volume and weight) and the horizontality of the legato discourse (or voices).

The four pieces of Opus 119 are the last four works Brahms wrote for solo piano. They are like a summing up of his life. The B Minor Intermezzo is a desolate and resigned expression full of unresolved dissonance, in short breathy phrases (again that sighing) and ending with a dissonant passage of descending thirds that seems to be headed for chaos and finally resolves at the very last bar, but in B minor. Brahms instructed Clara to play this as slowly as possible and only for herself— "an audience of even one is too many." The pianist must try to express that utter and complete resignation and sadness.

The E-flat Rhapsodie is massive and heroic, like the sonatas, with a short nostalgic interlude in the middle that sounds as though it were written to be strummed on a zither or some Hungarian folk instrument, with its rolled chords; and then there is an almost jolly parody of the heroic march theme.

Brahms presents the pianist with fistfuls of notes and copious chords, and sometimes you need to thread one fine line through all of those notes (as exemplified in the zitherlike section of the Rhapsodie in Opus 119, along with bits of a folk element in an otherwise heroic statement). In the same Rhapsodie the big theme comes back over and over, each time with different bass lines, different inversions of chords, sometimes even different harmonizations. Everywhere there is a struggle between major and minor, and even in the last lines of this Rhapsodie—Brahms' very last solo piano work—the struggle remains as he ends hugely, but in E-flat *minor.*

What makes Brahms "Brahms"? When Brahms came to Vienna as a young man of twenty-nine, he was considered a radical and musically unformed. He was intensely interested in new inventions—everything from Edison's phonograph to new developments in pianos construction and electricity. He read treatises about the ideal sound, the physics of sound, and the physiology and perception of sound—essays that explained the scientific interactions between harmony and dissonance. Brahms was looked for the connections between aesthetics and the science of sound and nature. He attended as many concerts as he could, including choral concerts; these deeply affected his short works for piano, many of which are in four-part writing. All his earnest pursuits fed into his composition.

And so it is difficult to understand all the early criticism that labeled Brahms as "lawless" and "formless." Yet before long he began to be valued for his originality. His links to the past melded together with his embrace of the new philosophies and redefinitions of everything that affected musical life. Even so, Brahms was in the end much more conservative than many of his contemporaries, such as Liszt and Wagner. In fact, it is the Classical element in his music, and those links to the past, that make his music so accessible to the ear. Brahms looked both backward and forward.

For Brahms, the most important goal was to be understood. To be heard, maybe even to be loved, was of much more concern to him than his technique in composition, since he felt that, as an end in itself, diminished creativity. Brahms' ideal audience was made up of those who could either play or understand him. In fact, he had a rather elitist view about musically discriminating audiences; he preferred those who, as one early twentieth-century critic put it, "could uncover the hidden soul of Brahms' world of sound."

But Brahms was a man of many contrasts. There is a strange, perplexing phenomenon in the music of Brahms: scarcely a great performer exists who would fail to list Brahms among the most beloved composers in the repertoire, and yet many listeners consider Brahms' music to be for connoisseurs and sophisticates, not as readily appealing to general audiences as that of the other Romantics.

The man had contradictory traits: he was very kind and generous to his friends, yet he often manifested a rude and coarse manner; he had great loyalty and love of family and friends, yet for some reason (and there are many theories) he never married. He seemed to be ambivalent about marriage and was quite prudish about the importance of maintaining respectable relationships, yet he was said to have visited houses of ill repute. He had unresolved love relationships— though probably not with Clara Schumann, with whom he had a long, affectionate, but complex friendship, and who he said "was present in all his music."

He was independent of spirit, yet strongly connected to his friends; he eventually became wealthy, but remained frugal; and his music contains both reserve and an overflowing bounty of emotions.

He could write a rustic Hungarian dance as well as the deepest, most refined utterances; in fact, his music has often been described as having healing and comforting qualities. Brahms had many friends, but he maintained a strong sense of privacy and resisted letting people get too close to him. Clara Schumann confessed that after fifty years of knowing him, she had no insight into his character or his way of thinking. He deliberately destroyed manuscripts and letters that would have revealed too much.

He often appeared disheveled and had a very nonconformist approach to his dress, although he was scrupulous about the details of his work. He enjoyed solitary pursuits, walking, reading the Bible, art books, and poetry, though he had no formal education (and was very touchy about that fact).

Like Chopin, he did not like to write letters, and though he claimed he was not good at expressing himself in words, his letters reveal him to have been extremely articulate, at least as far as I am concerned.

In 1983 I interviewed Detlef Kraus, president of the Brahms Society in Germany. As a North German from Hamburg, Brahms' birthplace, and a pianist who recorded and performed the complete Brahms piano works, he had a strong connection to the composer, and we devoted the discussion to unraveling and clarifying some of the enigmas about Brahms.

> The question of the reception of Brahms' music is one that has confounded me for a long time. A person must remember that it was the German Requiem and his vocal music that accounted for his initial acceptance and popularity. The German language was used more widely in continental Europe at Brahms' time especially in the big cities. Brahms' instrumental music is very tightly connected to his vocal music by means of motifs, phrasing, content, how it speaks, and what it says. It is not simply intriguing sound, but it has a "language" that is somehow more accessible when you relate it to German words. I have to confess, however, that even in my own country, there is a certain ambivalence about his music, except for the Second Piano Concerto, and the Handel Variations.

The Variations on a Theme of Händel, Opus 24, have been declared by musicians and critics, including Donald Francis Tovey, to be among the greatest variations ever written. Brahms wrote them in one stretch in 1861, when he was twenty-eight, dedicating them to "a dear friend" (Clara Schumann). Starting with a simple Baroque theme, each variation seems to unfurl into the next, gaining momentum, with just the right shifts of meter, ranging from Hungarian dance, to lullaby, to march, to song, and ending with a magnificent fugue, which is a rousing finale. In many of the variations, the phrasing and gestures required to express the right moods and rhythms are almost dancelike. The entire work is very orchestral and diverse, always challenging, and deeply pleasurable to play.

I asked Kraus why there is such a perplexing disparity between the pleasure a pianist gets from playing the piano and chamber works and the relatively limited audience, and he responded that it was actually the Hungarian Dances and music that is more accessible music to dilettantes that give most of us our initial exposure to Brahms; the instrumental music is very difficult both to play and to understand. Kraus made the strong point that there is a direct correlation between how the audience might respond to Brahms and how convincingly a performer offers it to them.

Kraus underscored the importance of a stability of tempo in performance as an essential component. There is a tendency to distort the tempo in Brahms—the most frequent error of interpretation. He added, "Another factor is that while pianists might know what f means, not so many know what p means. They go through it bang-bang, and that's their Brahms, and people applaud it; but you cannot play Brahms like you play Rachmaninoff."

When Kraus was young, he heard concerts conducted by a close friend of Brahms, who had the composer's full endorsement. Thus Kraus caught, what he calls, "the tip of the tail of Brahms' time."

As Kraus pointed out, Brahms' piano music is very erratic. There are three Sonatas, sixteen Intermezzi and Capricci, and a few Rhapsodies, which, along with the Hungarian Dances, variations, and miscellaneous pieces (Ballades, Romances, Variations, and so on), all belong to different periods. Many are rarely, if ever, played in concert. "Therefore, to single out a 'great Brahms pianist,' is a vain pursuit" (*Clavier*, "Two Gentlemen from Hamburg," December 1983).

According to Kraus, for Brahms in particular a performer must have great spontaneity, a sense of fantasy for color and phrasing, and a perception of the appropriate dynamics according to the size of the hall, much of which has been lost today because of electronic amplification. He stressed that the great legacy of such pianists as Wilhelm Kempff, Edwin Fischer, and Artur Schnabel is that they had to listen to themselves anew each time, without the benefit of technology.

The moment the subject of texture and inner voices was introduced into the conversation, Kraus' excitement and affection for what makes Brahms Brahms came into full flower. How can a pianist ever choose which inner voice to bring out, when there are so many beautiful things happening at once that intertwine with each other? Which voice should the pianist "love" the most?

Kraus exclaimed,

Why, that's precisely the point! You never can make a decision. If you think of the piece as a choral work, and you become, in a sense, the conductor of a choir, and say, "Now the altos, now the sopranos a little more," you can change as you wish with good sense and taste . . . and you might spontaneously choose to bring a new inner voice out.

The balance between treble and bass is a constant consideration, and there is no actual decision to make. You determine choices by all kinds of conditions which are always changing: the hall, the piano, the audience, the country, the time of day. Everything is always changing . . . so for students who cry out for recipes, there are none. In my own teaching, in master classes or at the Hochschule, I resist giving out formulas . . . they have to learn how to speak spontaneously, as they would to a person. Playing a concert is exactly the same thing: a kind of interaction with people. I do tell my students that the use of rubato in Brahms varies greatly from one artist to the next. You have to first find the finest tone, the right volume, and derive what you can from expressive phrasing, and do whatever you can within the framework of a stable tempo. And only after you exhaust all of these methods, should you alter the tempo—Tempo is the last thing you should change.

Kraus quoted Brahms, who was asked by his publisher, Simrock, for a metronome marking for the music: "You think I am such a donkey, that I play my music always the same way?!"

The little house in Baden-Baden in the Black Forest that was Brahms' retreat still exists. To this day anyone can trace the little path on which he walked for hours in the early morning before breakfast.

Once Brahms was asked how he happened to come upon a certain beautiful melody. "Well," he answered, "it took me two days of walking to get it." It is for this reason that when Brahms writes *andante*, it truly means he is walking (from *andare*, Italian for "to walk"). A good part of Brahms' inspiration came from his walks in nature, just as Beethoven's did. He had serenity and repose, but he also had a passionate and complex nature, both in his music and his relationships.

Brahms was an indispensable friend to both Robert and Clara Schumann, but that relationship was very complex. He was neither fish nor fowl—not quite a member of their family (caring for their children when Clara was on tour, protecting her after Robert's breakdown) and not quite a lover; both Brahms and Clara valued their privacy, and although each expressed love for the other in ardent letters back and forth after Robert's death, what exactly transpired between them is anyone's conjecture. It is more likely that his romantic involvements were with other women—Ottilie Ebner, for example, and another named Luise Dustmann.

Basically Brahms was a loner, although he was not lonely (he had so many friends that he was asked to be the godfather of sixteen children!), because he was a very devoted friend. And he dedicated many works to them. Dvořák said of Brahms: "Such a great man, such a great soul."

As a composer and a pianist, Brahms sought to avoid, almost shyly, all appearances of self-importance or pomposity, and he was constantly being compared, by critics and audiences alike, to his contemporary Franz Liszt, his direct opposite in many ways. Brahms wanted his compositions to speak for themselves, so his lack of bravura and visual flair was as impressive for its depth of meaning (the German word for it is *innigkeit*) as it was lacking in showmanship. It almost became a contest between virtue and virtuosity.

Brahms' build was short, square, and solid, unlike Liszt's tall, thin figure, but he presented an aspect of strength along with what was described as a "contemplative radiance from the inside." With Liszt there were many outward visual effects—drama, illusion, gestures—and with Brahms it was all inside the music (although later in his life Liszt became an abbé of the church and wrote very contemplative, deep, and complex music).

A pianist could alter Chopin, or Mozart, or Liszt, with an embellishment, because the music is basically melodic; but we could never change Brahms, because the music is so dense and organized. Brahms had a great desire to attain perfection—he even went back to emend an early Piano Trio in his old age.

His music is logical and perfect. For him the word *virtuosity* would mean "the basic ability to play the music faithfully"; and in this music there is both delicacy and monumentality. In order to achieve that monumentality, discussions of volume and intensity come up—and most students, if you ask them to play more intensely, play louder. I watched a DVD of a talented young piano quartet playing Brahms' Piano Quartet in C Minor, Opus 50, at the Verbier Music Festival being coached by the violinist Gábor Tákacs-Nagy. It wasn't until Tákacs-Nagy read them an excerpt from a letter Brahms sent to his publisher along with the score for publication that the students were able to delve deeper into their psyches and try to communicate the anguish and passion required to interpret this music. In the letter Brahms suggested that the publisher print an image on the cover of the score of a pistol pointed at a head—to inform performers about his state of mind while writing this work. In the end, as with all art, it is experiencing life that gives us the keys to interpretation, and sometimes even gifted young people don't get it or cannot get it.

Brahms cared not only about interpretation, but about matters of virtuosity and technique as well. He wrote fifty-one exercises that were practice aids for his own and others' performances and loved the technical challenges in his own music. In his own First Piano Concerto, in the first movement, there are octave trills that, as I mentioned, were too wide for my hand. So my teacher showed me a trick that sounded pretty good (which involved playing two notes with one finger—and that is all I will share here!). There are always subtle ways of getting around some of the more unplayable passages in any music; they are certainly not a reason to give up an entire piece. (And a whole essay can be written about the art of "faking" it!)

In middle age Brahms got very sloppy in his own playing; some of the reviews were bad, and Clara called him abominable. He hummed along, sometimes growling and howling to cover some of the difficulties, and one critic suggested that the composer must have surreptitiously acquired a dog.

Like all the great pianist-composers, Brahms had to grapple with the issue of pianos. When he was in Vienna he was provided with Streichers and Bösendorfers, and when in Germany he used Bechsteins and Steinways. In his apartment he had a Graf and a Streicher (which was modeled after a Steinway), and his earliest public performance on an American Steinway was in December 1865 in Mannheim. Brahms preferred the Steinway. In fact, for the premiere of his Second Piano Concerto, he said he would gladly pay for the shipping of an American Steinway; but, he went on, "I will not play again on some questionable or risky instrument!" Then, in 1881, Steinway opened a branch in Hamburg, making the pianos of his choice much more accessible.

Stylistically, no matter what the instrument, Brahms was said to have played without much emotional affect, as though he were playing for himself (it is often said that composers are the least effective interpreters of their own music). Since Brahms' time, his music has been performed with physicality and deep expressiveness. However, I remember my teacher once cautioning me, as Detlef Kraus was describing, that if I wanted to increase the intensity of the music, I must do it dynamically, and with expressive phrasing; the very last thing one should change, without an indication from the composer, would be the tempo.

With Brahms there came a new unique brand of fullness and beauty, of both harmony and melodic invention, and an inner nobility and sincerity. His musical masterpieces, of any length, even the shortest works, are microcosms of the composer's conception of the world. And that is the most enormous, most critical work for us: to try to get closer to that complicated core. In all of Brahms there is an underlying sense of sorrow and disillusionment, set off by passages of serenity, comfort, and consolation. But then, quite soon, within the same work, that mood can become overcast with a troubling unrest, as though something were brewing. Certainly his last piano works are filled with undeniable resignation and acceptance, if not despair.

I agree with Richard Goode, who told me that the time had come when everyone did not have to perform entire opuses—all twenty-four Chopin Preludes, or all the pieces in Opus 116 or 118 of Brahms—and I think it is entirely within reason and acceptability to make a "bouquet" of our own favorite Brahms works, choosing contrasting moods and keys, according to our own chemistry and taste. (Goodness knows there are a treasurable number of these luminous little masterworks.) We can only strive to get close to how *Stereo Review* described Radu Lupu's recordings of Opus 118 and Opus 119: "a glowing realization of what Brahms set down that leaves one at a loss for words and simply glad to have ears."

During an interview with Radu Lupu (*Clavier*, July–August 1992), the pianist, in a burst of enthusiasm, embarked on a fascinating discourse that gave me a glimpse of the detective work in which he engages in order to uncover the myriad permutations and combinations of Brahms' source material. Lupu remarked, "You have to make a balance just as you would between instruments. That's the most fascinating thing for us, looking at it, sweating it out mentally, and making those little decisions. I love doing that."

Certainly, for *all* pianists, that is the great joy of performing Brahms.

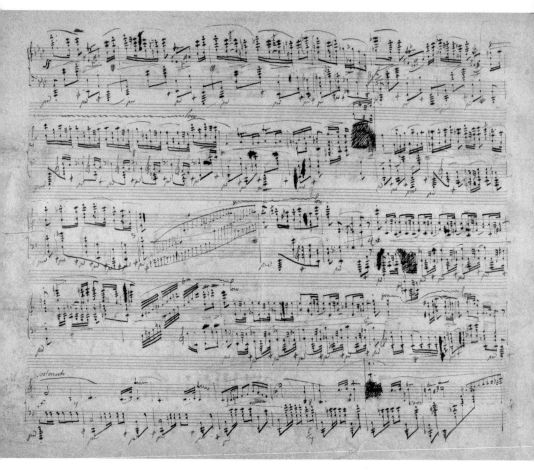

Frédéric Chopin, Polonaise in A-flat Major, Opus 53; autograph manuscript (1842?), page 2. The Pierpont Morgan Library, New York, Heineman MS 42.

7

CHOPIN (1810–1849)

One of Chopin's few requirements (which was quoted by his most famous student, Carl Mikuli) was that his students make it their duty to practice only on the best quality instruments.

For Chopin, then, that meant Pleyel, and sometimes Érard and Broadwood (from London). With advances in the English pianos, the pedals and more resonant bass strings encouraged Chopin to write his wonderfully rich and supple bass lines as accompaniments for his treble cantilena melodies, inspired in large part by Italian opera composers such as Vincenzo Bellini.

Mikuli said, "On those frail early pianos, *forte* could sound quite disagreeable, and Chopin called that strident sound 'a dog barking.' We have to strive for a round and deep sonority with substance." This was quoted by the Polish pianist and teacher Alexander Michailowski, a student of Mikuli; Michailowski was the teacher of my teacher Leopold Mittman. So reports of Chopin's frequent choice to play sotto voce, in a softer tone, can be attributed either to his pianos' limitations or his own ill health; but neither rationale allows us to deny the sometimes huge conceptions he penned in his heroic compositions. On the other hand, a frequent misinterpretation of Chopin is to bang out his *forte*s way beyond taste or style. For an overwhelming number of world-class concert pianists now, the Steinway action, although very different from those earlier pianos, has the ability to range between the vast sonorities and supreme delicacy that Chopin's music requires.

A very famous pianist once said to me, "I think it is harder to accept and love another pianist's interpretation of Chopin than is the case with any other composer." I think he meant that we personalize and poetize Chopin's music to the fullest extent, as though we were speaking and singing the melodies with our own voice, from the bottom of our hearts—and even then, as James Huneker, the great critic and writer, once said, "It can never be beautiful enough."

I believe that the two essential components for superlative Chopin playing (that is, after matters of the instrument and the requisite technical skills) are the ability to produce a deeply cantabile tone and a constant realization of Chopin's contrapuntal writing.

Chopin's connection and debt to Bach was enormous. We all know of his reverence—his instructions to his students to make of Bach their "daily bread"—and we can conjure up the touching image of Chopin's arrival on the island of Majorca, having been taken there by his companion George Sand to recover from tuberculosis. A small piano was carried up the mountain to the monastery at Valldemossa, and the only music he brought with him were his two beloved volumes of Bach's *Well-Tempered Clavier*, with its forty-eight preludes and fugues, which he then proceeded to copy, laboriously and lovingly, in his own hand.

Chopin's adoration of Bach led him to adapt many elements into his own music. Above all was the cantabile style, about which Bach had written treatises, although they seem to have been widely disregarded when one hears the percussive "typewriter" style of detached Bach playing that is so common. The contrapuntal writing, which we all readily identify with Bach, is the less-appreciated element in Chopin playing: for every beautiful melodic line in the right hand in Chopin, there is a perfectly crafted, equally melodic bass line, often embedded in repeated figures that appear to be simple accompaniments but contain hidden treasures within them. Often there are inner melodic tenor and alto lines as well.

The exquisite challenge that we face in Brahms' vocal choir–like piano pieces—choosing which voice to sustain above the others—is present in Chopin as well. (In both, the elements of spontaneity and improvisation ensure that we may choose one voice in one performance and a different voice the next time.)

It is a strange phenomenon that the "inevitable" quality we frequently describe and attribute to Mozart's compositions can be applied to Chopin's balanced voices. As chromatic and unexpected as his harmonies can be, one false note, even a different inversion of a chord, can, to the experienced musician's ear, sound incorrect.

Then there is the matter of rubato, also an integral part of Baroque performance—the ebb and flow of the tempo (accelerate a bit here, hold back there, and usually executed more in the melodic right hand against a more rhythmic bass line, which Chopin referred to as his *Kapellmeister*, toeing the mark and holding him within bounds).

Even the chromaticism in Chopin dates back to Bach. Aside from the obvious example of the Chromatic Fantasy and Fugue, there are the Preludes and Fugues from *The Well-Tempered Clavier*, which feel as though they are the most chromatic work you'll ever work on until the harmonies fall into place and you are left wondering at the forward-looking mind of someone writing in the late seventeenth and eighteenth centuries.

Chopin also carried on the long tradition of improvisational elements in his music: Bach, then Mozart, and finally Chopin were the masters of embellishment and improvisation. It was said that the improvising Chopin executed spontaneously when playing for friends was even more amazing and ravishing than any he ultimately notated into the Nocturnes or other compositions. Those ornamentations and embellishments have to sound as though we are inventing them ourselves at the moment of performance; but that takes practice and planning. When Chopin writes twenty-two notes in the right hand over two sets of sextuplets in the left hand (in the Nocturne in B-flat Minor, Opus 9 No. 1), he certainly does not expect the pianist to take out a slide rule and draw lines to ensure an equal distribution of melodic notes to harmonic accompaniment! And from one pianist to the next we will hear this passage done differently. However, many a student has had to be guided by a teacher to help these phrases to sound random, as Chopin would have wished.

Polyrhythms appear throughout Chopin's compositions, contributing greatly to the spontaneous flavor. They require perfect independence of hands for the harmonies to fall into place with the melodic line, and this too can be traced back to Bach.

Last, and maybe most important, one could even say that Chopin, as the ultimate tunesmith, was also nourished and inspired by his deep study of Bach's music. On one program, and in the accompanying CD, I juxtaposed the F-sharp Minor Prelude from Book 2 of *The Well-Tempered Clavier* alongside the F-sharp Nocturne, Opus 15 No. 2. It would be difficult to decide which piece is more lyrical.

One big difference between Bach and Chopin, or Mozart and Chopin, is that Bach and Mozart left huge swaths of music without a single marking in dynamics, phrasing, or articulation—partly, perhaps, because of the limitations of their early instruments, or even because of misplaced trust in the pianists who would someday perform their music. Chopin, on the other hand, left nothing unmarked. He thought of himself as a sort of classicist and was meticulous about communicating exactly what he wanted. His handwriting, as revealed in his manuscripts, is so very neat and pristine that even when he crossed something out, it was with the utmost artistic care and refinement, in exquisite crosshatching . . . quite beautiful to see!

Chopin indicated every shade of dynamic and emotional coloration, every pedal mark, every phrase mark, every articulation. Some of his phrases are among the longest lines a musician ever encounters. And that is one of the greatest difficulties in playing Chopin: striving to achieve a seamless line on the piano, which is, after all, a percussion instrument. Sometimes there is a wide swath of bars without a single pedal mark. This is not at all a careless omission (as it might have been in Beethoven or Mozart). After we try those bars without pedal and experience the contrast of the sustained harmonies in the pedaled bars and the suspended-in-space unpedaled passages, we will understand his intentions and feel the resulting textural effects, with an "aha!" moment.

Chopin elevated the art of fingering, even going so far, unusually, as to write it in. He once said, "Everything is a matter of knowing good fingering." First of all, he liberated the thumb as a full-fledged finger. Sometimes his fingering seems extremely strange and unconventional, not to mention uncomfortable—at first sight, or first try. But upon deeper examination, you find that it is all about the sound. If you finger a passage two different ways, it will sound different each way. Each of our fingers has a different strength and function, and Chopin made a serious and scholarly examination of such matters. We can fully appreciate the importance of choosing the right fingering in trills. Many times the unlikeliest pairing of 4 and 2, or 4 and 1, instead of the commonly used 3 and 1, or 3 and 2, will produce a better balanced trill, depending on whether a black note is involved; trying many combinations, and even angling the hand to find the best "center of gravity," is an important exercise.

Recently, I was teaching the Fourth Ballade to a student who was having some trouble with the double-third ascending chromatic scale passage on the next-to-last page. He was trying to adhere to Chopin's fingering, but it was not working well. I had another set of fingerings written in by one of my teachers, who was a real stickler for fingering; I didn't like those fingers either. The bottom line is that our hands are all different from one another's, and one set of fingers may not work for everyone. (Leopold Mittman once told me at a lesson, "If something is not working, change the fingering.") I set to the task and played the passages with my own, third set of fingering, which worked like a charm for my student as well. Chopin understood the intimate relationship between the hand and the keyboard, but in the fingering department, we do have options. And I love to help facilitate a problem passage for a student with a new improved set of fingerings.

If only students would realize how essential it is to practice with consistent fingering every time, especially in these most technically demanding passages! And that if they did, their success and accomplishment would come so much more readily than with random fingering.

Every Nocturne, Prelude, Ballade, Scherzo, and so on is filled with fresh melodies. Our mission is to shape and sing those melodic phrases. Those phrases, as in all music, have a beginning, an end, and contours in between, with high points and hierarchies of notes of relative importance that we have to think about and map and shape and execute, not to mention the relative importance of each of the simultaneous melodic lines.

And these high points and climaxes correspond to the emotional components, because music corresponds to speech. It is a language that has intonations, inflections, and accents, all appropriate to the meaning of the text.

Phrases, clauses, articulation, breathing points, long and short syllables—are all components of this transference of words into ideas and feelings, and then into speech, and then into singing. Of course, this all adds up to the idea of music as literature, in the largest sense—an idea that I like to keep uppermost in my mind and in my students' minds. And nowhere more than in Chopin, because he was such a student of the art of singing!

Chopin's Waltzes reflect, for the most part, the elegant, noble side of his character. Schumann declared that the dancers of these *valses* should be "at least countesses"; others have called them "faerie dances," suggesting that mortals are too clumsy to dance them. They are delightful specimens of his more capricious and joyful moods. Many of the waltzes have an undertone of melancholy and sadness; *żal* is the Polish word Chopin used to describe this element of regret or nostalgia that pervades even his more joyful music.

Chopin had been exposed to the waltzes of Johann Strauss Sr. and Joseph Lanner during his exile from Poland, in Vienna in 1830, before he came to Paris. This lusty, beer-garden variety of waltzes caused him to write with disgust about the vulgar tastes of the public. Chopin's own waltzes owe more to the genre of the *Ländler* of Schubert and Carl Maria von Weber. His waltz music was much more accessible to fashionable society than his more profound and significant works.

Nine out of the fifteen waltzes were published during Chopin's lifetime. Alfred Cortot categorized the waltzes into three groups: *valses brillantes* that conjure up whirling ballrooms; dreamy salon waltzes, which have a mazurkalike rhythm; and "allusive" waltzes, with weaker rhythms and more poetry. Possibly the waltzes received their ideal realization in the rarified atmosphere of the classical ballet *Les sylphides* rather than either the salon or the ballroom.

The discovery of manuscripts of a great composer's unpublished works is an event under any circumstances, and when the composer is Chopin, the discovery becomes more exciting, since there is so little surviving material evidence of the man and the way he worked. In 1979 I did an article for *Clavier* about Byron Janis' discoveries of unpublished earlier versions of Chopin waltz manuscripts. He socialized with Count Paul de La Panouse, who allowed him to browse in the family Château de Thoiry. There Janis found, among letters and other memorabilia in a trunk marked "old clothes," a folder marked "Written and given by Frederick Chopin, 1832." These were not rough drafts; they were finished versions of the *Grande valse brillante* in E-flat, Opus 18, and the G-flat Valse, Opus 70 No. 1; but they were quite different from the standard editions we know in his published collections of waltzes. The *Grande valse brillante* in E-flat was the first to be published in Chopin's lifetime. It is the most dancelike of his waltzes, and Schumann called it

Chopin's "body and soul inspiring valse enveloping the dancer deeper and deeper into its floods."

It is difficult to pinpoint just how Chopin wanted his compositions interpreted. "I never play a piece twice in the same way," he said once; his moods were so mercurial, and his playing so extemporaneous, that he frustrated his pupils with his constantly changing ideas.

The discovery of the waltz manuscripts by Janis, while not a monumental find, shed some light on Chopin's creative process, provided evidence of the evolving influences that bore upon his life and work, and account for the changes between his earlier and later inspirations.

Lines from a Browning poem come to mind:

> *That's the wise thrush: he sings his song twice over*
> *Lest you think he never could recapture*
> *The first fine careless rapture.*

Chopin, like the thrush, resang or rewrote many of his compositions.

Indeed, even the published versions often had profuse markings in the margins for proposed changes, but each statement was a finished creation in itself. The changes that Chopin made from one version of the waltz to the next require scrutiny with the three versions side by side. But in the end they amount to minimal changes in ornamentation and harmony that are too detailed to discuss here. Sometimes I suggest that a student choose between several editions.

Another small but great Chopin work, the Mazurka in F Minor, Opus 68 No. 4, has had a number of reincarnations and surgeries ever since the sketch for the work was discovered by Chopin's pupil Jane Stirling and his cellist friend Auguste Franchomme after Chopin's death in Paris in 1849. They described the sketch as indecipherable, but Franchomme rescued a page of it, the short, sixty-two bar version that was first published in 1855 and that still appears in most of the standard mazurka collections.

My friend Kingsley Day, pianist, composer, playwright, and former editor of *Clavier*, devoted himself to a deep survey of the work that had been done through the years by several musicologists and pianists, Polish and English. After carefully considering all their versions, Day determined that those fragments and previously omitted sketches could and should come together into a more complex, complete, and beautifully balanced 158-bar mazurka, inclusive of all parts that Chopin had not crosshatched out. Day also rethought tiny details such as slur indications and left-hand accompaniments (between a first simpler version, and the enhanced harmonies in a kind of *ossia* indication), and through what Day calls some "intelligent guesswork" he came forth with the resulting edition. It is a wonderful document reflecting the process of resurrection and interpretation of shorthand notation that is usually interpretable only by the composer himself. But these devotees who analyzed Chopin's ways of working, his past oeuvre, and any shred of evidence made informed choices that add bits of both evidence and beauty to our Chopin heritage.

Chopin's self-critical nature, along with his illness, were probable causes for the state of these fragments when they were found, and it remained for a devoted Chopin lover and performer to produce this latest fine edition, published by Hal Leonard.

These kinds of projects prove the passion of curious and dedicated musicians at the same time as they reveal the composer: Chopin emerges as a man who was tremendously self-scrutinizing and exacting, as well as ever-changing and growing. He may have instructed his friends to destroy all his unpublished works after his death, including the last waltzes and these remnant scraps they found in his apartment; yet pieces that he never considered worthy of publishing have become some of the best-loved works in the piano literature. Who knows what further changes he might have had in mind in now-familiar great works?

The basic trouble we face in our decisions about editions and accuracies comes from the discrepancies between the many editions that appeared, German, English, French, and Polish, sometimes all simultaneously published and often using different source material—sketches, engravers' manuscripts (even though they were rejected as inaccurate by Chopin), autographed "fair" copies, and "scribal" copies (those that evolved from "hearsay" or anecdotes from Chopin's many students). Chopin had little or no control over the publishing process in his lifetime, to say nothing of the posthumous editions. He himself was also the cause of many confusions—giving one version of a waltz as a gift to a cousin and another version to a student.

Years ago, when I was working on the large Chopin compositions such as the Sonatas, the *Barcarolle*, the *Fantaisie*, and so on, the edition of choice was the Paderewski edition; apparently the Poles thought they had a monopoly on understanding and sympathizing with what Chopin felt and thought, leading to overly ardent editing based primarily on conjecture. Even the much-touted Henle edition has been widely criticized for inaccuracies; more lately the new Peters edition has come out, which offers multiple choices taken from many editions, leaving the options to the pianist, and, most important, implying that there is no set, final, or unchallengeable way of performing these works.

Putting that issue of editions alongside the stark facts about the differences between our modern pianos, with their enormous sonority, and those used by Chopin, mainly Pleyel and Érard, we are forced to come to some striking conclusions: the pianos that Chopin used were capable of producing neither the volume level nor the current idea of what the term *allegro* implies in his music. Chopin's listeners had to pay closer attention to what was emerging from his instrument. Nowadays pianists strive for faster and stronger interpretations not only in his Études, but in all his music. Chopin's reality has gotten away from us.

I offer the following quotations from Chopin's own listeners and auditors of his classes, remarks that, to me, contradict the view that it was Chopin's frailty and illness that led to his delicate playing. I believe instead that Chopin mastered and was distinguished by a certain delicate but deeply expressive tone while shunning all exhibitionism; and I believe that as pianists we must always guard against slipping into too-flamboyant readings.

Hector Berlioz (in *Journal des débats*, 1841) wrote: "To grasp on the wing, this multitude of fine, delicate thoughts constituting Chopin's style (much of which has to necessarily pass unperceived in large halls and before a large public), we have to pay extremely close attention and have an exquisite musical intellect."

In another essay in *Le rénovateur*, Berlioz wrote,

> His execution is marbled with a thousand nuances of movement to which he holds the secret and which could not be notated. Unbelievable details abound in his mazurkas. Moreover he makes them doubly interesting by performing them with the ultimate degree of gentleness—the hammers graze the keys in the superlative of piano—so that we are tempted to approach the instrument and listen closely, as at a concert of sylphs and sprites.

From Chopin's student Émile Gaillard we have another observation:

> To strike is not to play. Chopin did not pound his piano, yet, under his fingers, everything emerged admirably. He seemed to caress the keyboard, and it is his soul, sensitive and pained, that rose up and wandered among us. When he had finished a nocturne, we wished only to hold our tongue to avoid breaking the enchantment where we had been taken.

The German poet Heinrich Heine observed, "Chopin takes no satisfaction in having his hands applauded for their agile dexterity. He aspired to a much finer success: his fingers are merely the servants of his soul, and his soul is applauded by those who listen not only with their ears, but with their heart."

Consider this excerpt from George Sand's autobiography, *Histoire de ma vie*, describing how Chopin worked. If his performance style was delicately wrought and peaceful, his composing was not:

> His ideas came to him spontaneously, miraculously; he found them without searching, or they resounded in his head and he rushed to listen to them on the instrument. But then began the most exhausting struggle . . . it was a special kind of effort, of uncertainty, of impatience, reshaping details. His grief at not finding the total perfection which he sought threw him into desperation. He locked himself in his room for days on end, weeping . . . changing one measure a hundred times, with a perseverance at once meticulous and frantic. Six weeks on one page . . .

Even with reminiscences such as this, there is a certain difficulty in piecing together the events of Chopin's life (just as there is in piecing together the fragments of an unpublished work). There are many errors and statements based on hearsay; there has also been a lamentable loss of personal effects. George Sand burned his letters in 1850, and in 1863, during the Russian invasion of Warsaw, more of his letters were destroyed by soldiers. In 1870 Maurycy Karasowski, one of Chopin's first biographers, was extremely careless with important letters and documents, losing some and tampering with others. In 1939 the Nazis destroyed still more of Chopin's letters along with more of his papers; during the 1944 Warsaw Uprising, even more papers were destroyed, and in 1950 a descendant of Chopin's pupil, friend, and helper Julian Fontana cleaned out her attic and threw out "useless papers."

Along with these unspeakably significant losses, we have the fact that unlike Schumann, Liszt, and Berlioz, to name just a few, Chopin never wrote about music; the sole comment on the art is the art itself. So a set of several evolving waltzes, or the evolving Chopin-Day version of the mazurka, is extremely valuable.

One of the most valuable resources we have is the reminiscences of his students—not only about his playing but about his teaching. I felt a deep measure of gratification when I realized that the standards and style of Chopin's interactions with his students are what we, as dedicated teachers, personally strive for as well. He taught between the years of 1832, when he was twenty-two, and 1849, when he died, giving equal energy to composing and to his students. He taught from a second piano, interrupting students when he wanted to make a point and demonstrating the preferred way; but was always encouraging, supportive of their egos, kind, and patient.

He used Bach's *Well-Tempered Clavier*, Clementi's etudes and pieces, Cramer's etudes, Beethoven's sonatas and concertos, Mendelssohn's *Songs Without Words*, works by Schumann, and others. Even though he was known to eschew programmatic imagery in his works, he recommended images to his students as metaphors if it helped them to produce the right sound. He cared about the personal lives of his students and their well-being, and he wanted them to be creative and courageous in their interpretations; and with the following advice, he uttered what is possibly one of the greatest piece of wisdom we can give our students:

> Forget you're being listened to, and listen to yourself. . . . When you are at the piano I give you full authority to do whatever you want; follow freely the ideal you have set for yourself and which you must feel within you; be bold and confident in your own powers and strength, and whatever you say will always be good.

Many of Chopin's students were from noble families. The young Chopin had been made to feel at home in aristocratic surroundings, and he loved the noblemen for their grace, elegance, and intellectually stimulating ideas. The aristocrats, in turn, were refreshed by the company of the profoundly artistic and introspective young man, a contrast to the superficial and charming "salon types."

But Chopin also had a strong instinct for both the rustic and the aristocratic elements, Polish and French. There isn't one piece of his music that doesn't reflect both of those influences. From his first Parisian concert appearance in 1832 and his earliest encounters in the Paris of the 1830s, with its band of artistically brilliant young men (Berlioz, Mendelssohn, Liszt, Eugène Delacroix, Alfred de Vigny, Alfred de Musset, Bellini), along with his wholehearted welcome into French noble society, his music became more and more imbued with a new intimacy that was better suited to salons than to concert halls.

Eventually he began to withdraw from society and reserve his art for a few sympathetic listeners rather than the general public.

It should be emphasized that Chopin was basically isolated from his peers even at twenty-two or twenty-three years of age. He kept his own style and was not enthusiastic about the music of the giants around him; despite the praises he received from Berlioz, he detested what he called the "brass bands" of his music. He didn't think much of Liszt's compositions and had little taste for Schumann, although all these men were sincere and generous admirers of his work. (And this includes the twenty-one-year-old Schumann's generous declaration, "Hats off, gentlemen, a genius!" after hearing Chopin's Variations on "Là ci darem la mano," a work that first sparked the public's interest.) Schumann also wrote:

> Chopin could publish anything anonymously. One would recognize him immediately . . . inherent in everything he does is that singular originality which, once displayed, leaves no doubt as to the master's identity. He produces, moreover, an abundance of new forms which, in their tenderness and daring alike, deserve admiration.

(Schumann's rave goes on and on for paragraphs; he was often ecstatic, even manic, in his writings; in any case, always magnanimous.)

No matter what the genre, at the same time he was creating poetic musical utterances, Chopin was deeply interested in the technical aspects of playing the piano. And no one understood the human hands on the piano better than Chopin.

In Chopin, music and technique cannot be extricated from one another. You cannot even practice the technical end of it effectively without considering the musical meaning. In fact, the secret of executing a challenging passage in Chopin (for example in the Études, each of which approaches a different technical problem) is first to find the music—and *that* will reveal the method.

Chopin conceived and notated each phrase with his own hand: in that gesture lay both the music and the technique. We must try to shape our own hands as he wanted (by following the phrasing, fingering, dynamics, etc.) and then define the technical means to execute the music. In other words, the process is to first identify the musical message and then follow the composer's own technical markings: these together will lead to the music's most completely meaningful realization. That being said, we all have different "equipment": different sizes and shapes, different bodies, including our hands, and different ways of "being" at the piano. Chopin wrote, "One needs only to study a certain positioning of the hand in relation to the keys to obtain with ease, the most beautiful quality of sound, to know how to play sustained notes, and to attain unlimited dexterity." He referred to the pure study of technique as "acrobatics."

We know very little about Chopin and his preferences from his own writings. He did try to write a "Projet de méthode" but complained that "the pen burns my fingers." It was a chore for him even to write a letter. If you saw the few pages he did scribble in preparation for his book, you would find them almost unreadable. Yet, as noted before, Chopin's music manuscript writing is among the most neat and pristine in all of music history.

He did not like to express himself about matters dear to his heart in written words—only in music. However, he did discuss matters of aesthetics and pedagogy with close friends and students. And so it is through those who have passed it directly down in quotes from Chopin's classes that we know anything about his ideas.

In Jean-Jacques Eigeldinger's most valuable book *Chopin: Pianist and Teacher, as Seen by His Pupils* (1986), Alexander Michailowski is often quoted. I love to think about the lineage of my great teacher Leopold Mittman and the insights and wisdom he derived from his teacher, Michailowski, which he received from Mikuli, who received them from Chopin. I think I learned from Mittman primarily by watching, listening, and absorbing, as if by osmosis. I can still "taste" his beautiful sound; I wanted it for myself and was determined to get it! It resides in my ear as exemplary, and I don't think I ever strike a note without trying, even subconsciously, to match it.

I remember how flat his hand was—almost spatulate. The pads of the fingers are the cushiony parts of the hands that can produce the most sensuous tones, and never a single strident tone. Playing on boney fingertips will not do it! And although almost all the cantabile and sostenuto passages are served by playing deeply into the key bed, there are those passages called *jeu perlé* (literally, "pearly playing") that require a superficial and rapid "floating" over the surface of the keys.

Souplesse! (suppleness, "to the tips of your toes!"), *facilement* (easily), *laissez tomber les mains* (let your hands fall). These are Chopin's quoted dicta to his students, and he constantly warned against fatigue, strain, and overpracticing.

> Caress the keys, sink and immerse yourself in the depths of the piano, drawing from it that sustained melancholy sound, as though your fingers are reluctant to leave the keys.
>
> Mould the keyboard with a velvet hand.

(Mittman's interpretation of that was to take my arm one day when I was quite young and press his finger into it, telling me to consider the keyboard as human flesh. Perhaps Chopin once took Mikuli's arm and impressed his fingers into his student's flesh to demonstrate touch in the same way. At any rate, since that moment I have never touched the piano the same way.)

The pedals are, of course, essential tools in Chopin, and pedaling is rarely taught thoroughly enough to young pianists. The pianist has to sit with both feet at the ready—at the left and right pedals. There are many incremental levels of depth (i.e., the depression of the damper pedal—a half, a quarter, an eighth), and microseconds involved in the act of catching a low bass note, clearing the sound between phrases, or rapidly changing the pedal in his fast, chromatic passages (flutter pedal). The *una corda* is not just a soft pedal. It is a great tool, if used discreetly, to create atmosphere—a veiled effect, or a mood of melancholy. But one should caution against its overuse, because then there is the danger of a cloying sweetness or even a muddied sound. The middle pedal, the sostenuto pedal, is rarely used unless we have to sustain a low bass and use both hands elsewhere.

One last caution, and that is to avoid overuse of the damper pedal (sometimes jestingly referred to as the "gas pedal"). Again, Chopin left wide passages of notes unpedaled; these were not omissions, but a deliberate tool for clarity and contrast in texture: a kind of "clearing" in the landscape of sound.

Chopin was a miniaturist. He was never interested in writing a symphony. His largest works are his two piano concertos, three piano sonatas, and a Sonata for Cello and Piano as well as a Trio. But these episodic works are not distinguished by their form; the charm and beauty are, again, in the melodies, the countermelodies, and the harmonies. There are those who refuse to take seriously any composer who did not write larger forms for larger ensembles. Anyone who complains about Chopin's legacy is an ingrate.

In the end, to fully understand Chopin, you have to appreciate the sense of him as a Polish émigré in France. All of his music is informed by both his homesickness (the Polish word for that peculiar form of melancholy is *żal*) and love for his homeland and all his folk roots along with the nobility and elegance he adopted from the high society he kept. But there was always the undertone of melancholy: "Today I finished the *Fantaisie*. The weather is beautiful, but I am sad at heart—not that it matters" (from a letter to Julian Ignace Fontana, Polish pianist, composer, lawyer, and loyal friend of Chopin, 1841).

Among the many pianists of the last several generations, not too many could hope to aspire to occupy the Chopin throne that was Arthur Rubinstein's particular territory. But the great pianist left in his will something very special to Krystian Zimerman: a certain gold button that he wore in his lapel at every concert. Since winning the Chopin Competition in Warsaw in 1975 at age nineteen, Zimerman has continued to have a distinguished career in a broad range of repertoire, but never losing his identification with Chopin. He is one of the few artists I have ever met who does not suffer from nervous tension, but rather feeds on the excitement and pleasure of live performance. Perhaps because of his closeness with Rubinstein, his focus is on tone quality: he has six pianos in his house and travels with one of his own whenever he tours.

I listen to a lot of recordings at home . . . and in my car while touring in Europe, and one day a strange thing happened. I was listening to many recordings in a row of the Chopin *Barcarolle*, without knowing whose they were; I had my secretary put them all on one tape; some were famous performances by say, Rubinstein or Argerich, others by lesser-known, even unknown artists. What surprised and delighted me was how all the recordings revealed beautiful things, and how little I could say, "This recording is preferable to that one" (except of course, that I recognized Rubinstein's tone and style immediately). When we listen not knowing who is playing, we find ourselves on another level of concentration. (*Clavier*, April 1988)

As a matter of fact, in 1983, I decided to try a different sort of project for *Clavier*. I took the *Barcarolle*, Opus 60, a Chopin work that I loved and was intimately familiar with, and spoke to seven different concert pianists about the same work, knowing in advance that there would be an astoundingly wide band of responses.

Because each artist has a distinctive chemistry with a composition, it is fascinating to explore the various ideas and responses different pianists have to the same work. Yet, given the plain frustration of translating feelings about music into words while steering clear of such technical details as fingering, I approached this project with mixed emotions: a sense of excitement about the potential revelations of those intangible qualities that distinguish one artist from the next, tinged with the fear that the results would be a conglomeration of cursory observations.

No matter what doubts I brought to each ensuing interview, there were constant reminders that the gifts and communicative powers of artists do not stop at their instruments. These artists think and live creatively, and, more, are generally eager to accept the challenge of defining and sharing their insights. Sometimes these viewpoints are, amusingly, diametrically opposed; but they are always marvelously original and inventive.

The *Barcarolle* is a difficult, enigmatic, and highly personal work. Whether the pianist secretly harbors an individual set of images or approaches it more abstractly, no two pianists will play it exactly alike; and it is precisely this provocative element that makes it excellent material for analysis. The *Barcarolle* is my own favorite Chopin work—it even inspired me to write a book centered on that work, *A Pianist's Journal in Venice*—and so the conversations with seven pianists focusing on the piece were of particular interest and value to me.

Then, some years later, taking another Chopin masterpiece, the Fourth Ballade, I interviewed another five fine pianists, and a similar article was published with all of their unique input. Instead of trying to excerpt parts of each conversation from my two collections of analyses and insert them into this chapter (which would be too cumbersome), I decided that these multiple discussions could be presented as appendices to this book. Both of these collections of talks yield a wealth of ideas about not only understanding these two works in particular, but also performing Chopin in general. My hope is that the reader will refer to the two projects in the appendices and find them a valuable resource.

In the "Composer's Landscape" series of performances, Chopin CD, I included a wide variety of works about which I will include some cursory remarks.

The *Berceuse*, Opus 57, is a tender and gentle lullaby, in many ways like a nocturne. (The original version did not have the two-bar introduction; rather, it started immediately with the third bar's theme.) When the manuscript was returned to Chopin for approval, he added the introduction and changed the title of the piece from the original *Variantes* to *Berceuse*. It is like a lullaby, with its hypnotic bass line; but it is also like a set of variations, with its many inventive embellishments written over that repetitive bass line. And it is also like a miniseries of etudes, because each little variation is another pianistic challenge—contrapuntal melodies, wide grace-note leaps, chords with the melodic line embedded, chromatic configurations, scales in double thirds, counterrhythms, and *jeu perlé* passages. If you listen carefully you might even hear the twelve chimes of a clock at midnight, a cuckoo's call, and even a "good night" in the final cadence. This delightful work requires an exquisitely controlled and *leggiero* touch, dexterity, and an imagination and ear for a wide variety of color shifts, even as the repeated bass figures unerringly hold the whole cavalcade of technical tricks together.

The *Fantaisie* in F Minor is a work that contrasts starkly with the *Berceuse*. The fantasy form differs greatly from one composer to the next, except that it is usually form*less*. This Chopin *Fantaisie*'s main characteristic is its erratic, episodic nature. It begins conventionally enough with an almost funereal March, but soon the *real Fantaisie* begins. There are sudden shifts in volume and key, contrasts in texture and rhythm, and in general, an extremely improvisatory character to the whole piece. It's a free-for-all, ranging from dream sequences juxtaposed against furious and passionate outbursts, with one extremely serene chorale occurring unexpectedly out of nowhere. Altogether a wonderful and mysterious piece.

The Ballades are stories. (Please see Appendix B for details about the Fourth Ballade.) The First Ballade, perhaps the most frequently played of all the larger Chopin works, is possibly the most abused. Students tend to play it more via the vague memory of how they think it *ought* to be played rather than by looking at the composer's indications and starting from scratch directly from the score. (André Watts once told me he thought it was the piece that was the most personal and the most difficult to love in someone else's interpretation.) Personally, I think that may be true for all of Chopin. I believe that even though the Ballades are thoughtful tales, they are frequently misused as showy vehicles, especially because they have very challenging coda sections that gallop to breathless endings.

The Scherzos are serious and ironic jokes, but with some of the most fluid and exquisite writing for the pianist: the B-flat Minor Scherzo is often the first big Chopin work given to students and is overplayed, and frequently without the *leggiero* and nuanced passagework it requires. The Fourth Scherzo in E is very Mendelssohnian in both the key choice and in character, with *leggiero* passages that are reminiscent of the Scherzo from *A Midsummer Night's Dream*.

The Polonaises range from the gloriously heroic to the reflective, from the Polish folk element to the military, from chauvinistic to melancholy. Schumann said it all: "If the mighty autocratic monarch in the north [Russia] could know that in Chopin's works, in the simple strains of his mazurkas, there lurks a dangerous enemy, he would place a ban on music. Chopin's works are cannons buried beneath roses."

The Études are the supreme tests in some conservatories that award their degrees and prizes based upon the proficiency of their execution.

But I have heard many a prizewinner who could, indeed, rattle off entire opuses of the Études, note perfect, and at demonic speeds, but while omitting the poetry in favor of the bravura.

It is the Mazurkas that are the most poetic and introspective of all Chopin's music. It is not enough to chalk these works off simply as nationalistic, nostalgic reminiscences. There are, according to most editions, about fifty-eight that have been published (with who knows how many unpublished ones waiting to be discovered in the drawers of the descendants of friends, students, and patrons). Some are simple enough to give to a student of intermediate technical ability, but to do them justice, most require of the pianist complete and utter refinement, with a superior sense of the delicate and subtle nuances that ebb and flow through the phrases. Although many of these little gems contain quite heroic sections almost approaching the spirit of the Polonaise, they also contain some of the most forward-looking and harmonically surprising explorations. The Mazurkas, along with the Preludes, which are his paean to Bach, are Chopin's crowning achievements in miniature form.

The Sonatas are consummate complex works that make up, in some ways, for the lack of chamber works from Chopin (with the exception of the Cello Sonata and the Trio). The two concertos have such negligible orchestral parts that in many sections the piano could do quite well without any orchestral accompaniment. The piano writing is so exquisite that we can never fault Chopin for any shortcomings, including the mundane orchestra writing, in which, he said, he had no interest. He compensated by giving us music that makes us feel more like pianists than any other.

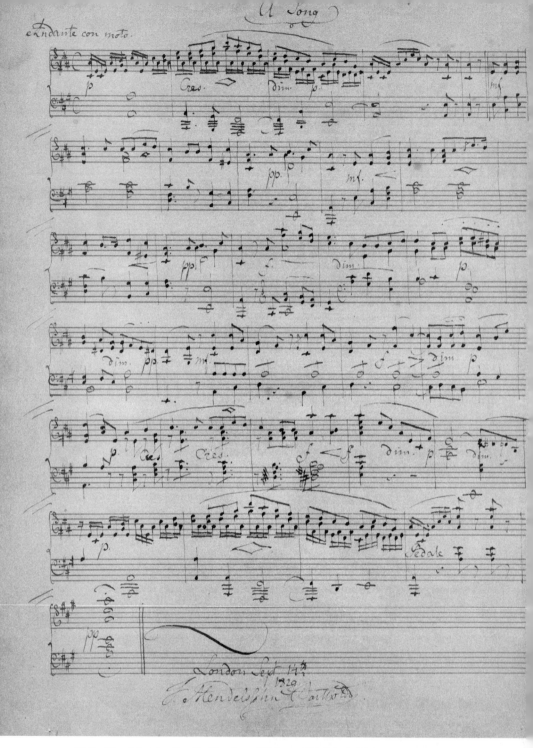

Felix Mendelssohn-Bartholdy, *Song Without Words* in A Major, Opus 19b No. 4;
autograph manuscript (September 14, 1829). The Pierpont Morgan Library,
New York, Heineman MS 144C.

8

MENDELSSOHN (1809–1847)

It is fascinating that between the years of 1809 and 1811, Mendelssohn, Chopin, Schumann, and Liszt were born. Mendelssohn died in 1847 at the age of thirty-eight.

George Bernard Shaw once said, "If you want to find out the weak places in a pianist's technique, ask him to play 10 bars of Mozart or Mendelssohn."

Shaw was a critic, not a pianist; but he was correct that Mendelssohn's music does require many of the same requisite technical skills as Mozart's—a certain clarity, dexterity, and refinement; it is even-tempered, discreet, lyrical, and balanced. Missing for some musicians is the impetuosity of Schumann, and the harmonic inventiveness of Chopin. But he could and did write impassioned music (as, for example, in his String Quartet in F Minor, Opus 80, composed as a tribute upon the death of his sister Fanny).

I believe that in Mendelssohn's case it is important to know as much about the man as possible. I think the refinement and reserve are present in both the works and his character, and I feel that his music has been somewhat underappreciated.

Mendelssohn was not narcissistic, nor was he, like Schumann, interested in constant self-reflection and self-revelation. It was in his letters that he was most likely to reveal his inner thoughts. Even though he uttered that famous phrase about music—that it was a much better expresser of thoughts and feelings than words—he could write in words very well too, and his letters to his family were articulate and colorful descriptions of his travel experiences, interspersed with exquisitely rendered sketches and watercolors of his surroundings when he traveled and snippets of compositions he had in his head, that were inspired by, for example, the Hebrides islands, Scotland, and, later, Italy.

Even in his music, Mendelssohn was more of an observer and a tone painter than an analyst. Some people find this description reductive, as though he "simply" made tone poems; but I believe he used the natural landscape as a metaphor for his inner landscape, such as the mysteries expressed in *Fingal's Cave*, the open joy of his experiences in the Scottish and Italian Symphonies, the playfulness of his incidental music for Shakespeare's *Midsummer Night's Dream*—all expressive of different states of mind.

He was an enormously gifted and cultivated person who could speak, read, and write at least five languages and was attracted to and inspired by literary works, as were Schumann and Schubert. He was not overly sentimental or self-indulgent; in fact, during all of his short life he had an ethic of hard work, even though he could quite comfortably have been complacent and never had to struggle to make a living.

Felix Mendelssohn was born into a very distinguished Jewish family, which is mentionable only because of the obstacles his family had to overcome (which cannot be underestimated). There is a record in Berlin's registry books of his grandfather, Moses Mendelssohn, a hunchbacked, impoverished son of a scribe, entering the city's servant's gate in 1743 at the age of fourteen, having walked eighty miles from Dessau: "six oxen, seven swine and one Jew." This malformed young pauper ultimately became one of Europe's greatest philosophers and scholars of the Enlightenment period.

Moses Mendelssohn was ultimately designated a *Schutz-Jude*, a "protected" Jew, which spared the family some of the humiliations visited upon Jews in Berlin. Still, Felix, Fanny, and their siblings were stoned in the streets, scorned, and derided, so that they had to ask their parents, "Is it shameful to be a Jew?"

After Felix's death, Richard Wagner wrote that the life and works of Mendelssohn clearly demonstrated that "no Jew, however gifted and cultural and honorable, was capable of creating art that moved the heart and soul"; and years later Wagner urged Germany to oust every Jew, offering the massacres in Russia as "an example worthy of imitation." Some fifty years afterward the Nazis destroyed the beautiful Mendelssohn monument in Leipzig, hacking it to pieces.

But in spite of having to endure and surmount rampant anti-Semitism, Felix and Fanny were able to grow up in an atmosphere of high culture within the compound of the Mendelssohn family estate; Felix's mother, Lea, was highly educated, played the piano very well, and read Homer in the original classical Greek, among her other many accomplishments. And the beautiful home that their father, Abraham, was able to purchase after establishing a very successful business attracted the greatest musicians, poets, artists, and thinkers of the age.

But Abraham had to convert the family to Lutheranism, adding the name Bartholdy, hyphenated after Mendelssohn, in order to be allowed to continue to reside in their home in Berlin. Felix later maintained his own prerogative and frequently omitted this appendage to his name; and because he rose to such a respected level, he flourished in spite of it.

Most music historians acknowledge that Mendelssohn was by far a more gifted child prodigy than Mozart. By sixteen Mendelssohn had composed some of his best work, including his Octet for Strings and the Piano Concerto in G Minor, with not only beautiful melodies and transparent textures but large-scale structures accomplished with ease and inherent grace; Mozart's early work, by contrast, is not really memorable. Also, Mendelssohn's early work sprang entirely from his own creative ability, whereas Mozart's early work was intensively coached and enhanced by his father. (Schumann wrote several rave reviews about Mendelssohn's compositions in his journals.)

The young Felix was taken to visit the great poet Goethe, who took the boy under his wing and relished every visit from the family to Weimar. In turn, Mendelssohn referred to Goethe as "the Imperial Sun of my life." One time, it is said, Goethe handed the young Felix a manuscript of a Mozart Adagio to play. (The poet had heard a seven-year-old Mozart sixty years earlier—and here was Felix playing Wolfgang to him!) But then Goethe, to stump the boy, handed him an unsigned manuscript of scribbles and blots and scratchings-out. Felix started reading and playing from the manuscript, then stopped and exclaimed, "This is Beethoven! I should know it anywhere!!" (Goethe, however, did not admire or understand Beethoven's music, so during one visit Mendelssohn insisted that the old poet sit and listen until he finally acknowledged that Beethoven was great.) Fanny pleased the elderly poet very much too, with her performance, during the first of several meetings with him, of twenty-four Bach Preludes from memory.

Mendelssohn is often mischaracterized as having had only bliss and no struggle in his life, but when one reads of the anti-Semitic attacks and threats to deport the family out of Berlin, they must disabuse critics of this rosy impression. I think that the most important of Mendelssohn's traits was that he was, on the whole, what we might refer to as an "ecstatic"—responding to the world around him at a high-pitched frequency of gratitude and gladness. This is the reason I respond to his music with love.

His piano music is distinguished by its lightness and capricious character—almost evoking the "kingdom of Oberon," as in his Overture and E Minor Scherzo for Shakespeare's *Midsummer Night's Dream*, where we can hear gossamer wings flitting all over the place—a quality we should strive for in playing his piano music. But his music is much more than playful and happy, as is evident in what is perhaps his greatest solo work, the *Variations sérieuses*.

Mendelssohn did have a basically sunny disposition, but he had his down periods as well—most notably when his operas, one after another, were not well received. He was being appreciated mostly for his pianism, along with his scholarship in bringing Bach's great choral works to light after they had lain ignored for a hundred years.

Mendelssohn could also fly into a rage when conducting an orchestra and having to deal with mediocre musicians playing out of tune. There are also descriptions of his piano classes at the conservatory and his furious response to carelessness or irreverence for the composer, along with his earnest reproaches for lack of sonority or of expressiveness.

Mendelssohn and Schumann were both deeply affected by late Beethoven, but Schumann was much closer to Beethoven in the uneven nature of his phrases. Perhaps it can be said that one of Mendelssohn's shortcomings was that his music was too well balanced. He rounded off the lengths of his phrases and kept things nice and tidy, resolved, happy, and clear, whereas the uneven lengths of Beethoven's phrasing provided unrest, tension, and passion. From Bach, Mendelssohn drew the element of recitative, which appears in a lot of his music. Even if Mendelssohn's music is less complex and more amiable, in his greatest works—the symphonies ("Scottish," "Italian," and "Reformation"), the choral music (*Elijah*), the *Variations sérieuses*, and so much of his chamber music—he found his own personal voice, with its own deeply expressive beauty. In any case, why should purity, simplicity, balance, and amiability be frowned upon?

Mendelssohn's favorite place to be was with his family in the garden at home in Leipzig, as he said over and over. However, he traveled extensively and gladly because he was invited to conduct and play all over Europe and enjoyed almost any city more than Berlin. When Mendelssohn went to England, his second home, he was accepted into and celebrated by the highest strata of society, including Queen Victoria and Prince Albert. The royal couple invited him to their palace, where he played for hours.

He also loved Italy and raved about Switzerland, where he reveled in nature and painted some of his loveliest watercolors. During one visit he painted at the same sites as J. M. W. Turner, John Ruskin, and Corot! Mendelssohn's paintings have a transparency analogous to the touch required for playing his music.

In fact, one of the greatest challenges of playing Mendelssohn concerns the touch. His scherzo effects, as found in the Rondo Capriccioso, the Octet, the *Midsummer Night's Dream* Scherzo, the concertos, and some of the variations in the *Variations sérieuses*, have an especially airy, light, staccato, buoyant movement, usually in the higher registers. The pianist has to strive for evenness, refinement, and clarity while keeping an unerring pulse. This is all a question of balance and control, along with contouring the lyrical phrases.

How can we apply the terms "balance and control" to Mendelssohn's music? Because there are so many notes, the first fact we have to deal with is that they are not all created equal. There are the beginning of a phrase, the end, and contours within the phrases. There are nuanced dynamic contrasts, even within the limited range of *leggiero* passagework, and the rubato must be minimal in order to keep the momentum.

It is essential to remember that the Romantic composers—Chopin, Schumann, Brahms, Liszt, and Mendelssohn—were punctilious in writing in generous indications for fluctuations in the tempo, sometimes using words such as *espressivo*, *sostenuto*, *ritenuto*, *allargando*, *accelerando*, *stretto*, and *calando*. All of these terms imply fluctuation, albeit approaching the idea from varying philosophical angles; so the pianist is well advised to keep his or her own impulses to a minimum. It is also, as I like to stress, important to know the exact Italian definitions of each indication on the score.

Many of Mendelssohn's piano pieces, whether for solo or ensemble, are, as mentioned, dense, with millions of notes for the pianist. (I recall playing the Sonata for Cello and Piano at Yale with my son, Dennis Parker, many years ago, and lamenting the number of notes to my friend the pianist Peter Frankl, who replied in jest, "I am *sure* Felix didn't mean for us to play *all* those notes!")

Actually, Mendelssohn understood the hand very well on the piano, and those patterns and intricate passages have to be practiced very slowly and patiently, with well-chosen fingerings, to cover "palms" of notes with the most natural and comfortable groupings; articulating and engraving them into the muscle memory of the hands while at the same time taking note of the harmonic constructions and modulations of bars in question, before we can dance our fingers around them at full tempo. Otherwise just executing the notes amounts to what I call "typing." In the end, with all our well-prepared technical achievement, we must be quite sure that the musical value and meaning are our prime goals. Again, the best way to practice technique is by keeping the musical lines and ideas behind every gesture even as we work out the kinks. It's my best advice. Mendelssohn abhorred virtuosic playing for its own sake: "These piano-acrobats give me less pleasure than rope-dancers or circus acrobats! They do not endanger their lives, but they endanger our ears!"

The *Variations sérieuses* require mastery of every technical trick in the book. In 1841 Mendelssohn wrote an excited letter to a friend: "Can you guess what I have just been composing—and passionately? Variations for piano! Eighteen of them on a theme in D minor, and I had such enormous fun writing them." (And it is just as much fun for the pianist to play them!)

He chose a humble, plaintive tune—he even called it peevish—and embroidered it in a "serious," sober way, building upon it with every conceivable novel idea. Others before him had certainly composed great and "serious" sets of variations—most notably Bach's Goldberg Variations, Beethoven's Diabelli and *Eroica* Variations, and Haydn's F Minor Variations. But most variations were shallow vehicles meant for nothing more substantial than brilliance for the sheer sake of virtuosic display. Chopin's Variations on "Là ci darem la mano" are pretty, but frivolous, and it is doubtful whether Mendelssohn had heard Schumann's *Symphonic Etudes*. And of course, Brahms' great variations were yet to come. Mendelssohn's *Variations sérieuses*, Opus 54, ranks with the finest variations and would influence such composers as Brahms and César Franck.

Many of these short variations are virtuosic and demanding; others are serene and spiritual, almost hymnlike. But none were intended for pure display, a goal Mendelssohn scorned. In fact, while practicing some of the most tricky variations, as usual the key to achieving technical ease was revealed in the music itself.

The eighteen variations are through-composed and merge together as an organic whole; the piece is so perfectly balanced and beautifully crafted that each variation's tempo and mood seem to emerge almost inevitably from the variation before and are beautifully set within the context of the entire set. It is a great, almost unbridled joy to play.

In 1828 Fanny wrote a letter to Felix describing her pleasure at receiving his birthday present: some "songs without words." Mendelssohn's eventual collection of more than fifty *Songs Without Words* became his most popular piano works, which does not make them any the less lyrical and fine. Probably no piano music has been performed more frequently, though sometimes quite perfunctorily and amateurishly, especially in the nineteenth-century drawing rooms of Europe. They have sometimes been called "slight" because they are miniatures (to be sure, some are greater than others), but they have never been labeled "insignificant," and some are strikingly original.

Mendelssohn objected to analytical discussions about the meanings of the songs: "What the music I love expresses to me, is not thought too *indefinite* to put into words, but on the contrary, too *definite*" (Mendelssohn's italics).

There have been many editions of the *Songs* since the first volumes were published by Breitkopf und Härtel between 1874 and 1877. Many had previously been published separately. In the nineteenth century, Kullak and Klindworth were among the editor-publishers of new editions, and in the twentieth century two other publishers, Ignaz Friedman and Henle, also came out with new editions. Imagine my delight when I stumbled upon a Ravel edition of the *Songs* while browsing in the *bouquinistes* (bookstalls) along the Seine!

These pieces have attracted many great composers and pianists because of their excellence and beauty. Franz Liszt composed his Grand Concert Piece on Mendelssohn's *Songs Without Words*, to be played by two pianists. A series of unfortunate events caused a performance of this work to be put off for a century: Liszt was to have performed it with a student in 1835, but he became ill, and the concert was canceled; Busoni died just before he and Egon Petri could perform it together as planned; but finally, in 1984, Richard and John Contiguglia, duo pianists, performed it at a Liszt Festival in Utrecht.

Many instrumentalists have been attracted to the songs and have transcribed it for their instruments with piano accompaniment, leaving the poor unsatisfied pianist to play everything but the most beautiful melodic lines.

The melodic lines in all of the *Songs* are singable; and in order to produce the cantabile, legato melodic line they require as songs, we have to use pedal. Mendelssohn instructs *sempre pedale*, but of course this is merely the instruction to the pianist to use the pedal. It remains for us, with an awareness of the differences between Mendelssohn's more delicate instrument and our powerful modern pianos, to use discreet pedal, in all degrees of depression, with relief between the phrases.

Most of the *Songs* have a Mozartean refinement, but without Mozart's operatic drama; a Schubertian lyricism, but without Schubert's intensity. There are many parallels, though, between the piano part in Schubert lieder and the Mendelssohn *Songs*, particularly in the depiction of water—streams or lakes—and in the lyric "story line," which we have to divine in the Mendelssohn pieces, as the titles—"May Breezes," "Duetto," "Spring Song," "Venetian Boat Song"—were added by the publisher. Nevertheless, the music is programmatic in many cases. In performance of these songs, we have the same task as lieder pianists: to depict the atmosphere with skill and imagination. In among the albums are barcarolles, spinning songs, folk songs, hunting songs, and so on. They are like little paintings or vignettes.

When asked what he meant by writing wordless songs, Mendelssohn replied:

> The song is just as it stands. Even if I had a particular word or words in mind, I would not want to tell anyone, because the same word means different things to different people. Only the song says the same thing, arouses the same feeling in everyone, a feeling that cannot be expressed in words.

(I am not certain any one song arouses the same feeling in everyone.)

It was Mendelssohn's aim, in his piano music, to rescue the piano from meaningless salon-type use and to invest even the smallest piece with dignity; indeed, these short works are often likened to miniature tone poems. I cannot think that Mendelssohn was referring to a lack of dignity or meaning in the short works of masters that preceded him; one can only conjecture that there were many lesser-ranking composers for piano who were contemporaries of his, and at whom he directed his "rescue mission"—Dreyschock, Thalberg, and so on. Mendelssohn also wrote several large tone poems, such as his *Hebrides Overture*, about which Brahms said, "I would gladly give all I have written to have composed something like the Hebrides overture."

Fanny Mendelssohn was Felix's soul mate, but he was conflicted about her professional life as a musician. Her enormous talents were largely stymied and unrecognized except by her husband, the artist Wilhelm Hensel, under whose name she published her songs rather than using her famous family name. She wrote over 460 pieces of music, and had the same musical education and probably equal gifts to her brother's. Her plight is perhaps best exhibited by words from her father in a letter talking about music as a profession:

Music will perhaps become [Felix's] profession, whilst for you, it can and must only be an ornament, never the root of your being and doing . . . he feels a vocation for it, whilst it does you credit that you have always shown yourself good and sensible in these matters . . . Remain true to these sentiments and to this line of conduct: they are feminine, and only what is truly feminine is an ornament to your sex.

The relationship between Felix and Fanny was close but complex. He was capable of tender love, as is evidenced in this letter (Munich, 1830):

My darling little Sister—

We have a young lady in our garden-house who has a certain different conception of music in her head from that of many ladies put together, and I thought I would write to her and send her my best love. It is clear that you are this young lady and I tell you, Fanny, that I have only to think of some of your pieces to become quite tender and sincere, in spite of the fact that one has to lie a great deal in South Germany. But you really know what God was thinking when He invented music, so it is no wonder that it makes one happy. You can play piano, too, and if you need a greater admirer than I, you can paint him, or have him paint you.

Fanny's husband, Wilhelm Hensel, was a painter, and Fanny had artistic skill as well.

Even if we consider the roles available to and the limits placed on women at that time, as well as the attitude toward Jews, it does Felix no credit that he wrote:

From my knowledge of Fanny I should say that she has neither inclination nor vocation for authorship. She is too much all that a woman ought to be for this. She regulates her house, and neither thinks of the public nor of the musical world, nor even of music at all, until her first duties are fulfilled. Publishing would only disturb her in these, and I cannot say that I approve of it.

Felix did, however, arrange with Fanny that some of her songs be published under his name, three in his Opus 8 and three more in his Opus 9 collections. This led to an embarrassing situation when Felix was visiting with Queen Victoria and Prince Albert at a musical soirée in her palace. Mendelssohn convinced the queen (who was quite a good musician) to sing one of his songs, and she unwittingly chose one of Fanny's, which had been published under Felix's name in his own opus. Felix, after accompanying her, diplomatically told the queen that the one she chose was one of his sister's songs and requested that perhaps now she might sing one of his! In Queen Victoria's old age, she was known to have boasted that Felix Mendelssohn had been her vocal coach.

Fanny once described her situation:

I have been composing a good deal lately, and have called my pi-ano pieces after the names of my favourite haunts, partly because they really came into my mind at these spots, partly because our pleasant excursions were in my mind while I was writing them. They will form a delightful souvenir, a kind of second diary. But do not imagine that I give these names when playing them in so-ciety; they are for home use entirely.

Fanny gave up too easily. (Around the same time there was the much more "liberated"—to use a twentieth-century term—Clara Schumann, in the full bloom of her ninth month of pregnancy *onstage* performing, albeit largely for economic considerations, in an era when women basically hid themselves at home during those months.)

Yet even considering the undercurrent of tension and the disparity between brother's and sister's views, Felix and Fanny were passionately fond of each other. In fact, some wondered whether he could ever love another woman as fondly. He did appear to have a happy marriage with Cécile Jeanrenaud, whom he married when she was only seventeen; they had five children.

But when Fanny died, Felix's own health began to decline, insidiously and mysteriously, as though the two souls had been connected by energies and currents linking their brains—and just a few months later, Felix died at the age of thirty-eight, from a mysterious brain condition and a ruptured blood vessel, similar to the stroke that took his father and his sister.

When the news spread to England that Mendelssohn died, Queen Victoria wrote in her journal:

> We were horrified, astounded and distressed to read in the papers of the death of Mendelssohn, the greatest musical genius since Mozart, and the most amiable man. He was quite worshipped by those who knew him intimately and we have so much appreciated and admired his wonderfully beautiful compositions. We liked and esteemed the excellent man, and looked up to and revered his wonderful genius, and the great mind, which I fear were too much for the frail and delicate body. With it all, he was so modest and simple.

A number of philosophical questions are often posed about Mendelssohn's music. Can a composer who has not struggled or suffered hardship produce complex masterpieces? Did, in fact, Mendelssohn have to overcome hardships? Some people feel that much of Mendelssohn "charms" the listener but does not astonish. Can we be content with "simple beauty" and "sheer happiness," with no conflict? For my part, I think that whatever the answers, there is a perfect place in this chaotic world for "simple beauty and sheer happiness."

AFTERTHOUGHTS

Whatever the exigencies may be for each composer, our work at the piano stays basically the same: certain words, such as *balance*, *taste*, *validity*, *intuition*, *touch*, and *contrast*, belong not only to all music, but to all of art, in the largest sense.

Any two pianists' readings of a score, though they be note for note identical and have all the indications in place, will be uniquely different from each other. That is what distinguishes a performance and makes it sparkle: those responses, ideas, and even "trinkets" that any single musician may find in the music, according to his or her own personality, ability, and individual life experience.

One element that I have not discussed is concentration, which, I believe, is in itself a talent that can affect performance. Some of the greatest musicians admit that they have trouble concentrating. Yet, unless we acknowledge that everything we do on the piano comes from the brain and goes from there to the rest of our selves, all our good intentions about technical and artistic elements will be limited. (I recall a certain amusing scold from a teacher: "Your fingers do not have brains in them! Your *brain* has to direct them!")

Can concentration be taught? It can be recommended, described, and reiterated constantly (to our students and ourselves), but we must each learn how to approach and cherish our time at the piano, whether it be a scant half hour or a long four hours. We must somehow manage to block out all the other extraneous matters that consume us all day long and then, for however long we have, give everything to the music at hand.

In viewing a score, whether for the second time or the hundredth, if we concentrate fully there is a chance we might notice a detail that had evaded us in previous readings, so dense and layered are the signals and intentions of any given composer.

The discussions in this book had to be limited to only a few works of each composer, but my hope is that the suggestions can be applied to most of their oeuvre. The "Composer's Landscape" series of audio-books will explore many more performances for each composer—with commentary.

I have listened to the lamentations of great artists after live concerts and when they heard their own performances recorded for "posterity." (And this includes those with worldwide reputations who have had the benefit of professional editing studios.) But because we are humans, and because we listen to ourselves so critically, we almost *never* feel that we play at the level these masters deserve; and therefore the impulse is to try again and again until we *do* feel good enough about our playing to share it.

If anything, I have an ever-increasing gratitude and appreciation for the masterworks from these composers; their scores are so much more than lines, spaces, and black dots cast onto manuscript paper. The deep-er we explore, the closer we can come to regarding every furrow of their landscapes—the aspects that evade description in words.

Simultaneously with my increasing experience and appreciation, I seem to have arrived, blissfully, at a point of acceptance of the human-ness in myself and others, and an affection for our humble and touch-ing attempts to communicate this great music. And so I offer this book and the music that follows without apologies, in the hope that it will be received with the understanding of how it was given—with hard work, courage, and love.

APPENDIX A

INTERPRETATIONS OF CHOPIN'S BARCAROLLE

[NOTE: This article, with interviews of distinguished pianists all conducted by the author, was originally published in *Clavier* magazine with the title "Chopin's *Barcarolle*" in two parts: the David Bar-Illan, Claude Frank, Byron Janis, and Nadia Reisenberg interviews appeared in the April 1983 issue; and the interviews with Gary Graffman, Rudolf Firkušný, and James Tocco appeared in the May–June 1983 issue. The author's introductory text has been adapted for this book, and all biographies have been updated.]

The *Barcarolle,* one of Chopin's last works, is considered by many to be one of his finest. After an introductory passage the lilting rhythm of the Venetian boat song is immediately established, and, except for one or two interludes, underlies the entire piece from its deceptively calm beginnings to the grand climactic pages. Written in F♯ major, it can be broadly described as "A-B-A" in form with the middle, or Trio section, slightly different in mood and figuration, and written in the contrasting key of A major.

Whether the *Barcarolle* was meant to be Chopin's own tribute to the glories that were Venice, or simply an episode of two lovers, or neither, can only be left to conjecture, and one artist's conception is as well-grounded as the next.

(For our discussion we used the Polish edition by Paderewski because the bars are numbered and facilitate making references.)

DAVID BAR-ILLAN

In his aesthetic and homey New York apartment David Bar-Illan communicated his enthusiasm for this beautiful work at once.

"In his last years, Chopin took a different direction in his composing, the two most outstanding examples being the *Barcarolle* and the Fourth Ballade. There is a new quality of added sophistication and an elaboration on techniques he had used earlier: more chromaticism, richer harmonies, less symmetry in phrases, an avoidance of cadences (foreshadowing Wagner), and much more importance given to the inner voices, a transferring of thematic material from one voice to the next. Also, there was less bravura for its own sake; the virtuoso parts are more in the service of the music.

"Obviously, Chopin lacked a middle sustaining pedal; if he hadn't, I think he would have used it to hold the opening C♯, thus allowing for more freedom of pedaling and more clarity in the opening bars. I think that the fourth and fifth bars should be played *pianissimo* so there is no worry about the pedaling as much as when playing it louder. Nothing should be notey. I do a lot of semi-pedaling and fluttering of the pedal to create legato and a misty atmosphere.

"Most performances start too fast and begin to sound too indifferent. I would say the metronome ought to be set around 54 = the dotted quarter. Then I pick it up at the poco più mosso at bar 35 and into the A major section, ignoring the editorial markings of rallentando and a tempo."

Most pianists like a color change in the A major section but what that color is varies greatly. Bar-Illan feels it is a veiled sound produced with both the una corda and damper pedals used liberally for the sotto voce effect. He also brings out the repeated bass notes as they change from A down to G♯ in bars 41–42 for a ". . . hypnotic, mercilessly monotonous pulsing.

The little figures that start in bar 43 are little wavelets or ripples.

I'm sure Chopin had that in mind; after all it is a boat song. There must be terraced dynamics. First the *sotto voce,* then *sempre piano,* then *forte*—each phrase building on the one before, which he helps by thickening the texture of the chords.

"I don't like programmatic scene-setting, at least I don't like to talk about it because it imposes my images on the listener; but there is one place where there is an obvious halting of the boat motion at the meno mosso at bar 72.

At least it is a moment of stillness and euphoria. Here I bring out the moving inner voice, and I pay special attention to the left hand staccatos. Then the momentum is regained little by little until the recapitulation at bar 84.

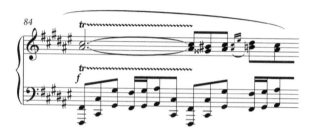

It's extraordinary how careful maintenance of the hypnotic pulse allows more freedom in the pauses, such as the one in bar 78.

"In the recapitulation most pianists pound the bass. It is simply a thickening of texture and not any more than an accompaniment to the cantilena in the right hand. The real climax is, of course, bar 93 and we must not vitiate its impact.

"Often performers ignore the *forte* in bar 103—the arrival of the tonic and the beginning of the coda. Chopin marks *sempre forte* at bar 107, almost anticipating a pianist's temptation to wind down in preparation for what is coming. I think this momentum and almost painful exultation, which has been growing since the più mosso until bar 103, is what makes the *Barcarolle* so great. If the performer plays the coda like a farewell, instead of with the full-bodied enthusiasm that still exists, he defeats the piece."

What about reports that Chopin, himself, played the last two pages quite softly? Would that lend a validity to the farewell type of interpretation? "I don't trust reports of performances. Anyone who has read three reviews of the same concert will see that no one account is reliable. People are usually so overwhelmed when a composer performs that they lose their objectivity and credibility as witnesses. Also, I don't trust composers as performers, especially because Chopin was so frail at the time. Most important is the internal evidence of the music, and what the music means to us now. I feel it is much more effective to make bar 110 a climax, from the F♯ pedal point in the coda, and not to let it die too soon. It should all be ferocious frothing until the codetta at bar 113, which is so much more effective after the huge breadth of the preceding passages. I don't even take the *piano* in bar 111 too literally. I play more a *mezzo forte* and use those two bars to wind down to a *pianissimo*. In bars 113–14 I bring out the thumb in the left hand because that is the singing line, and I do an almost Debussy-like leggiero in the right hand, using una corda and pedal."

Bar-Illan finished by bringing his ideas to life in a beautiful, spontaneous performance of the *Barcarolle*, punctuated by all sorts of commentary.

The late David Bar-Illan was born in Haifa, Israel, in 1930, and he attended the Juilliard School of Music in New York. His first stage appearance was in 1959 with the Israel Philharmonic, followed by his New York Philharmonic debut with Leonard Bernstein conducting. His first solo recital was at the John F. Kennedy Center for Performing Arts in Washington, DC. Bar-Illan was also a writer on mostly musical subjects. He eventually returned to his country to serve under Prime Minister Benjamin Netanyahu's administration.

CLAUDE FRANK

Claude Frank began by enthusiastically reporting, "I have just programmed the *Barcarolle* this season for the first time because of our discussions. I have studied it, but never played it publicly, so I cannot talk about battle experience. Performance of a work is essential to knowing it thoroughly. Some ideas are bound to change afterwards.

"The *Barcarolle* is a very difficult piece, but then, what isn't, if we want to play on the highest level? The most obvious difficulty in the *Barcarolle* is finding a mean between the architecture and the atmosphere. The first commitment is to sound, the piano sound itself, while quietly being aware of the architecture. It is a fantastically tightly woven piece which does not ramble; it has a very logical and important structure.

"The atmosphere is almost programmatic. That it is a boat song, there is no question; and that it is a love song, there is no question about that; that it, therefore, could be love-in-a-boat almost stares us in the face. In fact, if a person wanted to, they could be more graphic on certain pages. It's Tristan-like. Here we have to abstract the events and it would be silly to point to a passage and say this or that happens. Certainly Chopin would have been the first to categorically deny it.

"It is also difficult to make the extreme contrasts within the framework of this piece. We don't want to avoid the climactic passages; yet, the climax of a twenty-minute work is likely to be more quantitative than in an eight-minute work like this.

"Let's talk about the unusual time signature of $\frac{12}{8}$. Usually in music, $\frac{4}{4}$ meter has faster quarters than $\frac{2}{4}$, and $\frac{6}{8}$ meter will almost always move faster per eighth than $\frac{3}{8}$. Perhaps we can conclude that $\frac{12}{8}$ indicates a forward-moving tempo."

Regarding the rhythm, Frank has another theory, a highly original one. "Most people play the first bars 3–4 after the introduction instinctively, as though it were $\overset{>}{1}$ 2 3, $\overset{>}{4}$ 5 6, $\overset{>}{7}$ 8 9, $\overset{>}{10}$ 11 12, dividing the bar not only in half, but also further subdividing it into four groups of three eighths.

However, there is also another pulse, and that is 1̀ & 2̀ & 3̀ & 4̀ & 5̀ & 6̀ & accenting every other pulse, making six beats in the bar.

If you try it with that approach you will find that the stresses (the low F♯, then the G♯ thumb, and so on) create a seasick feeling, an effect of rolling over the waves, more than the more commonly played accents do. Some possible clues for this approach are both the $\frac{12}{8}$ time, which allows for this ($\frac{6}{8}$ would not) and the original Chopin pedaling, which shows a release of the pedal before the G♯, giving an emphasis and clarity to that note. Both rhythmic elements are there, creating a certain ambiguity that makes it full of unlimited possibilities. This gives us a modus operandi for the whole piece although it does not apply to the A major section at bar 39, where it is clearly in subdivisions of three."

Double trills, such as the ones in bars 23–24, are not often found in the piano literature, and Frank checked for other examples in Chopin. "Aside from the Double-trill Etude, there is only the *Polonaise-Fantaisie* where Chopin extemporizes for a moment in a sensual way with double, then triple trills.

"For me, the melody and feeling, beginning at bars 62–63 is almost Mozartean—like *Don Giovanni*. Without stretching it too much, the melody resembles the "Là ci darem la mano" duet in lilt ($\frac{6}{8}$), key (A major), and locale (Mediterranean).

from Mozart's "Là ci darem la mano"

It is perhaps the most intimate part of the piece. It's almost as though the boat were going into waters where no one else has been before. The melody in thirds is very Italian: like the bel canto writing for two sopranos singing a long cantilena line in parallel thirds. This is typically Mediterranean music: not only the melody, but the atmosphere of abandon. There is a pseudo-disorganization; although in reality, this piece has a Germanic organization. Even though Chopin was probably only in Majorca in Spain, Mediterranean is still Mediterranean, whether it is North Africa, Israel, Italy, Greece, or Spain."

The Italian word *sfogato*, which Chopin uses in bar 78 along with dolce, is almost impossible to define because music or Italian language dictionaries give all sorts of translations: "freely given out" in *The Oxford Companion to Music*; "ethereal, evaporated" in *Groves*; "vaporeux" or "fumeux" according to Cortot; "veiled," "effaced," "airy," or "exhaled" in various Italian dictionaries; and "letting everything go" or "utter release" according to a certain Italian teacher. Frank suggested that Chopin might purposely have chosen a word that had a certain illusory, nebulous quality. This word appears in the piece where all the motion suddenly stands still. It seems best to let the music dictate the meaning of the word.

"In connection with the architecture, I have a little anecdote to tell. When I once played this, over 30 years ago, for the American composer Arthur Farwell, he said to me, 'Do me one favor: make a point of playing bar 32 diminuendo, and bar 92 crescendo.

You must make that difference very clear because that's the whole idea of the piece.' From his composer's point of view, it was a structural idea, concerning form in the highest sense. It is the essential shape that is important, although perhaps he oversimplified a bit.

"Schnabel also used to think primarily from the composer's point of view. Not many people realize how beautifully he played Chopin. In his later years he didn't find the music polyphonic or unpredictable enough—there were too many four-measure periods. So many of his students, including me, have not played much Chopin as a result."

The interview was spiked with beautiful illustrative samples of Claude Frank's Chopin.

As a young child, Claude Frank escaped the Nazis with his mother by crossing the Pyrenees on foot. From Spain, he came to New York, studied with Artur Schnabel, and then with Karl Ulrich Schnabel and Maria Curcio. Frank has had a distinguished career, in both performance and teaching at prestigious universities, most recently at the Curtis Institute of Music in Philadelphia and the Yale School of Music. He has been most closely identified with the music of Beethoven. His wife, the late Lilian Kallir, was also a distinguished pianist, mostly a Chopin specialist, and his daughter, Pamela, is a noted violinist.

BYRON JANIS

Although Byron Janis was available only by phone, and we were both dubious about what such a conversation might yield, his own deep involvement with Chopin, along with the irresistible charms of the music, easily circumvented the distance. The jumping-off point was the possible imagery evoked by the work. "Of course, the thing about imagery is that it is never static. It is ever-changing, and a person cannot put a stamp on a phrase and say, 'This is what that means.' Not only may the images change from one pianist to the next, but, with the same artist, from one performance to the next. For me, the piece contains the barcarolle element, the Italian boat song aspect. A person could have fun with that idea about the two lovers; and maybe there might be something to it, but the very fact of saying it somewhat destroys the dream of the piece."

As we both consulted our scores (Janis was looking at the Cortot edition), he reflected on the opening bars. "It's a beautiful introduction, a prelude to a scene, whatever that scene may be; but it's more than that, because it's extremely lyrical. Chopin was fond of these introductions. Look at the First Ballade, the introduction before the 'song' starts. Even the third movement of the B minor Sonata has an introduction which is very harmonic and modulating." In fact, he noted that whole movement has a boat song feeling similar to the *Barcarolle*. "Yes, and he uses it again in the G major Nocturne, although I don't think Chopin was ever on more than two boats in his life. Chopin detested symbolism. He hated names put to his music, and I understand very well why; what a limitation. Whereas if you let yourself dream, you dream something different each time and the piece is a complete fantasy.

"What is also especially interesting about the piece is that it is a Nocturne, yet it is as big as any of the Ballades and it is like a Polonaise as well." I asked Janis to expound on that because the usual associations with the Polonaises are much more heroic. "When Chopin goes into the A major section at bar 39, after the beautiful transitional, cantilena passage, suddenly something very Polish enters the piece.

It becomes very much like the middle of the big A♭ Polonaise with the octaves in the bass. What he's done here is to give the whole theme a slightly martial quality because of the pattern of octaves in the bass. Also, like a polonaise, it's a bit processional. I feel the modulations are Polish as well. This progression in bars 41–42 that moves down by half-steps (A major to G♯ major, with sevenths added) seems to occur in his most Polish works.

"Look at that middle octave section of the A♭ Polonaise that I mentioned before, where the music moves from E major down to E♭ major in descending octaves. I don't know exactly what it is, but it's characteristically Polish. How elusive and inexplicable are the elements that unite to create a certain effect.

"The controversial question of just how much rubato ought to be used in Chopin (since the composer explicitly wrote in the ritards, rallentandos, and so on) is especially apropos in a piece such as the *Barcarolle* where the momentum and flow could easily be destroyed by overindulgence in the singing line without the stability of the even bass line. The whole secret of a good rubato is to seem to keep the flow no matter what. It is a give-and-take in which you are not actually giving back as much as you are taking, or vice versa. There is a slight discrepancy, but the illusion is still there. I always think of the example of the Greek Parthenon, which gives the illusion of perfect symmetry and beauty, and, of course, when it is measured, the sides are totally unequal. That building exemplifies what rubato should be."

Janis' extended research into the details of Chopin's private life sheds light on his work. In addition Janis' important discoveries of autograph manuscripts have given him insights into Chopin's process of composition.

"In the *Barcarolle* particularly, there are many differences from one edition to the next: for example in the tied (or untied) notes in the melodic line.

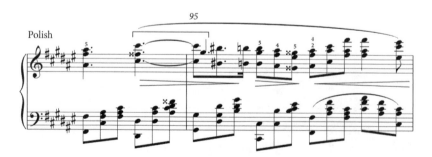

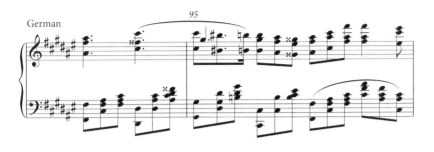

We can imagine what happened: first the manuscript written by Chopin was printed in Paris, for example. Often there are errors in the first printing, so in another edition—let us say the German, those 'errors' or 'supposed errors' were corrected by Chopin. Other errors were made by the printers and, in addition, Chopin often rewrote after printing. He even used to scribble changes in the margins of the printed music while students were playing. All this accounts for the many discrepancies."

How does a pianist choose? "You choose according to what you feel is the right one for you. Chopin had many thoughts on each work and his last versions were not necessarily the best ones. The *Barcarolle,* being one of the last works he wrote, was accomplished during a time when he was not feeling well and perhaps he was less careful or precise; who knows?"

To a final question of whether the *Barcarolle* is better saved for more intimate settings than a large concert hall, Janis objected, "Then a performer would also have to avoid the Mazurkas or anything of a more personal nature. The whole challenge of the artist is to try to provide the proper atmosphere, however intimate, no matter what the circumstances."

Byron Janis gave his first public recital at the age of nine in his home state of Pennsylvania. At that age he was already studying in New York with Josef and Rosina Lhévinne, and then he continued his studies with Adele Marcus. Later on he became the first student of Vladimir Horowitz. Since then Janis has appeared with every major orchestra in the world; he was the first pianist to travel to the Soviet Union at the beginning of the cultural exchange, and the first pianist to win the Grand Prix du Disque. In more recent years, because of a struggle with illness, he has focused on teaching.

NADIA REISENBERG

Sitting high above the city in an apartment conveniently located across from the Juilliard School, Nadia Reisenberg began by offering an overview of the *Barcarolle* as she feels it.

"If we start with the title, and if we take it literally, we see two elements: song and water. It is interesting that the work is so highly polyphonic. Chopin succeeded so marvelously in giving us the song throughout the piece while weaving around it a network of voices— sometimes melodic, sometimes as a response to a melodic statement. Along with this are all sorts of configurations which suggest water. In the A major section, beginning at bar 39, the inner voice is a sort of 'water-line' which must be kept constant. The monotony of those triplets, along with the bass line underlies the melody, which is not only in the upper voice at bar 42, but also in the inner voice at the reassertion of the theme.

"Chopin takes the same theme and treats it differently by giving it different surroundings. For example, the theme is first offered simply, in thirds with the bass line (another rolling motion suggestive of water).

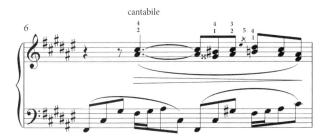

However, that same theme is offered again at bar 84 with the octaves in the bass and fuller chords in the right hand.

The theme at bar 62 is like a simple Italian street song,

but watch what happens when Chopin puts the same theme into F♯

major at bar 93 with its rich harmonic structure and swells in the bass.
These are like enormous waves.

There is so much more volume and richness to it. So it is not necessarily
the tune itself which suggests or determines a feeling, but the setting
and all that surrounds it. Of course the key of F♯ is so different from A
major, so that offers a change in color, too.

"The opening in bars 1–3 is a complete, cadenza-like introduction
which should not be divided but should be played under one long,
uninterrupted line (indicated clearly by the long phrase-mark) with
subtle subdivisions.

For example, the second quarter of the second bar is a sort of resting place. I like a little rubato at the beginning and more at the end, with perhaps a slight pushing forward in the middle of the passage. It is very much like a rubber band that you can stretch knowing it will go back into shape without distortion. I use a lot of semi- and quarter-pedaling in this passage. Then there is that beautiful rest. Only then does the piece start.

"A definite tempo must begin in bar 4. How does Allegretto differ from Andantino? It is more a question of mood than of tempo. If the music said molto espressivo I would probably play it more slowly than cantabile. The qualification is so important. Brahms often wrote simply *giocoso* or *teneramente* because it was more important to get the mood than the speed. Any sensitive musician will be able to establish an appropriate tempo.

"Another example of a subtle subdivision of a long phrase would be in bars 6 and 7 where, in order to avoid an ugly accenting on the beats in the melodic line, one breath would come after the first beat of bar 7, and the second (as though we were singing) would be the rest of that phrase. Again, I want to stress it is not a division, but only a subtle and musical subdivision."

Also in bar 6, Reisenberg (who was now at the piano) gave special importance to the first bass note of that bar, a low F♯. In fact she stressed the importance of bringing out the bass notes which are on the beats, especially those where there is a tied note in the right hand.

"When I played the Chopin B minor Sonata, I compared seven editions and finally made an eighth: my own. Chopin made so many changes that we are actually free to choose what works best for us. We can't ask Chopin what his preference was.

"I often play the trills by twice striking the same note, which is characteristically Chopinesque. In bar 11 I strike the G♯ twice. In bar 13 I play a very short trill; in bar 16 I play the F♯ appoggiatura on the beat, but in bar 17, I make a particular point of the E♮. Also in bar 17

I would put a B in after the G♯ and A♯ making a triplet before the trill. In bar 23, with the double trill, I trill from the upper note."

Jumping ahead to bar 78 where Chopin writes the indication *dolce sfogato*, Reisenberg asked some Italian friends and gathered from them that the meaning has to do with breathing—perhaps suggesting a state of ecstasy or enchantment—a holding of breath. "That whole interlude is like a Nocturne for me. It is so tender and lyrical that a person wants to hear it without any noise or distractions.

"I don't rush bar 93, in spite of the più mosso marking, because of the breadth of character in this section and because there must be a full, rich, open sound without ever being percussive."

Reisenberg feels the coda at bar 103 is noble and broader and should be played with generous rubatos, and a definite easing of the intensity of the preceding più mosso, as clearly indicated by the direction *tempo primo*. She cautions about the text in bar 106 where the trills are in whole steps, and underscores what she feels to be an error in the Polish edition in bar 108 in the second triplet in the right hand: the last D♮ she believes ought to be a C♯ according to the natural harmonic progression of that passage.

Reisenberg does not see bar 110 as any kind of climactic moment, but merely a leggiero extension of what has come before, winding down to the calando. Her romantic and thoughtful reading of the work is obviously a combination of keen Russian instincts along with educated comparisons of the various editions. It is a pity that her beautiful on-the-spot performance cannot be shared with readers. Nadia Reisenberg has, however, recorded the *Barcarolle* for Musical Heritage.

Nadia Reisenberg was born in Vilnius, Lithuania, and died in New York in 1983. She studied at the Imperial Conservatory in St. Petersburg. She and her family left Europe and settled in New York in 1922. Her teachers were Leonid Nikolaieff and Josef Hofmann. Reisenberg taught at the Curtis Institute, the Juilliard School, Queens College, and the Mannes College of Music and was a frequent juror for various competitions.

GARY GRAFFMAN

A conversation in the Graffman apartment, with its wonderful collection of oriental art and the grand view of Carnegie Hall, provides many thought-provoking insights.

"The *Barcarolle* is like Chopin's Ballades, although it is more intimate than any of the four of them. The *Barcarolle* and the Ballades are fantasies and both the elements of ballade and fantasy exist over the rhythm of the *Barcarolle*. This piece is a great example of the whole 'rubato business.' The left hand more or less keeps time and the right hand plays extremely freely, as though improvising. However, there should be more rhythmic constraint in this piece than in the Ballades."

The conversation took a tangential turn to the subject of style. "Until the generation before mine, pianists' views took precedence over the composer's and the player generally took great license in performance, even distorting the music at times. In this country the students of my generation were influenced in the other extreme. They were taught to pay more attention to the staccato over the note than to the point of the whole phrase. I'm sorry to say that nowadays although there are a few great artists, what is done is often for the sake of being different. This tendency is encouraged by critics who write about the over-played pieces in the piano repertoire. The *Barcarolle* is a masterpiece by one of the greatest composers. Any pianist with a feeling for Chopin will play the *Barcarolle* or his life will not be complete.

"In bars four and five, the performer has to establish the tempo, mood, and atmosphere by imagining himself in the setting laid out by the boat-song rhythm. A common error many pianists make is at bar six where the double-voiced cantabile enters. (Perhaps we have two singers?) Performers make a break or hiccup in the left hand rhythm instead of flowing right along. Bellini and the whole bel canto style had a great effect on Chopin's compositions. This piece lends itself particularly well to this style, which can be described as something between Neapolitan and Venetian. It is good to ask, 'How would a great singer sing that phrase?'

"Chopin was also much influenced by Bach and Mozart, so I think the trills or appoggiaturas, as in bar 16, should be approached traditionally. Vengerova, who was a student of Leschetizky, taught me to treat the appoggiaturas like a grace-note (the F♯ first and then the chord). Then I experimented with it, and because I have never had to make a solid decision (for a recording, for instance), I have played it several ways in performance. Whether the trills start from the auxiliary note or not (bar 11) is not so important. In this case I would start on the note itself because we are coming from the higher note in the melody, but if a gifted student could convince me of the opposite, I would accept it. I don't know if there is a rule. It is said that Chopin probably trilled from the top, but it is possible that in five years, research will find the opposite is true."

In bars 20 to 22 the pianist can stress either the left or right hand as they are equally important and independent.

"I love the left hand part and I bring that out, but never at the expense of the right hand. Each voice has a life of its own. In that place there are five voices. If you orchestrate it you can readily see which lines are in supporting roles and which are moving. If that E♯ were the viola part, surely it would be brought out. It is also good to notice that in the left hand there is a diminuendo sign while the right hand has crescendo, then diminuendo; so they reach their peaks at different times. I would practice each voice separately in that spot. This will make clear what your choices are and you can zero in on what you want."

A punctilious inspector of the written markings, Graffman examined the transition to the A major section (bars 35–38): "It tells us right there how much we are allowed to step up the tempo, poco più mosso, a little." He then discussed the differences between the first three editions— French, German, and English, and the manuscript, pointing out that the differences lie mainly in the phrasing, and that each is equally valid. "The whole value of the Polish edition is not the printed music, but the

remarks bar by bar in the back of the score which give references to the
other editions, and lay out your options.

"However, a pianist who has made a lifetime musicological study
of all of this can give a most uninteresting performance and I'd much
rather hear a great artist who has made arbitrary decisions but gives an
inspired performance.

"In the A major section beginning at bar 39 the bass changes from
the flowing pattern of 12 eighth notes to shorter phrases, creating a
churning, unrestful, ominous feeling that something is about to explode,
which does eventually happen. The upper voice in bars 47–49 is so
painful that it should be brought out.

In bar 62 this poco più mosso is more flowing and has longer phrases
than anything before.

"Bar 78 should sound like a singer improvising: basically in tempo,
but inspired and free. By the time you get to bars 82–84 the rhythm of
those incomplete left hand figures returns.

"Then comes the expanded recapitulation with sometimes three
voices in the right hand. Bar 93 should be even faster than 62: one

is poco più mosso, the other più mosso. In general I like to give the composer the benefit of the doubt. If he writes something, he usually has a good reason. Whether you play the più mosso in a headlong way, in longer phrases, or broken up in shorter groups, it should be breathless. The left hand is not as even and stable as it was; now with different patterns it is more an accompaniment than a line with a life of its own as in earlier pages.

"That coda! Everything begs to be highlighted; the dissonances like the F♯ in the bass in bar 105 with the G major in the right hand; bar 109 with its inner chromatic progression; the harmonic changes that occur with each eighth-note. It's pure genius.

I think bar 107 should be even bigger than bar 103. Look at the intensification in the melodic line. This time Chopin raises the third quarter of the bar, instead of having it three times the same.

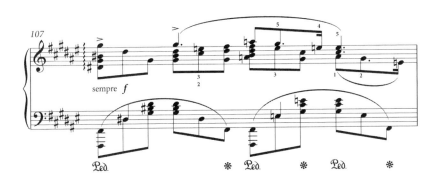

"The levels of dynamics need planning, yet the diminuendo to bar 106 followed by the crescendo should sound like the most natural thing in the world. After the cadenza beginning at bar 110, you finally arrive at a clean F♯ at bar 111. Then you can wind down. The bass line in bar 113 is a very long, legato line and the right hand is a leggiero accompaniment. Don't forget the last bar with its two statements. They are not equal: one is two eighth-notes, the other an eighth-note and a quarter.

Too many pianists ignore that.

"In short, a successful performance of this piece should sound as though you are composing the music on the spot, but coincidentally following the instructions of the composer."

Born in New York City, Gary Graffman won a scholarship at the age of seven to study at the Curtis Institute of Music with Isabelle Vengerova in 1936. He made his professional solo debut with Eugene Ormandy and the Philadelphia Orchestra at eighteen, and by age twenty, he had already established a fine career, winning prestigious prizes. After a year in Europe on a Fulbright scholarship, he returned to work intensively with Horowitz and, in the summers, with Rudolf Serkin at Marlboro in Vermont. His concerts and recordings attest to the huge contributions he has made to the piano world. All of this, unhappily, was cut short in 1979 by an injury to a finger on his right hand, limiting his performances to the literature for left hand alone, including works that were written for him. In 1980, he joined the faculty at the Curtis Institute, becoming the school's director in 1986 and its president in 1995, a position he held until 2006. He remains on the faculty there.

RUDOLF FIRKUŠNÝ

Rudolf Firkušný is a musician who prefers playing music to talking about it. He protests that there are no rules that tell how to play the *Barcarolle*, but that is exactly what this series of conversations shows: the variety of approaches and options. He began by extolling the *Barcarolle*. "It's one of the greatest. There's hardly anything to discuss because if you follow what's in the score, you find the answer. Chopin was very literal in his compositions. You don't have to 'do' anything. Obviously we all have our differences and these will come out by themselves. We have a kind of duty to bring something of ourselves into the music, but with control and without exaggeration. This piece has a certain chasteness or purity, and we have to be careful not to vulgarize or cheapen the music.

"This was one of the pieces that Chopin played himself. He never liked to play in big halls: he was extremely shy about appearing and was much more at home playing for a small group. Chopin played the *Barcarolle* at his last concert, probably at Pleyel, a small hall, before a small audience. Perhaps this accounts for the suggestion (by Tausig, I think) that the *Barcarolle* was meant to be played for only several people at a time. However, tradition has a way of becoming exaggerated and unrealistic and I don't think in this case there is any validity to that notion.

"At that time Chopin was quite ill and according to some accounts he played the coda *pianissimo* even though the text, which was corrected by him, shows the coda marked *forte*. So, number one, I think it is necessary to take the text literally; number two, he was the composer and had the right to do anything he wanted to; number three, due to his lack of physical strength he could not effect the big climaxes he meant to have.

"On the other hand, it is my own personal belief that Chopin was probably such a fantastic pianist that his *mezzo forte* was tantamount to a *forte*. He adjusted his tone to his own physical capabilities and that within the framework of his performance, with his many gradations of shading he projected his *mezzo forte*s as *forte*s to the listener. So even if he did play the coda *pianissimo* he probably still was able to sustain the tension carried over from the previous section."

Firkušný quoted an amusing remark he heard Artur Schnabel make to a student who was working on the *Barcarolle*. "'My dear, don't forget: this is not a motor boat. It is a gondola.' I think this is particularly wonderful because it says to me that it doesn't matter what your approach is, whether you play this way or that, so long as you create the gentle, rolling of the gondola and the special atmosphere around it.

"For me, the most problematic section in the piece starts at bar 39—the A major section. Some pianists think of it as only an interlude leading to the very Italian melodies at bar 62. Others think it is some kind of dance—perhaps a slow tarantella in the distant streets of Venice. I myself consider it as a purely coloristic shift in sound, like an unclear, misty vision slowly developing and gaining breadth. The rhythmic figures in the left hand must be kept constant throughout.

"Of course, the most magical place is at bar 78 where the feeling of the interpreter is the guide. It is one of the few places where we really have a free hand and can be quite improvisational. Just as the key of A major has built-in, automatic differences in personality from F♯ major, the gorgeous C♯ major in bar 78 is not at all the D♭ major of his *Berceuse*. Look at that wonderful modulation from C♯ major through bars 82 and 83 back to F♯ major in the recapitulation at bar 84.

"The *fortissimo* in bar 93 should not be overpowering as it would be in Liszt. Rather, it should be a kind of ecstatic playing, up through that fantastic, climactic chord in bar 102 and then because the ecstasy is over, it goes down at the tempo primo and down and down.

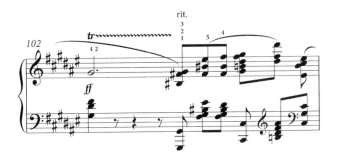

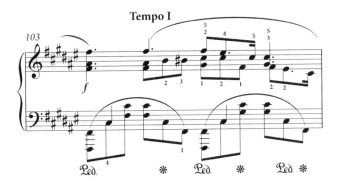

"That coda is the most extraordinary piece of music with its dissonances and richness of harmony. This step-down of dynamics is clearly there in the music: the *forte* in bar 103 as compared to the *fortissimo* in bar 93 through 102. I see this coda as a sort of glow of the sun. Whereas it was shining brightly in the preceding section, now it is setting; but there is still that glow. I have a similar feeling about the ending of the first movement of the Chopin B minor Sonata.

"Some pianists interpret certain Chopin works in a virtuosic, Lisztian style. In my opinion bar 110, for example, is not a virtuoso passage; it is a musical one and leads into the calando. The coda doesn't have to be loud to be intense. You must give the feeling that each note is there and talks. The very last cadenza-like passage at bar 115 doesn't build up velocity until one-third of the way into the measure. Those first few gruppettos are simply an extension of the leggiero 32nd note passage that came before. There's the same pattern we had before in bars 113–114, just repeated in this cadenza.

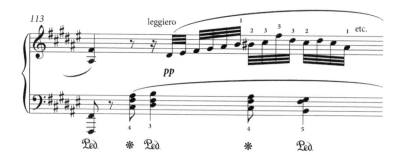

Sometimes the smaller notes are misunderstood in Chopin. For me, it is not a virtuoso passage, but rather like a cascade of water which starts slowly and gains momentum on its descent."

Rudolf Firkušný was born in Czechoslovakia. By the time he was five, the composer Leoš Janáček had taken him under his wing and "opened for [him] the gates of music." Firkušný considered Janáček to be his musical father. He made his debut at age ten, playing a Mozart Concerto with the Prague Philharmonic Orchestra. After studies with Artur Schnabel, Firkušný fled the Nazis, coming to the United States and eventually becoming a U.S. citizen. His first U.S. tour was in 1938. Firkušný had a broad repertoire, but after his performance of the Dvořák Piano Concerto (which had been unplayed in this country for sixty-five years), he became known primarily for his performances of the Czech composers, some of whom wrote works for him. Firkušný taught at the Juilliard School.

JAMES TOCCO

James Tocco established his affinity for the *Barcarolle* at once by playing and remarking on the dolce sfogato passage starting at bar 78. "This wonderful spot where all activity ceases reminds me of the mood of the Chopin *Berceuse*—with its idealized reverie. I usually play both pieces together on a program with the *Berceuse* first because I feel that even though they have a different spirit, they are closely allied by tone color and key (if you consider the D♭ of the *Berceuse* as the enharmonic equivalent of C♯, and therefore the dominant of the F♯ of the *Barcarolle*)."

Tocco demonstrated by playing the last few lines of the *Berceuse* followed by the opening bars of the *Barcarolle,* and it was certainly a prolongation of the reverie. Expressing my concern about the listener's overexposure to groups of three eighths, Tocco pointed out that as most of Chopin's compositions are in three, any Chopin group or all-Chopin recital will always have this as a factor. "The rhythmic movement is very different in both pieces: in the *Berceuse* it is hypnotic and static, whereas the *Barcarolle* is more fluid, supple, and therefore more flexible. I'm not even so sure that there's any difference psychologically between the feeling of the D♭ of the *Berceuse* and the C♯ of the dolce section in the *Barcarolle*. I don't know of too many examples where Chopin wrote in C♯ major, but he did use D♭ in many works. He was very much a classicist and a purist in his approach to the written language of music, so for the convenience of notation or for the correctness, he put it into C♯ major.

"Consider what has just occurred. We have had the constant rhythm in the bass, and then suddenly we have in bar 71 the trill on E with an E pedal point. Gradually the pedal point dissolves to D in bar 75, then to the dominant C♯ in bar 76, enhanced in bar 77 with the Neapolitan second (the D major chord), and floating in suspense from bar 78 onward.

I really think this is a recall of the idealized, suspended animation of the *Berceuse*. There is also the proximity of the writing: the *Berceuse* being Opus 57, the *Barcarolle,* Opus 60. So this is a basic factor in my approach, and I try to center everything around that.

"In the opening bars we have a good example of how Chopin often likes to suddenly leap very high, and then float down over a much longer time span. The leap is from the low C♯ all the way up to high G♯, and this leisurely floating effect resolves to the very last beautiful chord, a dominant 13th. In my pedaling I try to prolong the basses as long as possible and let all those harmonic suspensions work over the implied pedal point of C♯. This takes us into the actual movement itself.

"After bar four the music begins a supple flow. Chopin called the left hand the 'Kapellmeister,' while the right hand may be more flexible. There is very little thematic material in those Alberti basses; they simply provide the movement.

"Whereas a lesser composer might have written the following,

Chopin's basses were more extended and inventive.

He enriched them by putting in non-harmonic tones like the G♯ in the

first and third group of three eighths. He might simply have repeated the two-beat pattern making the second and fourth beats identical. Instead, he subtly extends the pattern over the full four beats of the measure by shifting the last C♯ up an octave. Whereas the lower C♯ at the end of the second beat swings back into the tonic F♯, the higher C♯ at the end of the bar leaves us in abeyance or suspension." Tocco played some examples from other Chopin works, including the B minor Sonata, where these same ingenious, suspenseful bass patterns are employed.

"Chopin didn't use thirds in very many of his compositions so that is another reason why I feel this piece is very close to the *Berceuse*. Thirds exist in the second movement of the First Concerto, the *Barcarolle*-like G major Nocturne, the Etude in Thirds, and the *Berceuse*. Of course, the *Barcarolle* sets forth in thirds, then moves to 'disguised thirds' in the form of sixths as in bar 10. Where the alto voice is independent, of course I take great pains to let it have its full say not only in the more obvious bar 11, but on into bars 12 and 13. Then the alto joins the soprano voice in bar 14, and becomes as one voice.

"Another interesting thing to note is how Chopin often put his breathing-places in unexpected places, not necessarily between phrases. For example, in bar 7 he precludes a breather after the A♯, the last note of the phrase, by creating that connecting line in the alto voice, leading to the D♯ in the first arpeggiated chord in bar 8 which, for me, begins the next phrase. See how he puts not one, but two eighth-note rests, separating the first note of the phrase, breathily, from the rest as he so often does." (Again, Tocco rustled up with ease several beautiful examples of this characteristic in Chopin to make his point.)

"I used to begin the A major section with a full sound on that tenuto A in bar 39 because I was concerned about keeping the A sounding over the basses. It is valid, but I changed it recently because of the tonal relationship between the F♯ minor and the A major. I don't feel that the A major is brighter than the F♯ minor. On the contrary, I feel that the general character of the music is lifted into the more weightless environment of A major. It is a very deceptive cadence. D major might be expected perhaps—but A major?"

Tocco's reaction to following the *Barcarolle* with another large Chopin piece was decidedly negative. "The *Barcarolle* is certainly not a miniature or minor work at all. It is one of the major works of Chopin, and it has, at the end, after those wonderful, clashing harmonies of the coda, what is perhaps the most ecstatic climax.

"In the coda the alto has a wonderfully reaffirmative role; it reiterates the upper voice in bars 107–108, and even though there is a reduction in dynamics from *fortissimo* to *forte* at the tempo primo, I feel that the F♯ pedal point, the harmonic complexity, and the *sempre forte* (Chopin's warning not to relent) all sustain the tension. I do a lot with agogic accents: for example, sitting on a particularly dissonant chord such as the first and third beats of bar 107 to create the impression of *fortissimo*.

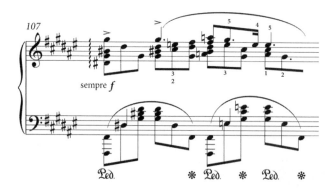

"The cadenza at bar 110 is, for me, like a sort of water vapor settling on everything and filtering out the sunlight."

It was a perfect chance to ask the obvious question: to what extent does Tocco draw from secret imagery to help determine color changes? "Of course I have imagery! I think it is, first of all, very important to have experiences, then to relate the music to these experiences (the visions, sounds, drama, literature, daily incidents) in an idealized way.

"Those last two bars—when I play them I feel they are so 'right.' They sum up everything. I don't spare any feeling or power at the end. It must be overwhelming."

James Tocco's musical studies began at age six, and he made his orchestral debut performing the Second Piano Concerto by Beethoven at twelve. He studied under scholarship at the Salzburg Mozarteum and in Paris with the flamboyant Brazilian-French pianist Magda Tagliaferro (who had studied with Cortot and toured with Gabriel Fauré, the director of the Paris Conservatoire). Tocco also worked with Claudio Arrau in New York. A career break came when he replaced Arturo Benedetti Michelangeli as guest soloist for the Tschaikovsky First Piano Concerto at the last moment at the Vienna Festival. In addition to concertizing, he is on the faculties of the University of Cincinnati College-Conservatory of Music, the Manhattan School of Music, and the Musikhochschule in Lübeck, Germany.

APPENDIX B

INTERPRETATIONS OF CHOPIN'S BALLADE NO. 4

[NOTE: This article, consisting of five analyses by celebrated pianists, was originally published in *Clavier* magazine in two parts: Paul Schenly, Ruth Laredo, and Jerome Lowenthal's pieces appeared in the December 1994 issue; and Garrick Ohlsson and Harris Goldsmith's pieces appeared in the January 1995 issue. The author's introductory text has been adapted for this book, and all biographies have been updated.]

Frédéric Chopin's Fourth Ballade, Op. 52 in F minor, is a dramatic work, ranging between delicately poetic and tumultuous extremes of emotion; it is not only the most strenuous and technically demanding of the four ballades but also one of the composer's finest late works, with several motives, brilliant harmonic treatments, and plenty of room for the performer's imagination to flower.

Not every artist studies a work in the same way. Some think about the structure and the form before sitting down at the keyboard; others eschew analysis of a piece and simply play, allowing the music to evolve. Some artists describe this process with ease, while others balk at expressing in words what they do at the piano. While using different approaches to the same work, artists sometimes arrive at similar musical conclusions, but sometimes those who use much the same process produce amazingly different results. The music they make ultimately reveals much more than words, but five distinguished pianists express some fascinating ideas about this great composition, Ballade No. 4, Op. 52.

PAUL SCHENLY

Every competition contestant who plays this Ballade dreads that the jury will say, "Thank you, would you please skip to the coda?" It is important to set the mood of the themes, so I relate the work to a literary ballad. When the theme enters after the introduction, Chopin seems to be thinking in terms of balance between the lines and the stanzas. For example, the opening lines of an old English ballad has the same repetitive structure that Chopin uses in his theme:

> *O Where hae ye been Lord Randal my son*
> *O Where hae ye been my handsome young man*

Although the verse does not translate into $\frac{6}{8}$ meter, there is the same kind of chanting. The story in a literary ballad unfolds with no commentary or interjection by the author. Events are the result of supernatural forces, destructive elements, or taboos, even in such romantic adaptations as Coleridge's *The Rime of the Ancient Mariner.* I believe Chopin thought generically, and used elements that are universal to all ballads.

The argument might be made that music is more specific than words. Certainly Mendelssohn said this about his *Songs Without Words.* I read that Chopin published this Ballade with the title *Ballade Without Words,* implying that he intentionally omitted words as Brahms did with his

"*Edward*" *Ballades*, Op. 10. I believe Chopin thought of this Ballade as a personal dream with supernatural or mythological tendencies.

The opening should be warm and natural without being sentimental. Unlike a nocturne in which pianists try to do something different each time the theme reappears, that repetitive quality here should suggest an incantation, almost a dreamscape. The danger is having too many tempos in a piece that is uninterrupted and with momentum that is built through active rhythms, rising sequences, volume, and even more speed at the end, although increased tempo is built in through the addition of sixteenths; I do not make a point of speeding up; the music intensifies through the diversity of the writing.

Many of the seeds (motives) of the theme, such as the repeated notes, appear in the introduction. One approach is to imagine Chopin playing with the repeated Gs out of which emerged a theme in an improvisatory style. Once the theme begins, pianists are in an archaic land. The *mezza voce* starts with the chanting of the theme in measure 8 rather than at the beginning, which I take with a bolder tone. Open octaves such as these, or as in the opening of the Liszt Sonata, suggest thought rather than song. The dynamic marking in measure 11 is important: the right hand should lift slightly after the first E♭ to play the next three as a vibration rebounding off the first one. Keep the crescendo up to the fourth E♭ before making the diminuendo.

The main theme (measures 8–10) F, E♮ D♭, C, and B♭ reflects the descending F minor scale suggested in the introduction. The variations on the theme should be played expressively, as in the tied notes of measures 24–29. Bring out the alto voice in measures 45 and 46 to unify the music with the repetition in the bass (measures 48–49).

Chopin uses much thematic transformation and inversion. The ballade form was an attempt to create one long piece with different ideas, instead of dividing the music into movements. This is in a sonata form with a development section and the second theme in the subdominant (measures 84–86). I think of it as a theme with variations because the theme returns in measure 58 with the beautiful alto material that is a commentary on the main theme. It should not be louder than the soprano, but I try to bring it out. Its presence adds to the excitement without increasing the tempo.

In measures 51–52 a dance-like idea seems reminiscent of Chopin's native Poland, from which he was exiled. At the same time there is a descending-scale motive (measures 8–10) that laces through the piece. Pianists who go faster here sacrifice overall unity. In measure 53 the G♭, F, G♮, G♭ in the alto voice form another motive that appears in measure 72 in the right hand.

Vary the phrasing of the theme in measure 64 by starting it two six-teenths before it usually begins.

The motivic material that begins in measure 72 weaves in and out with descending scales, fragments of the theme, and so on. Avoid succumbing to the temptation to be a virtuoso here, but treat it all melodically, without too much *accelerando*. Measures 74 and 75 seem to vibrate around G♭ and G♮, but then all the material resolves melodically. Without bringing out each motive, it is important to show the design of the music. These passages are never an end in themselves but are connective tissue.

In measure 80 go back to the main tempo. The second theme in measure 84, marked *dolce*, is a force of conflict. Although it is the essence of peace, conflict arises because the theme is separate from the narrative and foreshadows the conflict when it reappears in measures 169 and 177.

A repeated motive (measures 100–102) is played in the bass against the descending harmonic line in the right hand. Chopin combines two themes, which restrains pianists from rushing mindlessly through the music.

Another dance-like section begins at measure 108, followed by a development in measure 121, with the main theme in the left hand.

After a series of surges, the introduction returns in measure 129. In measure 134 there is a bit of supernatural or magical fantasy, followed by measure 135 that contains an allusion to Bach, who was important to Chopin. It has a kind of "Where am I" quality. More magical developmental material provides a bridge back to the recapitulation around measure 144. At measure 146 I would firmly re-establish the tempo.

Chopin introduces a more flowing accompaniment with 16th notes in measure 152; here it is not necessary to go faster. Bring out some of the bass, such as the low F, F♭, and E♭ in measure 154. Against that use the soft right-hand motion to phrase the music almost by itself. In measure 169 the second theme appears now in D♭ instead of B♭, with a D♭ pedal point. When played beautifully, the music speaks for itself.

The randomly placed melodic notes create a built-in rubato in measure 175, while the left-hand thumb in measures 181–183 plays a lovely idea that should be brought out.

I drop the volume quite a bit in measure 186 in order to build up again; after the sforzando in measures 191–194 there are important accents on the first and fourth beat.

The chords in measures 198–201 are melodic staccatos, lightly pedaled. I haven't decided whether to pedal the last low C in measure 202. It can be hair-raisingly beautiful, but because it was not written, I am not sure that I have the courage to do it. The descending melodic line at the top of the chords in measures 203–207 is a recollection of the introduction.

In the coda I bring out the descending alto voice in the first half of the bar and the descending minor scale in the soprano in the second half. In measures 212 and 214 the bass crescendos and the chromatic scales are important because they foreshadow the right-hand chromatic scales in measures 215–216. A descending minor scale appears in measure 217 at the top and in 219, played by the left-hand thumb.

Danger lies in performing the octaves in measure 224 to sound like the Tschaikovsky concerto. They are all melodies and motives, as in measure 68, that we have heard before. Look for the design in a measure like 227, being careful not to make it sound like a stick rattling along a picket fence.

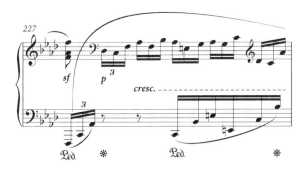

This piece can easily be interpreted in a cheap and vulgar way by shameless emotional display. When Chopin called it a "ballade without words," he didn't mean a ballade without clothes.

Winner of the prestigious Avery Fisher Prize, Paul Schenly is presently the head of the piano department at the Cleveland Institute of Music, the founder and director of the summer music festival Pianofest in the Hamptons on Long Island, and the artistic director of the Cleveland International Piano Competition. Schenly has been a soloist with a number of major American orchestras. He is on the nominating committee for the Gilmore Piano Foundation and has recorded for Sine Qua Non and RCA.

RUTH LAREDO

I learned the four Ballades at an early age as an essential part of the repertoire, yet I never performed them. Now I appreciate how great they are. I don't usually like to analyze music verbally. This Ballade is a dark and tragic work. It is inventive and imaginative, all of which matters more now to me than when I studied it.

In terms of form, Chopin uses a loose style, similar to a rhapsody. In the beginning there doesn't seem to be a direction with the G octaves. The music seems to he in C major, but in measure 8 the F minor tonic appears, as though Chopin put an improvisation on paper. It is this extemporaneous quality that makes the work so extraordinary. I don't like to title the sections, but there are parts that resemble an introduction, a theme, and variations.

I take the *Andante con moto* at my own pace. This is a very personal piece and should not be played metronomically. The *mezza voce* theme is straightforward, whereas the embroidery and embellishments of the theme in the first variation, at measures 23 and 29, allow for more rubato.

Then Chopin gets to the rather flat section at measure 38.

This leads to measure 58, where the theme is more grandly varied and embellished. Emphasize the drama of the F minor theme throughout this section until measure 71. Make as much of a *ritenuto* as possible in measure 70 before the *fortissimo* of measure 71. There is ferocious spontaneity, with an accelerando leading to another *ritenuto* in measures 78–79 and a bridge to an entire new idea at measure 80. It must have been agonizing for Chopin to write these improvisatory ideas on paper. I picture Chopin as George Sand describes him, with his eyes wide open, practically tearing his hair out to get the music to sound freely improvised.

There are stormy dramatic parts and quiet chorale-like places as in measure 80 that return to a boiling point. A wonderful fugal section starts at measure 135, which should be played *misterioso*.

It is like walking from one room into another, each with different colors and moods. The most difficult timing is to envision the work as a whole. Although the tempos shift, they should be related. There are many places, such as the *dolcissimo* cadenza at measure 134, that are free flights of fancy. It takes a long time to hear something as a whole, so it is beneficial to learn it when you are young and come back to it later. The pitfalls are not just musical but technical; this is a virtuosic piece. Even the difficult coda has melodies weaving throughout, coming to a thunderous conclusion. I love to get past the technical work to be free to express the music. That is why I prefer Chopin to Liszt. I don't feel an affinity to all that glitter without as much of the inner message.

No matter what the intervals between the notes or the inversions of the melodies, intuition, experience, a good education, and a personal point of view will put you in touch with the beauty of the music. I once heard photographer Richard Avedon say that he never learns a thing the way that people expect him to. If he reads a book, he has to experience it obliquely. Analyzing every note of a work does little for me or my ability to play it. I went to music school and studied with fine teachers, learned counterpoint, harmony, and theory; but these do nothing to show me the message. I don't advocate closing our eyes to the elements that are there, but what is important is what we do with them. Only by planning the music carefully will it sound improvised.

Ruth Laredo, particularly known for her performances, recordings, and scholarship in the music of Scriabin and Rachmaninoff, gave her last concert at the Metropolitan Museum, as part of her Concerts with Commentary series, shortly before she died at age sixty-seven. She attended the Curtis Institute of Music in Philadelphia, where she studied with Rudolf Serkin, whose preference for Beethoven and the classics were in direct contrast to Laredo's preferred Russian repertoire. She debuted in 1962, with Leopold Stokowski conducting the American Symphony Orchestra at Carnegie Hall and then with the New York Philharmonic under Pierre Boulez, becoming one of the world's leading women pianists.

JEROME LOWENTHAL

It is interesting to ask students to identify the form of a large Chopin work. They know it has a recapitulation and a middle, and often incorrectly answer that this is an ABA form. It is not an ABA form. It is helpful to think of this Ballade as being in sonata form in which the variation idea plays a considerable role, as in Schubert's C minor posthumous Sonata. If it is a sonata form, the second theme appears in B♭ in measure 84 in the subdominant, taking the place of the dominant as is often the case in romantic works. It also happens in the Schumann *Fantasie* in C. The cadence of the exposition is in measure 99, and the development begins in measure 100, extending to the recapitulation in measure 146, as suggested for measure 135. Measure 152 is a continuation of the theme with the reintroduction of the second theme at measure 169; the flowing bars represent a variation. Even the coda is a variation on the first theme. If it is played *forte*, it is an onslaught; the key to interpreting Chopin dynamics is to assume that they represent either a general mood or an initial attack.

With this cursory outline of the form, look back at the beginning. As with the other ballades, this one begins as a kind of impersonation of an improvisor. It was carefully composed, of course, but Chopin's talent for improvisation is often apparent in his music.

The contrary dynamics between the hands are important in the repeated G octaves.

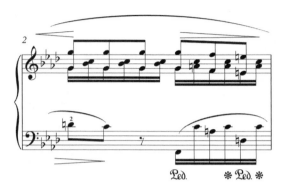

The theme begins in measure 2 and is repeated in measure 4. The main theme begins in measure 8, but notice how the last phrase with the repeated E♭s in measure 11 resembles measure 2 and the left hand in measure 1.

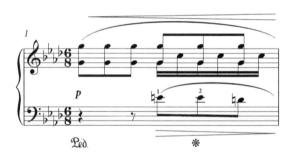

One of the great motives of the piece is the repeated notes, which find their final apotheosis in the three repeated Gs in measure 202. Pianists mistakenly play them using the old-fashioned, vulgar pedal to prolong the third chord.

There is an intervallic play between the three introductory notes played *mezza voce*, which return at measure 46.

Schirmer's Joseffy edition of the Ballade has a wonderful preface by James Huneker, who writes about a special Polish melancholy called *żal*. I always think of this melody that way, especially with the special poisoned quality of those intervals. The interplay and uncertainty of the intervals give it a peculiarly haunting sound.

The accompaniment represents a strumming plucked instrument, as in a serenade, and the melody should be played cantabile and emotionally, taking care to honor the rests as in measure 10. The more dialectic those two parts are, the better.

The piece builds with some variation to the first modulation in measure 38 to the Neapolitan. The left hand suggests, metrically, the main theme. Generally, whenever Chopin starts the theme with the second eighth of six, it suggests the melody. At the same time the right hand has three repeated notes, so this magical passage represents two motives. Then the music modulates down a whole tone to F♭. The climax comes at measures 55–56 with the repeated G♭s.

Many pianists back off of those notes instead of following Chopin's crescendo marking, because they are afraid of being shocking. Then comes the fullest variation in measure 58.

When I studied this work with Eduard Steuermann, he said, "Now comes the part when the whole audience listens to see how you blend the sonorities." He was so idealistic that he truly believed it. That blending is a challenge. The variation ends with the four G♭s in measures 70–71, and then dramatically breaks off.

In the following passage Chopin changes the minor second of the D♭ to C into a major second of the D♭ to C♭; it is a major transition to the calm second theme. In measure 80 a theme appears that is also a transition and modulation through the cadence in measures 83 and 84 to the second theme. Although this theme is less important, it includes the repeated notes, as in measure 80. Starting in measure 100 the development uses the motive of the descending minor second.

Measure 112 has a physical and emotional *légèreté* (lightness), while the left hand is playful. In the more serious part of the development, at measure 121, it is important to bring out the duet between the tenor and soprano voices that uses the two motives of the first theme. A grand restatement of the repeated notes occurs in measure 125.

Chopin moves with indecision in the wonderful modulation in measure 128 and the emotional turning in 131 to 133, which are among my favorite moments in the piece.

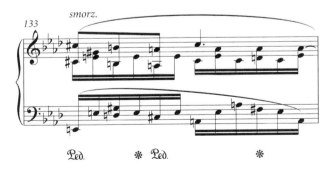

Then comes that gossamer cadential passage that exploits the descending minor second and turns it into the diminished third of the opening.

Measure 135 is like someone taking his first steps in a strange new world. It leads to the second half of the theme, with certainty, at measures 137–138, followed by that nebulous quality heard in the second half of the theme in 140–141. This material provides a way to slide back into the full recapitulation at measure 146.

It is important not to change the tempo in the next variation, measure 152, but to consider it as a continuation of the theme. The soprano part communicates the melodic continuity. Bring out the bass notes in measures 161–163. At measure 169 the second theme should maintain the same tempo with a caressing leggiero in the left hand. You can continue steadily with the crescendo bringing it to build to another climax, as in measures 181 and 183. The low B♭s in measures 185–187 are like funeral tollings; give a dark coloring to the chords. The D♭s lead to the bass, which moves toward a triumphant D♭ major harmony in measure 191.

Measures 191 to 195 have the repeated Fs bringing to mind the Ocean Etude. Consider emphasizing the harmonic changes in those arpeggios. It all ends on a second inversion chord at measure 195, leading to a chord sequence in the next measure, which contains the motive of the main theme.

I call measures 198–200 sleight-of-hand chromaticism, because all the enharmonic modulations and harmonic changes go nowhere. Niecks, a Chopin biographer, called that aspect of the composer's writing coloristic, implying chromaticism just for the sake of color. With the C bass of the F minor chord in second inversion at measure 195, feel the C pedal point. The dotted half-note chords in measures 203–210 prolong the dominant, as if holding a breath.

The coda is a final statement formed by a suggested variation of the theme in the root position of F minor. At measure 224 the right hand suggests the first motive of the opening theme. The last page is built mainly on the descending minor second. At measures 231–232 a last passionate statement of the repeated notes occurs in the left hand in a speeded-up version.

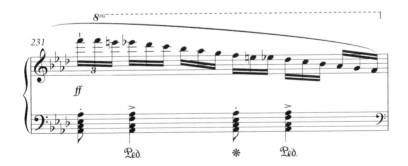

Chopin uses the interval of D♭ to C to the point that it becomes the basis of the last passage. If you can preserve the rhythm of those last bars, it is better than just playing as though you're falling down a flight of stairs. Chopin indicates no pedal.

I want to emphasize the pseudo-improvisatory character of this Ballade, which is presented in the beginning and continued by the serenade nature of the theme, the tight and rich use of motives, and the free sonata form with the secondary subject in B♭, the subdominant. Those are the things that anchor the piece for me.

Jerome Lowenthal teaches at the Juilliard School in New York, where he was also chair of the piano department for many years. Lowenthal is also on the faculty at Music Academy of the West in Santa Barbara, California, and the list of his students who have gone on to major careers is staggering. He made his debut at thirteen with the Philadelphia Orchestra and then in 1963, with the New York Philharmonic. His career has brought him solo appearances with great orchestras and conductors worldwide, and collaborations with distinguished colleagues, most recently with his companion, Ursula Oppens. One of his distinguishing characteristics is his pleasure in finding rare and lesser-known works and presenting them to the public. His teachers were William Kapell and Eduard Steuermann at the Juilliard School, and Alfred Cortot at the École Normale de Musique de Paris. A prizewinner at Queen Elisabeth Music Competition in Brussels and the Busoni Competition, he is on the juries of many of the world's top competitions today.

GARRICK OHLSSON

I use every edition I can get my hands on when studying Chopin except the 19th-century Augner edition, where editors changed notes if they offended the ear. The publishers assumed that some of Chopin's bold dissonances were wrong because he was too refined to write what they viewed as brutal discords. The variants in Chopin's manuscripts offer insights into the way he thought. The old Oxford edition was the first scholarly project, edited by Edouard Ganche and based on the original French editions; there are some interesting phrasings in it. The Paderewski edition is valuable because it contains annotations of the differences between the French (Schlesinger), the German (Breitkopf and Härtel) and the English (Wessel) editions. The Mikuli and Joseffy editions are authentic.

Chopin was so popular during his lifetime that publishers produced simultaneous editions in France, England, and Germany. Chopin or his copyists might prepare three manuscripts at once, possibly altering a note here or there as each saw fit. Therefore it is possible to have three first editions of the same work.

Chopin's Ballade #4 has an introduction and a long, beautiful melody, which is internal, and then rises in waves, which eventually climax. Gathering intensity, the music almost explodes but never resolves itself. A version of the second subject appears in measure 84, but Chopin writes with such a continuous flow, it is hard to say that one particular note begins a melody. A second climactic development occurs around measure 125, which is not as tumultuous as the first; it gathers steam, reaching a cataclysmic explosion in measure 202. Finally there is the difficult coda with its active demons. Chopin's architecture is precise, but his sense of form is fluid and organic, like a living plant, with every leaf different and each limb leading into the next branch.

William Hibbard, the 20th-century 12-tone composer, offered an interesting analysis of this work and wondered why the G♮ in measure 22 resonated so magically. He looked at the music and discovered that in the long ruminative melody there was no G♮ until that one moment, although there are G♮s in the harmony. Part of the magic is the way Chopin resolves that phrase to the dominant seventh on a diminuendo, which pushes the music forward. Chopin is an upbeat composer, always leading you forward, whereas Stravinsky, for example, is downbeat.

On a more subtle level, look at where Chopin puts such suspensions as the tied D♭ in measure 9 or the F♭ in measures 13–14. They become pungent dissonances suspended over a new harmony in the bass, yearning to be resolved. It is a wonderful ache that draws us forward.

The difficult left-hand accompaniment has two components. First, the left hand functions as a *lieder* accompaniment. To get a slightly lilting barcarolle feel, play the first and fourth beats of each bar with the left hand, and the chords in between with the right hand. Second, there is the bass line with pedaled staccato Fs, which is no accident. A sophisticated orchestrator like Debussy might have half of the cellos play pizzicato and the other a half-bowed F for a sustained, yet articulated sound, which is exactly what Chopin wanted. Pedal the Fs and play with a slightly faster attack and a little extra life. Try to play the melody in the right hand, and only the Fs in the left hand; it is hard to control. After adding and balancing the chords, you will understand the difficulty of the passage.

Some pianists tend to release the pedal as a series of hiccups on the third and sixth beats of each measure in the theme. In the original manuscript the pedal releases are not regularly placed. I often do a quick change of the pedal on the third beat. Practice the left-hand accompaniment with two hands, listening attentively to the balance between the chords and the tones you want to bring out. Then transfer the section to the left hand alone.

This *mezza voce* melody is an inward tune, almost unformed, that is invented as it goes along, like humming. Chopin leaves much to the artist as far as improvisation. For example, the melody repeats at measures 8–10, which can be felt as an attenuation. Make a point of releasing the D♭ in measure 10 to contrast with the tied D♭ in measure 9.

The four repeated E♭s in measure 11 are a typical Chopin sound that makes the piano vibrate. Each E♭ has its own sound with no accents. Pianists might climax at the fourth E♭ eighth note because it is the high-point, but Chopin suggests stepping back from it. In the Oxford edition there is a decrescendo mark over the line at the same time as the crescendo appears in the middle of the bar. The staccatos in the bass of measure 11 are not played as traditional staccatos, but are not dull either; they are an orchestration at the piano without assigning specific instruments. At age 46 I am finally getting smart enough to sing these phrases to myself. Most piano teachers tell their students to make the piano sing. I pretend to be a fine opera singer because singing the line gets me away from certain mannerisms I do with my fingers. Even swaying or moving to a melody gives pianists an expanded sense of the music, and conducting yourself is interesting. Music is singing, dancing, even talking; it should speak with a certain eloquence. All of these activities are fun and can solve musical problems.

There are many beautiful details to discover, such as the F♭ in the bass of measure 25, which is mirrored in measure 27. In measure 38 the repeated G♭s are reminiscent of the repeated notes of the first subject and predict the second subject. Sink to *pianissimo*; it's magical and not quite earthly, an unexpected glance toward heaven.

In measure 45 there is a deliberate crescendo where the inclination is to make a diminuendo. In measures 53–54 there are lovely inner alto voices. Follow the dynamic markings and bring out the G♭ to the F, and the G♮ to the G♭.

In measure 58 the thickness of texture reminds me of the beginning of a Bach Passion, with its counterpoint and intense sound. Musicians can almost hear the oboes.

In measures 59–60 there is no accent on the fourth E♭ in the melodic line, and in measure 65 all four G♭s are accented. On the other hand there ought to be a decrescendo in measure 61 to make another crescendo leading to the *forte* in measure 62.

Even an endless crescendo in Beethoven doesn't mean each note is louder than the one before; these dynamics come in waves and with a crescendo over ten or so bars; we do have to allow our hearts to beat. In measures 70–71 there is an enormous crescendo. I fast-pedal the first half of measure 70 and gather all those descending octaves in the second half of the bar on one pedal, releasing it before the *fortissimo*.

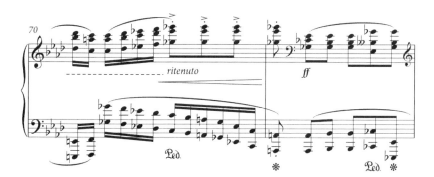

The ritenuto is like a boulder in the middle of the street that stops the music. Chopin used the pedal not only to sustain but also for sound effects. It allowed him to combine sounds in imaginative ways.

Next the music becomes wild, but evaporates in measure 74. This is a strenuous piece to play and practice, both physically and emotionally.

The pedal from the end of measure 74 is released at various spots in different editions. I like to make the touch a bit thinner and more staccato around measure 76 to get that *jeu perlé*, a Chopinesque sound.

Jumping ahead to measure 107, I bring out the three accents in the right hand as throbs leading to the mazurka section. This is sadly graceful music, transforming into a joyful but slightly quivery and manic state in measure 114. Chopin had volatile, emotional energy, and his writing is like the stream of consciousness from such a person. The section cadences beautifully in measures 120–121, and it darkens with the theme in the bass at measure 121.

I leave the pedal down at measure 134 from the fermata on A and lift it exactly where Chopin indicates, treating each note like harmonics. The theme reconstitutes itself at measure 146; it is the only time Chopin doesn't tie the two halves of the theme together. Pianists should observe the rest in measure 148.

The last variation of the theme is at measure 152. I play it lyrically, with the passion growing out of the music. At measure 154 Chopin wrote complicated rhythms, 6 against 4 and 10 against 6. Don't delineate these rhythms exactly as written. There is wild rubato here, with the four sets of three in the bass, making the measures slightly rocky, as though the earth shifts a bit. It happens again at measure 161.

At the accelerando in measure 163, the music gets desperate and doesn't know how to resolve; it dies down in measure 169. The passions are underground, erupting in the beautiful rising left-hand scales at measure 169. My favorite bars in the piece are 175 and 176. This place should sound like a rambling rubato, but playing it exactly as Chopin wrote it takes your breath away. I get shivers when I play those bars. It is as though Chopin suspends gravity for that moment. Paul Creston loved to lecture about Chopin as one of the most gifted rhythmic composers and used these measures as an example. The permutations include

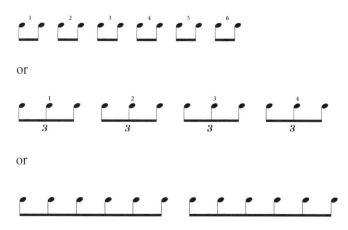

as well as two against three

or a 9 superimposed over both bars.

At measure 191 I like to emphasize the steady rhythm of the accents at the beginning and mid-point of the measure and the implied accents at the harmonic changes (A♭, A♮, B♭, B♮) imbedded in the passages. The melodic climax that builds from measures 169 to 191 is a magnificent long line, almost Wagnerian in its endless volcanic passion. In measure 191 there is tension and frustration in the lack of resolution, even in a place like measures 201–202. After the climactic writing, it is almost as though Chopin says, "Yes, but no." Then there is a sense of stability in measures 203–210, a magical place. The coda's passionate risoluto reminds me of the coda in Beethoven's Appassionata, seizing fate by the throat, although the coda is more hysterical. The coda has to be passionate and fast; but if it's a garble, the implied melody, harmonic information, and dissonance get lost. To make it sound faster, play all the notes clearly and bring them out. The high D♭ in measure 212 is important as the first note of that descending line, just as the bass line leads up to another D♭.

To establish the right tempo, start slowly for two measures, and repeat them at faster tempos until you maintain the elements without losing the music. In measure 215, save energy by not making a crescendo in the second set of ascending chromatic thirds. Measures 221 and 222 have one of the last gasps of melody in the top line. There's no calm left at this point.

At bar 223 I take the middle right-hand notes in the left hand. Generally, I agree with Claudio Arrau, who believed there were good musical reasons behind a composer's decisions, and he advocated not rearranging fingerings. Sometimes the original fingering creates a struggle and simplifying it takes the grit out. As a realist, I find that the struggle in this case makes you lose the chaotic distance between the intervals. This is an impossible passage where everything should be brought out and still make a fantastic sweeping crescendo. The octaves in measure 224 are not Tschaikovsky octaves; they are big, but not bombastic, and there is still a lot of music there. Measure 226 is a reinforced climax, and I fight an accelerando before 227. Then I spread the accelerando out over four bars. Don't forget to bring out those beautiful melodic high points in 231 and 232 at the A♭ s.

The last four chords are a formal ending, without any ritard. I do the Wilhelm Furtwängler trick: he drove an ending on and on without relenting and then held back before the last chord.

A good interpreter can make a beautiful phrase out of any three notes in Chopin. The real challenge comes in gathering all these beautiful moments into a whole. You still have to pick the daisies along the way, and that's why I like to find the special touches that say something about the whole.

Garrick Ohlsson has been revered for his Chopin playing ever since he became the first American to win the Gold Medal at the 1970 International Frédéric Chopin Piano Competition. Since then he has recorded and performed the entire Chopin oeuvre, and he has become one of the most highly respected pianists of our time in a vast and varied spectrum of the piano repertoire. Ohlsson also won first prize at the Busoni Competition in Italy and the Montreal Piano Competition in Canada, and he was awarded the Avery Fisher Prize in 1994. He had a succession of noted teachers, including Claudio Arrau, Sascha Gorodnitzki, Rosina Lhévinne and Irma Wolpe.

HARRIS GOLDSMITH

The first thing that occurs to me is the number of Chopin's works having a narrative quality that are not called ballades; for example, the *Polonaise-Fantaisie*. Some say Ballades have legends attached to them. The third Ballade is about Ondine, the water nymph, and there are two stories associated with the fourth. One is from the Polish poet Adam Mickiewicz, who says the Ballade is about two brothers who search the world for their brides. The other fascinates me more: it is about the Canker and the Rose. You hear that cankerous strain right from the beginning and watch it wind through the piece, erupting finally in the coda.

During the first three lines, it is not clear what the piece is about or the key until the fermata in measure 7. Suddenly the C, which seemed to be the tonic, becomes the dominant. Although the fermata is over the C major chord, the C in the treble should follow *attacca*, without lingering, and the fermata should be placed over the upper C. The *a tempo* appears so close to the bar line that Chopin may have wanted it to apply to the C as well. Don't forget the fermata applies to the alto E that overlaps the soprano C. This is one of the most telling moments of the entire piece; the uncertainty is ominous. That C is followed by an upper neighbor, D♭, and a lower neighbor, B♮, that introduces the chromaticism with its sort of sickly quality that is the canker. Each time it returns, that sickly quality is increasingly virulent.

I see this piece as an interrupted theme with variations. It is a mistake to use too much rubato in the first statement of the theme. It should be measured and rather severe and stark with a sense of moving forward without dawdling as in the beginning of the *alla marcia* of the F minor *Fantaisie*. When an artist inadvertently puts variants in the first statement of the theme, as in measure 24, it shows a lack of understanding or concentration. This variant is just a bit more intensified.

In measure 12 of the theme the left hand leads to a low A♭ in a chordal passage. Chopin doesn't use that material at the corresponding place in the first variation, but he uses a similar transition in the left hand of measures 36–37 that leads to the first episode in measure 38. The theme drops in pitch in measure 42.

These changes should be in color and dynamics, not tempo. In measure 46 Chopin develops elements of the theme working to the climax in measure 55. In measure 58 he arrives at the second variation where the chromaticism leads to double thirds in textured phrases. This variation is more than a restatement of the theme because it pushes toward a second theme and goes through a sort of delirium that starts in measure 72 and leads to the key change of B♭ at measure 80. Play the accelerandos in measures 74 and 163 keeping in mind that all the variants on the theme have the same basic pulse. Finding an *Andante con moto* to accommodate all the variants without rushing or slowing is important. I superimpose the basic theme on a variation, as in measure 152, when I'm teaching the work to encourage students to think of the theme underlying the florid writing.

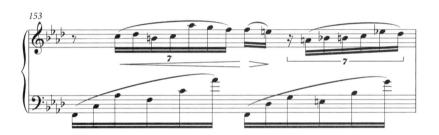

This Ballade is not just a theme and variations but a theme and variations interrupted strategically by a desire not to be a theme and variations.

The second theme, which begins in measure 84 with its lilting $\frac{6}{8}$ rhythm, is a reference to a similar theme in the second and third Ballades. After the nebulous feeling at measures 80–84, the dolce theme offers a change of color after the sickly first theme. The second theme is healthy, open, and straightforward, although its ending at measure 99 seems inconclusive, even though it is in the same key of B♭.

It seems that Chopin created the diversion in measure 100 just as Shakespeare might have done to heighten the tension or to relieve it before the dénouement. The composer presents two great conflicting ideas, only to suddenly include this giddy interlude. There is a sense that the piece is trying to escape from the F minor theme, but that it is doomed to keep returning.

At measure 121 Chopin weaves a tapestry of thematic fragments that is a development section, though not in the sense of traditional sonata-allegro form. The section continues for a full page until the A major harmony in measure 134, then it returns to that fraught moment at measure 8. The overlapping and stretto (measures 135–138) become a variation of sorts.

Then the music finally settles in B♭ minor, in measure 145.

In measure 149 Chopin uses the first variant, and in 152 the final variation appears where the canker is already virulent. It is a tormented and tumultuous moment, with the music progressively working into a frenzy. This variation is incomplete, breaking away in measures 164 through 168. By singing the skeletal version of the theme along with playing the final embellished variation, it becomes obvious that there is no resolution of the last phrase as in measures 15–16. At measure 169 a new airborne version of the second theme appears in D♭. Measure 181 is a triumphant moment, yet the piece keeps building. By measure 186 the music has not broken away from its intensity; then Chopin starts a new sequence in measure 187 and by 191 there is another triumphant moment in D♭, similar to the "Ocean Etude."

The F minor chord appears again in 195, with deceptive ascending chords, which lead to the high C, the only dominant. In measures 201–202, the pianist finds himself in ruins.

Chopin carefully plotted to end in ruins. In measure 202 some pianists pedal because they don't want the audience to applaud, but certainly, there should not be any pedal at that fermata.

At the coda in measure 212 there is a trace of Baroque notation: the 32nd note following the third 16th of the triplets. The 32nd note should not be played squarely on the third note of the triplets. In measure 219 there is a string of 32nds. Think of the 32nd note in relation to the following dotted 16th, not the preceding one.

In measure 223 many students play the middle note of the triplet with the left hand. I disagree with that practice because the chromaticism in the alto voice (G♯, A–D♮, E♭–G♯, A) gets lost along with the feeling of the dotted figure in the bass. By fingering the music as written, it is impossible to play at breakneck speed.

The left-hand octaves in measures 224 and 226 are a transformation of the left-hand octaves in measure 68. Do not lose the rhythm of the triplets in the last bar. Just practice hard and pray.

Harris Goldsmith is a pianist, author, critic, and musicologist. He studied at the Manhattan School of Music with Robert Goldsand and Verna Brown, and later with Claudio Arrau and Karl Ulrich Schnabel. Goldsmith has coached, taught, and performed at various universities and festivals, and since 1994 he has taught Music Literature and Chamber Music at the Mannes College of Music. He has recorded for RCA, CBS, and Musical Heritage Society.

BIBLIOGRAPHY

Avins, Styra, sel. and annot. *Johannes Brahms: Life and Letters*. Oxford: Oxford University Press, 1997.

Bettmann, Otto L. *Johann Sebastian Bach as His World Knew Him*. New York: Birch Lane Press, 1995.

Blunt, Wilfrid. *On Wings of Song: A Biography of Felix Mendelssohn*. New York: Charles Scribner's Sons, 1974.

Brendel, Alfred. *Musical Thoughts and After-thoughts*. Princeton, NJ: Princeton University Press, 1976.

Brendel, Alfred. *Music Sounded Out*. New York: Farrar Straus Giroux, 1990.

Chissell, Joan. *Clara Schumann: Dedicated Spirit; A Study of Her Life and Work*. New York: Taplinger, 1983.

Comini, Alessandra. *The Changing Image of Beethoven: A Study in Mythmaking*. New York: Rizzoli International, 1987.

Eigeldinger, Jean-Jacques. *Chopin: Pianist and Teacher, as Seen by His Pupils*. New York: Cambridge University Press, 1986.

Frisch, Walter, and Kevin C. Karnes, eds. *Brahms and His World*. Princeton, NJ: Princeton University Press, 2009.

Geiringer, Karl. *Brahms: His Life and Work*. 2nd ed. New York: Oxford University Press, 1947.

Gutman, Robert W. *Mozart: A Cultural Biography*. New York: Harvest-Harcourt, 1999.

Hildesheimer, Wolfgang. *Mozart*. London: J. M. Dent and Sons, 1982.

Huneker, James. *Chopin: The Man and His Music*. Cambridge, MA: Charles Scribner's Sons, 1900.

Kirkpatrick, Ralph. *Interpreting Bach's Well-Tempered Clavier: A Performer's Discourse and Method.* New Haven: Yale University Press, 1984.

Kochovitsky, George A. *Performing Bach's Keyboard Music.* White Plains, NY: Pro Am Music Resources, 1996.

Lockwood, Lewis. *Beethoven: The Music and the Life.* New York: W. W. Norton, 2003.

Marek, George R., and Maria Gordon-Smith. *Chopin.* New York: Harper and Row, 1978.

Marston, Nicholas. *Schumann: Fantasie, Opus 17.* Cambridge: Cambridge University Press, 1992.

Methuen-Campbell, James. *Chopin Playing—From the Composer to the Present Day.* New York: Taplinger, 1981.

Neuhaus, Heinrich. *The Art of Piano Playing.* London: Barrie & Jenkins, 1973.

Newman, William S. *Beethoven on Beethoven: Playing Piano Music His Way.* New York: W. W. Norton, 1988.

Reed, John. *Schubert.* Totowa, NJ: J. M. Dent and Sons, 1987.

Rosen, Charles. *Beethoven's Piano Sonatas: A Short Companion.* New Haven: Yale University Press, 2002.

Rosen, Charles. *The Romantic Generation.* Cambridge, MA: Harvard University Press, 1995.

Schumann, Robert. *Schumann on Music: A Selection from the Writings.* Translated and edited by Henry Pleasants. New York: Dover, 1965.

Schweitzer, Albert. *J. S. Bach.* Vol. 1. Translated by Ernest Newman. New York: Dover, 1966.

Selden-Goth, G., ed. *Felix Mendelssohn: Letters.* New York: Vienna House, 1973.

Taylor, Ronald. *Robert Schumann: His Life and Work.* New York: Universe Books, 1982.

Wechsberg, Joseph. *Schubert: His Life, His Work, His Time.* New York: Rizzoli, 1977.

INDEX

CD TRACK LISTING

All performances are by Carol Montparker, pianist.

1. BACH: Prelude and Fugue in C Major, from the *Well-Tempered Clavier*, Book 2 (4:20)
2. BACH: Prelude and Fugue in F-sharp Minor, from the *Well-Tempered Clavier*, Book 2 (7:19)
3. CHOPIN: Nocturne in F-sharp Major, Opus 15 No. 2 (3:35)
4. CHOPIN: Impromptu in F-sharp Major, Opus 36 (4:50)
5. MOZART: Six Variations on an Allegretto Theme in F Major, K. 54 (6:41)
6. SCHUBERT: *Moment musical* in C Major, Opus 94 No. 1 (4:57)
7. SCHUBERT: *Moment musical* in F Minor, Opus 94 No. 5 (2:01)
8. SCHUBERT: Impromptu in F Minor, Opus 142 No. 4 (7:18)
9. BRAHMS: Capriccio in G Minor, from *Fantasien*, Opus 116 No. 3 (3:39)
10. BRAHMS: Intermezzo in E Major, from *Fantasien*, Opus 116 No. 6 (2:43)
11. BRAHMS: Capriccio in D Minor, from *Fantasien*, Opus 116 No. 7 (2:33)
12. BEETHOVEN: Sonata No. 24 in F-sharp Major, Opus 78: Adagio cantabile—Allegro ma non troppo (4:58)
13. BEETHOVEN: Sonata No. 24 in F-sharp Major, Opus 78: Allegro vivace (3:09)
14. SCHUMANN: Romanze in F-sharp Major, Opus 28 No. 2 (3:59)
15. SCHUMANN: "Des Abends," from *Fantasiestücke*, Opus 12 No. 1 (4:30)
16. SCHUMANN: "Aufschwung," from *Fantasiestücke*, Opus 12 No. 2 (4:14)